Berlitz HANDBOOK

IRELAND

Contents

Top 25 attractions	4
Ireland fact file	10
Trip planner	12
UNIQUE EXPERIENCES	20
Sporting experiences	22
Exploring ancient sites	32
Song and dance	38
Walking the wilderness	44
The Irish pub	50
Literary Ireland	54
PLACES	60
Getting your bearings	62
Dublin	64
South of the Liffey:	
Georgian Dublin	64
Georgian Dublin walk	72
Central Dublin	75
North of the Liffey	78
West and north of city centre	82
South of Dublin –	
County Wicklow	83
North of Dublin – County Meath	85
West of Dublin – County Kildare	86
Listings	88

The southeast	96
Counties Wexford and Waterford	96
Kilkenny and Tipperary	100
Nore Valley drive	102
The Vee Gap to Lismore	105
Listings	107
County Cork	112
Cork city	113
Around Cork city	115
West Cork	117
Bantry Bay drive	118
Skibbereen area	120
Listings	123
The southwest	128
Killarney	129
The Ring of Kerry	131
Horse trading	134
The Dingle Peninsula	138
Tralee and North Kerry	140
Listings	142
Limerick and the Shannon	150
Limerick city	151
South of Limerick city	153
County Clare	155

4 **Trinity College** Wander through this haven of academic tranquillity in Dublin's city centre *(see p.65)*

5 **National Museum of Ireland, Dublin** Explore the world's largest collection of Celtic antiquities *(see p.70)*

6 **Blarney Castle, Co. Cork** Every rock has a legend attached at this huge tower house's gardens *(see p.116)*

7 **Ulster-American Folk Park, Omagh** Open-air museum and reconstructed homes from Ireland's past *(see p.240)*

8 **Newgrange, Co. Meath** Visit the biggest of a cluster of these important Neolithic burial mounds *(see p.86)*

9 **Guinness Storehouse**, **Dublin** The brewery's visitor tour culminates in a complimentary pint *(see p.78)*

10 **Ring of Kerry** See colourful villages and glorious sea views on this famous scenic drive *(see p.131)*

11 **Croagh Patrick, Co. Mayo** Follow the well-worn pilgrims' path up this imposing mountain *(see p.177)*

12 **Glendalough, Co. Wicklow** Absorb the atmosphere of this 6th-century monastic settlement *(see p.84)*

13 **Crown Liquor Saloon** Sup a pint in the ornate interior of Belfast's grand Victorian pub *(see p.222)*

Top **25** attractions

1 **Georgian Dublin** You can still glimpse the Dublin Mountains from the city's 18th-century Georgian squares, as when they were built *(see p.64)*

2 **Cliffs of Moher, Co. Clare** Stand on the very edge of Europe and watch the Atlantic rollers pounding in some 216m (158ft) below *(see p.158)*

3 **Giant's Causeway, Co. Antrim** See why the 37,000-plus basalt pillars of this geological curiosity, and their legends, have fascinated travellers for centuries *(see p.251)*

🚗 The Burren drive	160	
Listings	*165*	
▪ The West – Galway & Mayo	170	
Galway city and Bay	171	
The Aran Islands	173	
Connemara	175	
County Mayo	177	
⭐ Festival fever	178	
Listings	*182*	
▪ Inland Ireland	188	
The southwest Midlands	189	
The southeast Midlands	192	
⭐ The Irish big house	194	
The north Midlands	196	
Listings	*198*	
▪ The northwest	202	
Sligo	203	
Northwest Lakelands	206	
Donegal	207	
⭐ Fortified Ireland	208	
Listings	*213*	
▪ Belfast	218	
The city centre	218	

🚶 Queen's quarter walk	224
University area	226
Listings	*229*
▪ Northern Ireland	234
Derry/Londonderry	234
Inland to Tyrone and	
Fermanagh	238
In and around Armagh	242
⭐ On the trail of St Patrick	244
County Antrim	248
Listings	*252*
▪ PRACTICAL ADVICE	256
Accommodation	258
Transport	261
Health and safety	268
Money and budgeting	270
Responsible travel	273
Family holidays	274
▪ SETTING THE SCENE	276
History	278
Culture	286
Food and drink	292
INDEX	298

15 **Strandhill, Co. Sligo** Hire a wetsuit and board and discover the thrill of huge Atlantic swells *(see p.31)*

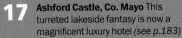

14 **Grafton Street** Dublin's chic shopping street is famous for its buskers and lively ambience *(see p.69)*

16 **The Aran Islands** Glimpse the older ways of rural Ireland amid the stony landscape of Aran *(see p.173)*

17 **Ashford Castle, Co. Mayo** This turreted lakeside fantasy is now a magnificent luxury hotel *(see p.183)*

18 **Kinsale Gourmet Festival** Taste great dishes at this Co. Cork seaside resort with an annual eating festival (see p.127)

19 **Yeats Country, Co. Sligo** Find your poetic soul in the enchanting lake and mountain landscape celebrated by the poet (see p.205)

20 **Slea Head, Dingle Peninsula** Wild Atlantic scenery, deserted beaches and megalithic remains never fail to enthrall (see p.139)

21 **Strokestown Park Famine Museum** A sobering introduction to the 1845 famine (see p.196)

22 **Galway city** Explore the compact historic centre on foot, while browsing boutiques and bars (see p.171)

23 **Bloomsday** Join the Dubliners as they celebrate James Joyce's *Ulysses* on 16 June (see p.56)

24 **The K-Club, Co. Kildare** One of Ireland's best golf courses, with a luxurious hotel at its core (see p.25)

25 **Sheep's Head Way, Co. Cork** Walk, bike or drive the way-marked route for great views (see p.118)

Ireland fact file

Ireland is Europe's most westerly outpost and is known for its physical beauty, with vast areas of unspoilt wilderness, dotted with romantic ruins. The country also boasts one of Europe's liveliest capital cities, Dublin, where the population is becoming more diverse, adding new strands to its already thriving arts and music scene. Belfast and Cork are also packed with busy bars and restaurants, and live entertainment.

BASICS

The island of Ireland contains two separate countries: the Republic of Ireland (ROI) and Northern Ireland (NI). The latter, in the northeastern corner of the island, is part of the UK

Population: ROI: 4.2m (NI: 1.7m)

Area: 84,288 sq km (32,544 sq miles)

Official language(s): Irish, English (latter is the second official language in ROI)

State religion: none; majority Christian

Capital city: ROI: Dublin (NI: Belfast)

President: ROI: Mary McAleese (NI: none; subject to the British Crown)

National anthem: ROI: *Amhrán na bhFíann* (The Soldier's Song) (NI: *God Save the Queen*)

National symbol(s): the harp, the colour green

National sports/art forms: hurling, Gaelic football

National airline: ROI: Aer Lingus (NI: British Airways)

CURRENCY

ROI: Euro (€)

1 euro = 100 cents (c)

NI: Pound Sterling (£)

1 pound = 100 pence

The following figures are approximate:

£1 = €1.15

US$1 = €0.75

US$1 = £0.64

TIME ZONE
GMT
GMT + 1 (late March to late October)

In January:

New York: 8am
London: noon
Dublin/Belfast: noon
Sydney: 10pm
Auckland: midnight

In July:

New York: 7am
London: noon
Dublin/Belfast: noon
Sydney: 9pm
Auckland: 11pm

IMPORTANT TELEPHONE NUMBERS
Country code: ROI: +353 (NI: +44)
International calls: 00 + country code + number
Police: ROI: 112 or 999 (NI: 999)
Ambulance: ROI: 112 or 999 (NI: 999)
Fire: ROI: 112 or 999 (NI: 999)

AGE RESTRICTIONS
Driving: 17
Drinking: 18
Age of Consent: ROI: 17 (NI: 16)

Smoking
Banned in all workplaces (including pubs, restaurants, hotels and clubs) and on all public transport, including taxis

ELECTRICITY
ROI: 220 volts, 3-pin plug, European-style (NI: 240 volts AC)

OPENING HOURS
Banks: Mon–Fri 10am–4pm, 5pm one day a week
Shops: Mon–Sat 9am–5.30pm. Most places have a convenience store open until 9pm, and many supermarkets and city centre shops open from 11am on Sundays

POSTAL SERVICES
ROI: An Post (NI: Royal Mail)
Post offices: Mon–Fri 9am–5pm, Sat 9am–1pm
Post boxes: ROI: green (NI: red)
Standard post: 55c (NI: 46p)
Airmail: 82c (NI: 68p)

PRIDE

Trip planner

WHEN TO GO

Climate

Although Ireland lies at roughly the same northerly latitude as Newfoundland, it has a mild, moist climate, because of the prevailing southwesterly winds and the influence of the warm Gulf Stream along its western coast. As no part of the island is more than 110km (70 miles) from the sea, temperatures are fairly uniform over the whole country.

Average temperatures in the coldest months, January and February, are between 4–7°C (39–45°F) and in the warmest months, July and August, between 14–16°C (57–61°F), occasionally reaching as high as 25°C (77°F). The sunniest months are May and June, with an average of 5½–6½ hours of sunshine a day over most of the country. The sunniest region is the extreme southeast.

Public holidays	
1 January	New Year's Day
17 March	St Patrick's Day
12 July	Orangeman's Day
	(NI only)
25 December	Christmas Day
26 December	St Stephen's Day
	(NI: Boxing Day)

Movable dates in Republic of Ireland
Easter Monday, May Day (first Monday in May), June Bank Holiday (first Monday in June), August Bank Holiday (first Monday in August), October Bank Holiday (last Monday in October)
Movable dates in Northern Ireland:
Good Friday, Easter Monday, Spring Bank Holiday (last Monday in May), Summer Bank Holiday (last Monday in August)
Government offices, banks, post offices and shops will be closed.
In the ROI all pubs are closed on Good Friday and Christmas Day and no alcohol is sold in shops. In parts of Northern Ireland pubs do not open on Sundays.

Cliffs of Moher, Co. Clare

Parts of the west of the country are twice as wet as the east because of the prevailing Atlantic winds, with annual rainfall averaging 1,500mm (59 inches).

Rural Ireland is best avoided from November to February, as cold and rainy weather can persist everywhere, and the daylight hours are short, running from about 8.30am to 4.30pm. However, city breaks at that time of year can be very enjoyable,

Enjoying some summer surf at Strandhill, Co. Sligo

Trip planner

with open fires in many pubs and restaurants adding to the ambience.

High/low season

July and August are the high season for Irish family holidays, and also see the greatest influx of holidaying families from the UK. Prices and pressure on facilities rise accordingly. The best times to visit are late spring and early autumn. There are some excellent bed and breakfast rates to be had outside the high season, especially if you stay two or more nights. Seaside destinations will be crowded in the summer, while in the more remote areas, including the Ring of Kerry and Connemara, many smaller guesthouses and restaurants close from October or November to mid-March or April.

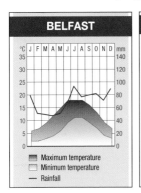

BELFAST

Maximum temperature
Minimum temperature
— Rainfall

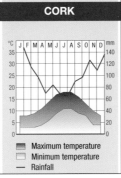

CORK

Maximum temperature
Minimum temperature
— Rainfall

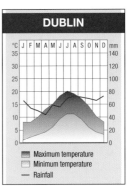

DUBLIN

Maximum temperature
Minimum temperature
— Rainfall

ESSENTIAL EVENTS

The St Patrick's Day Festival parade in Dublin

February

Dublin International Film Festival.
Hosts world premières and the best in
Irish and international filmmaking.

March

St Patrick's Day Festival. Ireland
celebrates on 17 March and the nearest weekend with a major parade of
marching bands in central Dublin.

April

**Cuirt International Festival of Litera-
ture.** An international cast of leading
writers and poets congregate in
Galway city for five days in mid-April.

May

Cathedral Quarter Arts Festival.
Starting on the May Day bank holiday
and continuing for a week beyond,
Belfast's city centre is abuzz with arts
events, from readings to concerts.
Cork International Choral Festival.
A jam-packed programme featuring
the very best of international vocal
music with gala concerts, competitions and master classes.
Fleadh Nua Music Festival.
Traditional musicians flock to Ennis
in County Clare in the last week of
May. Official competition programme
and a lively fringe.

June

Bloomsday. Dubliners celebrate
James Joyce's novel *Ulysses* on 16
June by dressing in Edwardian finery
and re-enacting scenes from the
novel. Readings, performances and
guided walks.
Cork Midsummer Festival. Centred
around Midsummer Day, Cork city
hosts a feast of site-specific theatre,
live music and other arts events.
Irish Derby. Smartly dressed punters watch the cream of the world's
bloodstock compete at the Curragh
race course, County Kildare, on the
last weekend in June.

July

West Cork Chamber Music Festival.
For 10 days from the last Friday in
June, international virtuosi perform

around 60 concerts in the intimate surroundings of Bantry House and the town church.

Galway Arts Festival. The city comes alive in the third week of July with myriad arts events, including a big top for concerts and a street parade.

Dublin International Horse Show. Highlight of Ireland's equestrian and social year, held in Ballsbridge, Dublin, in the first week of the month: international showjumping for teams and individuals.

Kilkenny Arts Festival. Long-established multi-arts festival in the compact medieval town during the second week in August, especially strong on visual arts.

Oul' Lammas Fair. Believed to be one of Ireland's oldest traditional fairs, with horse-dealing and free entertainment in the streets of Ballycastle, County Antrim.

September

Clarenbridge Oyster Festival. The opening of the Galway oyster season is marked on the first weekend by demonstrations, competitions and free entertainment.

Lisdoonvarna Matchmaking Festival. Traditional harvest festival where matchmakers in the tiny Clare village pair up singletons amid music and dancing.

October

Dublin Theatre Festival. Theatrical companies from all over the world play alongside new Irish productions for two weeks in late September–October.

Cork Jazz Festival. Major stars of the jazz scene pack the city on the last weekend in October.

Belfast Festival at Queen's. One of the biggest arts festivals on the island is centred on Belfast's university in mid-late October.

Trip planner

Tuck into Galway Bay oysters at the Clarenbridge Oyster Festival

ITINERARIES

Ireland looks small and compact on a map, and the temptation to try to cover too much in too short a time is strong. The distances between towns are not great, but once off the main roads travel can be slow, and signposting is famously erratic. Spend some time in Dublin, Cork or Belfast without a car, then opt to explore just one or two different regions – northwest, west or southwest – rather than attempting to visit everywhere with a tight schedule. Much of the charm of rural Ireland lies in the slower pace of life and the unpredictability of everything (including the weather), so slow down and be flexible.

Two-week highlights tour

Days 1–2: **Dublin.** Use the hop-on-hop-off bus to visit the city centre's highlights, starting at Trinity College and the Book of Kells.

Days 3–4: **Cork.** Drive south to Cork city, stopping at the Rock of Cashel en route. Next day, explore the city centre on foot, then drive out to Blarney Castle to kiss the famous stone, or visit seaside Kinsale.

Days 5–7: **Killarney and the Ring of Kerry.** Explore Killarney's lakes, and the next day, drive the coastal route round the Ring of Kerry.

Days 8–10: **The Cliffs of Moher.** Head north through Limerick, stopping at Bunratty Castle, and on to the famous cliffs, then head north again to stay overnight in Galway.

Days 11–14: **Galway–Connemara.** Walk the compact city centre, then

Local produce for sale at the roadside in the Ring of Kerry

Walking in the Giant's Causeway

drive out to the wilds of Connemara, spending two nights in Clifden, before returning home via Dublin or Shannon airport.

A long weekend in Northern Ireland

Day 1: **Belfast**. Walk the city centre, allowing plenty of time for the Titanic Quarter.

Days 2–3: **The Antrim Coast**. Drive north along the Antrim coast, through the picturesque Glens to pretty Cushendun.

Day 4: **The Giant's Causeway**. Explore the sensational Causeway Coast, with its basalt pillars, rope bridge and romantic ruins. Stay overnight in Bushmills and sample some of the local whiskey.

Day 5: **Derry**. Walk the historic city walls of Derry (also known as Londonderry) before returning to Belfast.

A week of stunning scenery

Day 1: **Connemara**. Drive into the heart of Connemara's wilderness, past Lough Corrib and through Clifden to Letterfrack and Connemara National Park.

Days 2–4: **Westport to Sligo**. Take the scenic Doolough Pass from Leenane north to Westport past the towering bulk of the conical mountain Croaghpatrick. Drive around Achill Island and across the eerily empty bogland of North Mayo through Bangor to the blowholes and wide vista of Downpatrick Head, and on to Sligo.

Days 5–7: **Donegal**. After exploring Sligo town, and admiring Ben Bulben's great bulk, head north along the coast to the Donegal Highlands and on to Bloody Foreland for huge empty beaches and spectacular sunsets.

BEFORE YOU LEAVE

Visas and entry requirements

Passports are required by everyone visiting the Republic except British citizens (though most airlines insist on a passport for ID). Visas are not required by citizens of EU countries, Australia, Canada or the USA. Citizens of these countries can enter Ireland for three months with just a passport (see www.inis.gov.ie), and Northern Ireland for six months (see www.fco.gov.uk).

Nationality	Visa required
UK	✗
US	✗
Canada	✗
Australia	✗
New Zealand	✗
Ireland	✗
South Africa	✗

Embassies and consulates
Dublin
Australia: Fitzwilton House, Wilton Terrace, Dublin 2; tel: 01-664 5300; www.ireland.embassy.gov.au
Britain: 29 Merrion Rd, Dublin 4; tel: 01-205 3700; www.britishem bassyinireland.fco.gov.uk
Canada: 7–8 Wilton Terrace, Dublin 2; tel: 01-231 4000; www.canada.ie
New Zealand: None. www.nz embassy.com/united-kingdom
South Africa: 2nd Floor, Alexandra House, Earlsfort Centre, Earlsfort Terrace, Dublin 2; tel: 01-661 5553; www.dfa.gov.za/foreign/bilateral/ireland.html
US: 42 Elgin Rd, Dublin 4; tel: 01-668 8777; www.usembassy.ie

Belfast
American Consulate General, 223 Stranmillis Road, Belfast; tel: 028-9038 6100; http://london.us embassy.gov/nireland

Tourist information
Irish Tourist Board (Fáilte Ireland)
General enquiries: Fáilte Ireland,

88–95 Amiens Street, Dublin 1;, tel: 01-884 7700 (within Republic: tel: 1850-230 330; 0808-234 2009 in UK); www.discoverireland.com
Dublin: Dublin Tourism, Suffolk Street (near Grafton Street), Dublin 2; tel: 01-605 7700 (0800-039 7000 in UK), accommodation reservations tel: 1800-363 626; www.visitdublin.com

Northern Ireland Tourist Board
47 Donegall Place, Belfast BT1 5AD; tel: 028-9024 6609; www.discover northernireland.com
Belfast: 59 North Street, Belfast BT1 1NB; tel: 028-9023 1221
Dublin: 16 Nassau Street, Dublin 2; tel: 01-679 1977

Tourism Ireland offices abroad
For information on the whole island.
Australia: 5th level, 36 Carrington Street, Sydney 2000, NSW; tel: 02-9299 6177
Britain: Nations House, 103 Wigmore Street, London W1U 1QS; tel: 020-7518 0800
Canada: 2 Bloor Street West, Suite 3403, Toronto, ON M4W; tel: 800-223 6470/416-925 6368
New Zealand: Level 7, Citibank Building, 23 Customs St East,

Winding roads in County Donegal

Auckland 1010; tel: +649-977 2255
US: 345 Park Avenue, New York, NY 10154; tel: +1-800-2223 6470/ 212-418 0800
South Africa: Development Promotions, 62 Hume Road, Dunkeld, PO Box 30615, Braamfontein 2017, Johannesberg; tel: +27-11-442 0824

Maps
If you intend to do the sort of driving that takes you off the main routes, it is worth buying the *Complete Road Atlas of Ireland* (Ordnance Survey Ireland and Ordnance Survery of Northern Ireland), which sells for about €9.99. Cyclists and walkers may want smaller-scale maps: these can be bought locally from Tourist Information Centres, newsagents and bookshops.

Websites
http://entertainment.ie
Find out what's going on
www.discovernorthernireland.com
Northern Ireland Tourist Board
www.heritageireland.ie
Heritage of Ireland

www.hostels-ireland.com Tourist Board-approved holiday hostels
www.discoverireland.ie
Irish Tourist Board
www.goireland.com Book a hotel
www.ireland.com Information on things to do in Ireland
www.met.ie For the latest forecast
www.irishtimes.com National daily
www.rte.ie National broadcaster for podcasts and free downloads
www.visitdublin.com Best way to find a bed in Dublin. Link to free Visit Dublin App
www.overheardindublin.com Get a handle on the local sense of humour

Books

- *A Place Apart* by Dervla Murphy (John Murray). Her 1978 account of Northern Ireland is still first-rate.
- *Collected Short Stories* by William Trevor (Penguin). Set in both England and Ireland. Trevor is a master of the quiet epiphany.
- *McCarthy's Bar* by Pete McCarthy (Sceptre). Humorous account of an Englishman's discovery of his Irish roots. Excellent on pubs.
- *Penguin Book of Contemporary Irish Poetry* edited by Peter Fallon and Derek Mahon (Penguin). Well-balanced selection of today's poets.
- *Ship of Fools – How Stupidity and Corruption Sank the Celtic Tiger* by Fintan O'Toole (Faber & Faber). Ireland's economic catastrophe analysed in a tightly argued polemic.
- *Troubles* by J.G. Farrell (Penguin). Booker Prize-winner's wry, atmospheric account of sitting out the Civil War in a crumbling hotel.

Trip planner

UNIQUE EXPERIENCES

Sporting experiences – *p.22* **Exploring ancient sites** – *p.32*
Song and dance – *p.38* **Walking the wilderness** – *p.44*
The Irish pub – *p.50* **Literary Ireland** – *p.54*

ESTD 1759

GUINNESS'

Sporting experiences

The Irish are proud of their reputation as a sports-mad nation, whether as spectators or participants. People are as passionate about watching team games that feature a ball or a spot of horse racing as they are about their own activities, particularly golf, angling and cycling, while recently surfing and kayaking have grown enormously in popularity.

Sports enthusiasts will have a field day in Ireland. Exciting spectator sports abound, and the country's landscape is made for all the activity that can be thrown at it.

All of the international sports are played with a passion, especially rugby, while football (soccer) is also well supported and there are many people who play at local level. The build-up to national and international finals is mighty. Native games, such as hurling and Gaelic football, are unique to Ireland, and attending a live match, whether on a local pitch or on the hallowed ground of Dublin's Croke Park, should be a priority of any sport-lover's trip. These are fast-paced, thrilling, high-voltage games of skill, amateur in nature, under the control of the Gaelic Athletic Association (GAA), with wildly partisan spectators adding to the excitement.

Golf, probably introduced to Ireland by the Ulster Scots, is a democratic sport in Ireland, with affordable public courses for everybody and over 400 clubs. These include some of the world's best links courses and prestigious parkland courses. Similarly, the Irish racing scene lacks the snobbery that it has acquired elsewhere, and going to the races is a hugely popular day out. In Ireland, the horse is

Cyclists pause for refreshment outside the Dew Drop Inn in Galway city

a national obsession, and race meetings are frequent, affordable and fun. Meanwhile, for anglers Ireland can offer deep-sea, coarse and game fishing, with a minimum of bureacratic formality. Indeed, there are so many lakes and rivers that you will soon get accustomed to having a prime spot all to yourself.

It is quite easy to base an entire holiday around an activity. A riding holiday is one of the best ways to experience the Irish countryside and make new friends. Cycling holidays are also possible; the sport grew popular in the 1980s when Sean Kelly dominated professional cycling and Stephen Roche won the Tour de France. Today, there are many trails and places to hire bicycles.

Watersports are also becoming increasingly mainstream. Kayaking is perfectly suited to the Irish coast; kayaks are widely available for hire, and escorted trips, especially in the moonlight, have proved popular. And in recent years, international surfing stars have been discovering Ireland's Atlantic coast, surfing its huge waves, and inspiring locals to do the same.

Hurling is a fast-paced and occasionally rough sport

Gaelic games

The GAA was founded in 1884 in Thurles, County Tipperary, to revive native games under native control at a time when Ireland was still under British rule. Teams were organised around the parish, the county and the province. Because of its local roots, the GAA worked in a similar way to American football in creating a strong local identity, and pride of place, through sporting rivalry. When two parishes or counties meet in a final, passions run high: the teams' colours are worn – some even paint their cars in the local colours – and flags fly from every home and business.

Hurling has been played in Ireland since prehistoric times. It's the fastest of all field games, played with a hurley – a stick with a flat head, made from ash – and its rules are relatively simple, although watching it for the first

time can be a dizzying, bewildering experience. The ball hurtles around at breakneck speed and players bat their hurleys about, narrowly missing teeth and foreheads. The small ball, called a *sliotar*, is hard and ridged. The object

Sporting experiences

Gaelic games vs garrison games

Gaelic games – hurling and Gaelic football – have been played since time immemorial, but because of poor communications in troubled 19th-century Ireland, there were no agreed rules until the founding of the GAA in 1884. Football was known as a 'garrison game', as it was introduced to Ireland by the British army for recreation. A hundred years ago the only people in Ireland who knew the rules of this sort of football were soldiers. Until 2005, it was forbidden to play 'foreign games', ie football and rugby, on GAA pitches.

of the game is to score a goal (three points) by getting the ball between the posts and under the bar. A single point is scored when the ball goes between the posts and over the bar. The main traditional hurling areas remain south of a line from Dublin to Galway, with a small pocket in the Glens of Antrim. Cork and Kilkenny are the top hurling counties. The best places to see a game are Croke Park in Dublin, Páirc Uí Chaoimh in Cork and Semple Stadium in Tipperary. Tickets can be bought through the the GAA website: **www. gaa.ie.** Book well in advance; finals are usually booked solid by supporters, but there should be tickets for other games.

Like hurling, Gaelic football is played by teams of 15 a side, with a round ball similar to that used in football; it shares some features with Australian Rules football. It's fast and chaotic, a spectacular game, and attracts the biggest crowds of any sporting event in Ireland. The high point of the GAA year is in September with the All-Ireland hurling and football Finals in Dublin's 80,000-seater **Croke Park** (tel: 01-819 2300; www. crokepark.ie), which incorporates a museum devoted to Irish sports. Details of fixtures can be found at www.gaa.ie.

Horse racing
Among the things that make Irish race meetings so different and so much fun are the national love of horses and people's familiarity with them, the carnival atmosphere, and the optimism of the punters who are forever thinking they will place a winning bet. There is no dress code, very few 'exclusive' areas, and the entrance fee is nominal.

Betting becomes a national obsession at certain times of year, including the National Hunt meeting at Cheltenham, which happens over St Patrick's Day, and the Irish Grand National, which is held on Easter Monday.

Races are great people-watching occasions, whether you opt for a wintry National Hunt meeting, at which fences or hurdles are jumped, or the flat, where races are shorter, and the betting more likely to follow form (in theory). Learn more from **Horse Racing Ireland** (www.goracing.ie), the national body for the promotion of the sport, which includes a witty glossary of racing terms.

Golf
Ireland's golf courses continue to be a major magnet for visitors, its traditional

A local blacksmith with a customer

Highlights of the racing calendar

- **Irish Grand National**, Easter Monday at Fairyhouse, County Meath. A long-awaited race to determine the year's new champion.
- **Irish National Hunt Festival**, April at Punchestown, County Kildare. Five days of exciting racing over jumps and hurdles.
- **Irish Derby**, late June or early July at The Curragh, County Kildare. A day of classic flat racing, the dressiest of all race meetings.
- **Downpatrick, Galway, Killarney, Listowel, Sligo** and **Tramore** all hold sociable summer racing festivals in August and September. Ladies Day is a highlight for its best-dressed prizes.

Ballybunion's golf courses are famous for good reason

Sporting experiences

links courses now joined by major new developments, such as the Jack Nicklaus-designed parkland course at Mount Juliet. Ireland has over 400 courses around the island, including over 30 percent of the world's natural links courses, perched on cliff tops or meandering among sand dunes. While dealing with the challenge of Ireland's major courses, you will also be amazed at the beauty of the scenery, and the relative lack of crowds. The Irish are keen golfers, and it is generally seen as an accessible sport of the people, rather than a status symbol.

The majority of Irish clubs are unstuffy places that welcome visitors, who are usually pleasantly surprised at the low price of green fees. Exceptions to this are the more expensive parkland courses at the **K-Club** (tel: 01-601 7200; www.kclub.com), **Adare Manor** (tel: 061-396 566; www.

adaremanor.com) and **Mount Juliet** (tel: 056-777 3064; www.mountjuliet. ie), and some of the more famous links courses like **Ballybunion** (tel: 068-27611; www.ballybuniongolfclub. ie) and **Waterville** (tel: 066-947 4102; www.watervillegolflinks.ie).

Northern Ireland has numerous 18-hole golf courses, but the two most prestigious (and expensive) are the **Royal County Down** at Newcastle, County Down (tel: 028-4372 2419; www.royalcountydown.org) and **Royal Portrush** (tel: 028-7082 2311; www.royalportrushgolfclub.com). Many golf clubs offer cheaper rates, so it's best to check with the local tourist information offices or www.discover northernireland.com/golfing.

Irish Golf Holidays (tel: 061-366 999; www.irishgolfholidays.com) is a family-run company based in Shannon that will organise all details of

- **The K-Club**, County Kildare. Two parkland courses. The choice of plutocrats.
- **Portmarnock**, Dublin. On a sandy peninsula north of Dublin; still holding out against women members.
- **Ballybunion**, County Kerry. Tiger Woods warms up on the Old Course for a European tour.
- **Killarney Golf and Fishing Club**, Killarney. Choice of three courses amid stunning lake and mountain scenery.
- **Lahinch**, County Clare. Challenging links course on the shores of the Atlantic, famed for its massive bunkers.
- **Royal County Down**, near Mourne Mountains. A tough course.
- **Royal Portrush**, County Antrim. The only Irish club to have hosted a British Open. Fine coastal location.

your golfing holiday in a customised package, with accommodation and tee times pre-booked, and an itinerary, with hire car or private minibus and driver, and airport greeting. **Tailor Made Golf Tours** (tel: 065-682 1593; www.tailormadegolftours.com) is owned and operated by three avid golfers based near Shannon airport, who will advise and organise every detail of your golfing holiday.

For a full list of courses and to put your own package together, see **www.golf.discoverireland.ie**.

Angling

Ireland has a profusion of cold- and warm-water fish species, so there is a broad range of experiences on offer, including salmon fishing, pike fishing, trout fly fishing and sea angling. Stay in one of Ireland's **Great Fishing Houses** (www.irelandflyfishing.com), and you can share tips with fellow enthusiasts at the end of the day.

Coarse fishing is not popular with the locals, so the freshwaters are teeming with species like pike, bream, tench, eel and rudd. Thanks to the haunting beauty of the often empty landscapes, coarse fishing in Ireland is contemplative and tranquil. If your interest lies in a gourmet dinner, you could opt for a showdown with a pink-fleshed salmon (which holds an honoured place in Irish culture and folklore), trout

Perfect your putting until the sun goes down

River angling in Connemara

or sea trout (the ultimate delicacy). You'll need a licence, and a knowledge of current conservation laws: **Fisheries Ireland** (www.fisheriesireland.ie) has details.

Sea fishing is a real thrill, with over 6,437km (4,000 miles) of coastline, from the crashing Atlantic on the west to the gentler waters of the southeast. There are over 80 species in the water, from spring to autumn. Whether you choose languid wreck-fishing, or a fun bout of deep-sea fishing in lively company on a charter boat, you're guaranteed an exciting and enjoyable time – and possibly a delicious supper of ling, pollack or monkfish. To join a chartered boat in Clew Bay near Westport, contact Marie Gavin-Hughes of **Clew Bay Angling** (tel: 098-41562; www.clewbayangling.com). Kinsale, County Cork, is a popular deep-sea angling centre, with easy access to

wreck fishing; contact **Willem-Jan Van Dijk** (tel: 021-477 8944; www.solcon.nl/kinsale). For a full list of boat charter companies all around Ireland, and news on the latest topics of interest to sea anglers, see **www.sea-angling-ireland.org**.

County Fermanagh, with its large lakelands offering mixed coarse and game fishing, is one of the main attractions of Northern Ireland. Each year many angling events are held in the county, the main one being the **Waterways Ireland Classic Fishing Festival** (tel: 028-6632 3110; www.fermanaghlakelands.com), one of Europe's premier fishing festivals in the spring.

Horse riding

Ireland breeds some of the world's finest horses, from million-dollar racehorses to good-natured, long-haired ponies. Irish horses are often felt to be truly special by equine fans, and

Unique experiences

A question of breeding

Ireland excels at breeding thoroughbred racehorses, with long pedigrees and high price tags. The Irish Sport Horse is a cross between a thoroughbred and an Irish Draught, a heavier animal descended from the all-purpose farm horse which could also be ridden to hounds. The Irish and British mounted police both like Irish Draught horses for their calm temperament. The Sport Horse, valued for its intelligence, athleticism and good nature, is ideal for showjumping, eventing and dressage, as well as general hacking. Beginners often prefer an Irish cob, a heavier horse known for its good nature. The Irish coloured horse, associated with the travelling community, and previously dismissed for its 'lack of breeding', combines aspects of the cob and the Sport Horse in unpredictable measures, and has become enormously popular as a riding horse in both Ireland and the UK.

the opportunity to ride an Irish horse on its home territory should not be missed. Whether you choose a residential riding holiday with tuition on a challenging cross-country course, a pleasant amble around quiet lanes on a hairy pony, or an exhilarating gallop along a sandy beach, be honest about your abilities, so that the stable can match you with the right horse.

Dartfield Horse Museum and Park (Loughrea, County Galway; tel: 091-843 968; www.dartfield.com) is the base for Willie Leahy's riding trails and horse holidays. Willie is a legendary horseman, currently master of the famous Galway Blazers. He will organise anything horse-related, be it an hour's ride, a residential holiday for children and adults, with cross-country challenges, to a day out with the Blazers on one of his 400 Irish-bred horses. He also operates the **Connemara and Coast Trails**, six days riding through

Galloping on the shores is a real treat for horse riders

Cyclists enjoying the scenery in Connemara National Park

spectacular mountain scenery, suitable for beginners and experienced riders.

Clonshire Equestrian Centre (Adare, County Limerick; tel: 061-396 770; www.clonshire.com) is set in 48 hectares (120 acres) of private parkland. The centre offers top-class training in dressage, cross country and showjumping from novice to advanced level, with weatherproof indoor arena facilities. Self-catering apartments are available, and there is a holiday programme for unaccompanied children.

Alternatively, at **Westport Woods Hotel and Riding Centre** (tel: 098-25811; www.gotrekking.ie), Michael Lennon organises equestrian packages featuring mountain trekking beneath mystical Croagh Patrick, and thrilling beach rides, tailored to individual needs, with the use of the hotel's leisure centre and spa to recover from a day in the saddle.

For other equestrian holidays, **www.ehi.ie** is a useful resource.

Cycling

Ireland's vast network of small roads, many so small that they are unclassified, are ideal for the cyclist. Meandering roads and trails are framed by spectacular scenery, leading to small, friendly villages, with welcoming hostelries. Cyclists are a friendly bunch, and tend to congregate in the evening to swap stories and tips.

Sea views and heathery mountain slopes alternate on the quiet roads of the Beara Peninsula in west Cork and Kerry, which has a very popular cycling route (**www.bearatourism. com/cycleroute**). The small scenic roads of Kerry, Dingle, the Burren and Connemara are also popular with cyclists; in Northern Ireland the Mountains of Mourne and the Cooley Mountains provide beautiful but challenging terrain. Certain towns, including Skibereen, County Cork, Ballyshannon, County Donegal, Carrick-on-Suir, County Waterford, Achill Island and Westport in County Mayo have been designated 'cycling hubs', as they provide good accommodation and eating options, and have signposted looped cycling routes suitable for all fitness levels. See **www.discoverireland.ie/cycling**.

Organised cycling holidays are increasingly popular, either travelling in a group with a back-up van, or cycling independently to pre-booked accommodation, with baggage transfer. **Irish Cycle Hire** (tel: 041-685 3772; www.irishcyclehire.com) will rent you a bicycle, and also offer self-guided tours with luggage transfer. Dublin-based company **Irish Cycling Safaris** (tel: 01-260 0749; www.irishcyclingsafaris.com) offers routes on the Antrim coast, the highlands of Donegal, the Ring of Kerry, Wicklow and wild west Mayo, among others.

Ireland has a strong tradition of road racing, and there are races most weekends, organised by **Cycling Ireland** (tel: 01-855 1522; www.cyclingireland.ie).

Surfing

Beaches used to be empty in bad weather, except for a few dog-walkers. Now they are always busy with kitesurfers, windsurfers and, most numerous of all, surfers and boogie boards. When weather conditions are right, huge rollers pound in from the Atlantic. A wetsuit is essential, but it is a rare day when you will not find a rideable wave on the west coast. Surf schools offer tuition to beginners on the more benign beach breaks, and wetsuits are widely available for hire.

Notable spots for Atlantic swells, stimulating breezes and foaming

Strandhill beach is a great place to catch some waves

Unique experiences

surf are Strandhill and Easkey, both in County Sligo, and Lahinch in County Clare. Accredited surfing schools here and elsewhere in in counties Clare, Cork, Donegal, Kerry, Mayo, Sligo and Waterford can be found by contacting the **Irish Surfing Association** (www.isasurf.ie).

At Lahinch, the more advanced surfers are towed out by jet-ski, hoping to catch one of the biggest waves ever surfed in Europe, the Aileens. This thrilling and very dangerous challenge is only recommended for confident and experienced surfers, but it can be watched from the Cliffs of Moher, in essence creating a new spectator sport.

Kayaking off the Causeway Coast

The **Lahinch Surf School** (tel: 087-960 9667; www.lahinchsurfschool. com) will teach you to ride the waves, whatever your level of experience. Run by Irish Senior Champion John McCarthy, the first man to surf the Aileens, the school has a team of hardcore surf dudes at hand to instruct. All equipment is provided.

Sea kayaking

A sea kayak is ideal for exploring Ireland's many waterways, given the long rocky indented coastline, and the offshore islands. It's a great way to get up close to wildlife without disturbing it – you can enjoy close-up views of nesting seabirds in May and June, and basking seals sunbathing on the rocks from May to September. **Atlantic Sea Kayaking** (tel: 028-21058; www.atlantic seakayaking.com) is run by Jim Kennedy, a former Irish champion, who pioneered the sport in Ireland. Try a three-hour beginners' package, or join a moonlit cruise of Ireland's only seawater lake, Lough Ine.

For details of sea kayaking companies in Beara Peninsula, Clew Bay, Connemara, Galway Bay, Waterford and Wexford, see www.irishseakayak ingassociation.org.

Sporting experiences

A sporting destination

The Maharees is a 5km (3-mile) tombolo (sand spit) that divides Brandon Bay and Tralee Bay in County Kerry. Surfers delight in the Atlantic waves on the long sandy beaches, while the Maharees Islands attract sea anglers. There is a 19km (12-mile) stretch of the Dingle Way for walkers, parallel to the beach on Brandon Bay, where horse riding is also an option (Oí Connorís Trekking; tel: 066-713 9216). Tralee Golf Club (tel: 066-713-6379; www.traleegolfclub.com), a famous links course designed by Arnold Palmer, is only half an hour's drive away.

Exploring ancient sites

Visiting Ireland's Neolithic, Celtic and early Christian sites, among the oldest in Europe, offers a window into the distant past and takes you to some unusual and beautiful places. The Hill of Tara, seat of the Celtic High Kings, is steeped in mythology, while the peacefulness of Glendalough and the smaller monastic sites is unforgettable.

Located as it is on the western extremity of Europe, Ireland was never conquered by the Romans, so many ancient remains have been preserved, giving the island an unusually rich but enigmatic archaeological inheritance. The first human settlements are believed to date from about 8000BC, but it was not until the Neolithic period began around 4000–3500BC that there is evidence of skilled farmers with stone axes, capable of clearing forests to plant crops. The oldest tomb-form, the passage grave, dates from this era, and the most famous one is Newgrange.

The Bronze Age reached Ireland around 700BC, when the inhabitants adopted the Celtic culture and social system. Individual kingdoms formed part of larger fiefdoms, ruling each of the four provinces of Connacht (west), Leinster (east), Ulster (north) and Munster (south). The king of each province in turn was said to pay homage to the High King of Ireland at Tara. This folklore had great credence in the 19th and early 20th centuries, but is now generally dismissed as closer to myth than history.

Christianity arrived in Ireland in the 5th century, and the country was peacefully converted, with remnants of the pagan past being incorporated

St Mary's church graveyard in Glendalough, County Wicklow

into the new religion. Due to the collapse of the Roman Empire, and Ireland's isolation, the Irish Church developed its own character. Monasteries were established during the 6th and 7th centuries, and became important centres of learning and artistic enterprise, creating illuminated manuscripts, ornate metalwork and carved High Crosses and statuary. Glendalough, Clonmacnoise and other monasteries attracted students from England and Europe. This golden age gave Ireland its reputation as the 'Land of Saints and Scholars.'

From the late 9th century on, Ireland was attacked by Viking raiders, who targeted monasteries, as there were no towns. Anglo-Norman invaders brought the isolation of the Irish church to an end, introducing Cistercians and other orders from Europe. Eventually, most Irish monasteries were destroyed during Henry VIII's Protestant reformation in the mid-16th century, and have lain in ruins ever since.

Exploring the Neolithic, Celtic and early Christian sites that are dotted around Ireland and learning about their attendant mythology is a fascinating experience that enhances understanding of the island's distinctive culture.

Prehistoric and Celtic sites

While the huge stone monuments have survived, there is no documentation to enable us to know who built them, nor what beliefs lay behind the ritual burials that some of the tombs contained. Several of the passage graves and stone circles are oriented to

Early Christian monuments can be seen on Devenish Island

Exploring ancient sites

the rising or setting sun at the winter solstice, but nobody knows why. All sites, even the smaller ones, are marked on Ordnance Survey maps.

The Neolithic burial grounds at **Newgrange** (tel: 041-988 0300; charge; www.heritageireland.com; Nov–Feb 9.30am–5pm, 5.30pm Mar–Apr, 6.30pm May, late Sept–Oct, 7pm June–mid-Sept) are a Unesco World Heritage site and are older than the Egyptian Pyramids, pre-dating

---

Worth a visit

- **Scattery Island** (tel: 065-682 9100; www.heritageireland.ie) has the remains of a 6th-century monastery. Boats leave from Kilrush, County Clare, June–mid-Sept
- **Devenish Island**, Lower Lough Erne (tel: 028-6632 3110; www.doeni.gov.uk/nieaplaces_to_visit_home/historic-

monuments.htm), is an important early Christian site, visited by boat tours from Enniskillen
- **Inishmurray Island**, Mullaghmore, County Sligo (tel: 087-677-4522; www.sligoheritage.com/islandtours.htm) has a well-preserved 6th-century monastery. Boats run Apr–Sept

Stonehenge by 1,000 years. Consisting of three separate Neolithic burial mounds, two of which are open to the public, this is one of Europe's most important prehistoric clusters. Access is solely by tour from the **Brú na Bóinne Visitor Centre** near Donore.

Newgrange is the only monument where access is allowed to the interior passage and chamber. The latter is aligned so that the rising sun sends in a shaft of light at the winter solstice (entry on that day is by lottery). The sites are very busy in the summer and entry is not guaranteed, though the interpretative centre is some compensation. Go early, and allow at least three hours.

The **Hill of Tara,** famed in song and poems, is an impressive limestone ridge with views across the central plain of Ireland to distant mountain ranges. A Stone Age burial site, once the magnificent headquarters of the Celtic kings, it is unexcavated, and only the remains of ring forts and a standing stone mark the place that was Ireland's spiritual and cultural capital for millennia. Watch the 20-minute film at the Visitor Centre (tel: 046-902 5903; www.heritageireland.com; May–mid-Sept daily 10am–6pm; charge; Hill free), and follow the guided walk to get the full picture.

In the northwest of Ireland, at **Carrowmore** (tel: 071-916 1534; www.heritageireland.com; visitor centre Apr–Sept daily 10am–6pm; site free all year, charge for centre), near Sligo town, the 6,000-year-old Bronze Age graves of Ireland's largest megalithic graveyard are scattered across the fields. From here you can see **Knocknarea**, which stands 328m (1,078ft) above sea level. Drive south down the R292 to locate the signposted path leading to its enormous Neolithic tomb (70 by 11m/200 by 35ft), which is said to be the burial place of Queen Medb (Maeve), the warrior queen of Connacht in Celtic mythology. The ascent is steep but worth the climb: the magnificent view suggests why the Celts associated this part of Ireland with myth and magic.

In southwest Ireland, the **Burren National Park** in County Clare abounds with megalithic sites, the biggest being the **Poulnabrone Dolmen** (free), a distinctive 'portal dolmen' (burial tomb) with a huge capstone that has become a kind of logo of the area. It was built about 5,800 years ago, and when excavated contained

The mythical Hill of Tara

Unique experiences

the remains of 22 bodies, that were at least 1,500 years old.

Stone circles are a feature of west Cork and Kerry, usually with a burial site at their centre, and often with two upright pillars (the portal) opposite a recumbent altar stone. They are oriented to the setting sun at the winter solstice, and those that have been excavated have a ritual burial at their centre. The **Drombeg Stone Circle** (Glandore, County Cork; free), sited on a plateau with views of the distant sea, with 14 stones, is the biggest and most complete of the early Bronze Age remains. The burial at its centre was carbon-dated to 1124–794BC. Beside it is a cooking pit with full instructions.

In the megalithic cemetery at Carrowmore, Co. Sligo

Exploring ancient sites

If you are staying in Dublin, the best way to visit Newgrange and the Hill of Tara is on an organised tour. The tours have booked time slots to enter the tomb, and you are guaranteed entry without queuing. Buy your ticket in advance at the **Suffolk Street Tourist Information Office** (tel: 01-605 7700; www.visitdublin.ie) or on board. Other companies that offer trips include **Mary Gibbons Tours** (tel: 086-355 1355; www.newgrange tours.com), which has a daily tour

to both Newgrange and the Hill of Tara, and **Over the Top Tours** (tel: 01-860 0404; www.overthetoptours. com), which operates a Newgrange shuttle bus leaving the Suffolk Street Tourist Office in central Dublin daily at 8.45am and 11.45am. Alternatively take a guided minibus tour of Newgrange and the Hill of Tara. They also have a daily tour of Glendalough and the Wicklow Mountains.

A safe place

Round towers, the only form of architecture that is unique to Ireland, were built by the monks originally as watchtowers and belfries. They also served as physical landmarks for the location of a monastery, visible from great distances.

Today, 73 round towers survive. During Viking raids they were used as places of refuge for the monks, and for the monastery's valuables, which would include chalices and other altar vessels made of gold and jewels, as well as illuminated manuscripts. This is why round towers have their doorway (15ft/4.5m) above ground level. Once inside, the monks could pull up the ladder and be safe from the invaders.

Early Christian monastic sites

Early monks apparently appreciated good scenery, as they tended to build in the very best beauty spots: wooded glens, lake islands and river bends. The natural beauty of these settings is in turn enhanced by the simple stone monastic buildings still standing. A typical early Christian (AD525–1050) monastery usually includes a small dormitory, an oratory or church, many graves and a round tower (*see box, p.35*).

Glendalough (tel: 0404-45325; www.heritageireland.com; daily 9.30am–6pm, 5pm mid-Oct–mid-Mar; charge) is a good example of this – St Kevin's hermitage and church was founded in the 6th century in a steep-sided glacial valley between two lakes. Today's ruins– a 33m (110ft) round tower, stone churches and numerous stone crosses – date from the 11th century. Get there early in the morning, while the mist is still down, to experience the site's fullest impact. Glendalough is about 45 minutes south of Dublin on the R756. Tickets for organised tours can be obtained at the **Suffolk Street Tourist Information Office** (*see p.35*). Alternatively, **Gray Line** (tel: 01-458 0054; www.irishcitytours. com) runs a daily Wicklow tour that includes Glendalough. From April to October it runs a tour to Newgrange four times a week.

Clonmacnoise (tel: 090-967 4195; www.heritageireland.com; daily mid-Mar–mid-May and mid-Sept–Oct

High crosses and one of the round towers at Clonmacnoise

10am–6pm, mid-May–mid-Sept 9am–7pm, Nov–mid-Mar 10am–5.30pm), near Athlone in central Ireland, was founded by St Kieran and built on a natural gravel ridge on a bend of the River Shannon, and is the biggest monastic site in Ireland. It has the ruins of a cathedral, seven churches (dating from the 10th–13th century), two round towers, three high crosses and numerous graves. There are several Irish Romanesque doorways and arches. Today it is way off the beaten track, but in AD545 the Shannon was an important waterway.

Ardmore Cathedral and Round Tower (County Waterford; free) is a cliff-top site in southeast Ireland on a narrow promontory with extensive sea views, a stunning location for the ruined 12th-century cathedral. Its sturdy Hiberno-Romanesque arches contrast with the slender, conical-roofed round tower. St Declan's Oratory and Well nearby date from the 9th century, and are still visited by pilgrims annually on 24 July.

In the southwest, **Innisfallen Island** on Killarney's Lough Leane

Skellig Michael has a dramatic location

can be reached by rowing boat from **Ross Castle** (tel: 064-663 1633; charge). The romantic ruins on the wooded island date from the 7th century. You can walk the footpath around the island's perimeter in about 20 minutes, enjoying the lake views. The last High King of Ireland, Brian Ború, is said to have been educated by the monks here.

Exploring ancient sites

Skellig Michael

Skellig Michael, set 13km (8 miles) off the Kerry coast, is dramatically situated on a barren rocky island and can be visited by boat, weather permitting, between May and August. Dating from around AD800, the tiny monastery was built under twin peaks on a saddle of rock at the top of 600 stone steps. Six beehive huts, in which the monks lived, and two rectangular oratories, where they prayed, were built dry stone on a cliff edge around a small garden area. They are surprisingly well preserved, given the exposed Altantic location. Its distinctive silhouette seems to follow you around, as you drive the Ring of Kerry and the Dingle Peninsula, hovering offshore. There are no facilities on the island, and it is rough underfoot. Visit with **Sea Quest** (Portmagee; tel: 066-947 6214; www.skelligsrock.com), leaving Portmagee around 10.30am, returning about 2pm.

Song and dance

In spite of the international success of U2, Van Morrison and Westlife, at home traditional music still rules. All over Ireland you will encounter free live music, often in pubs, part of a long tradition of community entertainment. Step dancing is booming post-*Riverdance*, and the easier, barn-dance-like set dancing is enjoyed by many.

Irish traditional music has long been part of everyday life, and hornpipes and reels have never gone out of fashion. Traditionally, people gathered in each other's homes to create their own entertainment, making music on small, inexpensive portable instruments *(see box, p.41)*. New words were set to haunting old airs, and passed down through generations in an oral tradition. Distinctive local styles developed, and still survive. Notably, a different scale of intervals is used in the older music, and *séan nós* (literally 'old style') sounds more like Arab or Indian music than mainstream European sounds.

Jigs, polkas, and waltzes were imported from Europe and acquired a distinctive Irish flavour. Emigrants settling in America and Australia took their music with them, and it was absorbed into the culture of their destination. The result is that a fiddle player from the Appalachians would probably feel quite at home in a Donegal pub, and vice versa. Irish immigrants in fact often preserved traditions that died out at home, and music collected in America has greatly enriched the repertoire of Irish-based musicians.

Today Irish music and dance is widely taught in schools and has many enthusiasts. Young performers

A performance at a Fleadh Cheoil

compete for medals for singing, dancing and instrumental solos at a big gathering called a Fleadh Cheoil, literally 'feast of music'. Free displays of Irish dancing can be seen at most Irish outdoor summer events.

In the early 20th century, the depressed economy and widespread emigration, combined with the Church's objections to dancing as an incitement to immorality, threatened the survival of the Irish musical tradition. However, the folk-song boom, which originated in the USA with the Clancy Brothers, did much to revive it. The Dubliners re-established the city's lusty ballad and rebel song traditions, while bands like the Chieftains also recreated an authentic sound from days gone by. In the 1970s traditional groups like the Bothy Band and Planxty used modern recording techniques to create romantic 'Celtic' music, a path also followed by De Danaan, Enya and Altan, while the band Kila has added the beat of world music to the Irish sound.

Music in pubs

The impromptu 'session', in which a group of musicians improvise in a pub, is the best way to hear Irish music, and can happen at any time. Strongholds of traditional music are to be found in Donegal, Galway, Clare, Dingle and Slieve Luachra on the Cork–Kerry border. In addition, most cities have a few pubs specialising in traditional music, where a core

The Irish pub is often the place to find traditional Irish music – and great craic

group of musicians is employed on particular nights. Scheduled sessions usually start around 9.30 or 10pm.

A wide range of ages is to be found in the best of Irish sessions, with the younger musicians and singers learning from the older ones. Musicians usually perform 'sets', for example, two

Traditional Irish songs

Irish songs closely mirror the history of Ireland's people. The tradition of composing humorous or satirical ballads commemorating specific people or events (*Finnegans Wake*, for example), is alive and well. The older songs, with words in English or Irish, are generally love songs, like *She Moved through the Fair* (as recorded by Sinead O'Connor in 1997), and drinking songs, like *A Jug of Punch*. Rousing sea shanties, like *Fiddler's Green* and *The Holy Ground*, are perennially popular.

The 19th-century struggle for independence gave rise to 'Rebel Songs' and started with *A Nation Once Again*. These emotive songs are still sung with great fervour.

Emigration led to sad songs of yearning for home: *The Fields of Athenry*, *Carrickfergus*, *The Mountains of Mourne*. The words of the last are sung to an ancient Irish air, *Carrigdhoun*. *Danny Boy*, the saddest song of all, is sung to *The Londonderry Air*.

jigs, followed by a reel, the excitement building as the music speeds up. The musicians decide the order of play, and often take solo turns.

There is an etiquette to attending a pub session. You are expected to listen quietly and not to stare at the soloist: most people look at the floor. If you are enjoying an extended small session it is a courtesy to buy a round of drinks for the musicians. Everyone is expected to contribute to the entertainment on these occasions, so make sure someone in your group has a song prepared.

Certain pubs are especially good for hearing traditional music on a regular basis. In Dublin, **O'Donoghue's** (15 Merrion Row; tel: 01-676 2807; www.donoghues.ie) was the launching pad for The Dubliners and has sessions nightly from 9.30pm. **Hughes** (19 Chancery Street; tel: 01-872 6450) has sessions nightly from 10pm and is probably the best bet for good-quality music.

In Cork, the **Mills Inn** (Ballyvourney; tel: 026-45237), midway between Cork and Killarney, is a favourite with local Irish-speaking musicians, including Peadar Ó Riada. **Sin É** (Coburg Street; tel: 021-450 2266) in Cork city is known for live Irish music.

In the Galway area, pubs worth investigating include **Taafe's** (tel: 091-564 066) or **An Pucán** (tel: 091-561 528) in Galway city, or **Winkles Hotel** (tel: 091-637 137) at Kinvara on Galway Bay, which is famed for its music and big names, including local Sharon Shannon.

In County Clare, the village of **Doolin** has grown up around its three pubs all equally famous for traditional music. Start your pub crawl at **O'Connor's** (tel: 065-707 4168; www. oconnorspubdoolin.com). **Ennis** is also a small town with a strong musical

Matt Molloy's bar in Westport has an especially strong traditional music heritage

tradition. Try **Cruise's** (tel: 065-682 8693) or **Knox's** (tel: 065-682 9264).

Elsewhere in the country, **The Corner Bar** (tel: 074-954 1736) in Ardara, County Donegal, has music nightly in summer. **O'Flaherty's** (tel: 066-915 1983) in Dingle, County Kerry, has music most nights. **Matt Molloy's** (tel: 098-26655) in Westport, County Mayo, is owned by The Chieftains' flute player, Matt Molloy, and is renowned for great sessions.

Traditional music is less prevalent in Northern Ireland, but **White's Tavern** (2–12 Winecellar Entry; tel: 028-9024 3080; www.whitestavern.co.uk) in Belfast has traditional Irish sessions on Friday and Saturday nights.

If you are not near any of these pubs, try the website of traditional music specialists, **Comhaltas Ceoltóiri Eireann** (http://comhaltas. ie), which lists a network of local contacts for fans of traditional music.

Music at Fleadhs and festivals

Comhaltas Ceoltóiri Eireann runs the **Fleadh Cheoil** Irish music

Playing the harp at a Fleadh

competitions, which provide a huge array of free entertainment, both in competition and in street and pub sessions. The biggest is the **All-Ireland**, **Fleadh Cheoil na h Éireann** (www.fleadh2011.ie), a three-day event held in August in a different location every year, attracting around 10,000 musicians, many from overseas.

Song and dance

Musical instruments

The **harp** is a small triangular instrument, like the one in the logo for Guinness, held on the knee. **Tin whistles** are sold in souvenir shops, along with music. The **flute** is a simple wooden one. **Uilleann pipes** (pronounced ill-un), literally elbow pipes, are bagpipes, played with the bellows under one arm. They can create a beautiful, wistful sound, but are temperamental, and need careful 'warming up'. **Squeeze box** is the Irish term for a range of melodeons, accordions and concertinas, popular for dance music. The **fiddle**, usually played in a distinctive local style, is identical to the classical violin. The **bodhrán** (pronounced bow-*raun*) is a hand-held goatskin drum, reintroduced in the 1960s. **Spoons** (from the table) make a great percussion instrument. **Guitars**, **banjos** and **bazoukis** may also feature, but are shunned by the purists.

Many Irish singers and musicians got their first break playing Irish cabaret, which is put on during the summer, aimed firmly at visitors. It is a glitzy show of song, dance and comedy, featuring an impressive array of talent. Expect to pay about €55 a head for a four-course meal and two hours of good-natured live entertainment.

Medieval banquets with cabaret are held nightly at **Bunratty Castle, Knappogue Castle** and **Dungauire Castle** (tel: 061-360 788; www.shannonheritage. com; May–Sept). The same company also puts on a **Traditional Irish Night** at **Bunratty Folk Park**. They are very popular: book in advance online for the best deals.

In Dublin a traditional Irish cabaret night, with or without dinner, is held at a huge thatched pub, **Taylor's Three Rock** (Grange Road, Rathfarnham; tel: 01-494 2311; www.taylorsirishcabaret.ie; May–Sept).

In May every year, Ennis, County Clare, hosts the **Fleadh Nua** (www.flea dhnua.com), an eight-day celebration of dance and song, with workshops, concerts, competitions and ceilidhs. The main venue for concerts and competitions is **Glór Irish Music Centre** (tel: 065-684 3103; www.glor.ie). Check their schedule outside festival time.

Traditional Irish dancing in Galway

The Gathering (www.thegathering. ie) is a pre-St Patrick's Day weekend in Killarney with big-name concerts, ceilidh, set dancing workshops and numerous pub sessions.

The **Baltimore Fiddle Fair** takes place on the first weekend in May in intimate settings in this beautiful west Cork seaside village. These are concerts, workshops and sessions from an international array of musicians; www.fiddlefair.com.

The **Willie Clancy Summer School** (tel: 065-708 4148; www.oac.ie), held at Miltown Malbay in west Clare in early July, is the biggest traditional music summer school, with daily workshops and evening entertainment.

Ballyshannon Folk and Traditional Music Festival (www.ballyshannon folkfestival.com) in County Donegal showcases the best of Irish traditional and folk music over the first weekend in August.

Irish dancing

Irish dancing was reinvented by *Riverdance* in 1994 when its Chicago-born star Michael Flatley undid

A set dancing event in Co. Limerick

150 years of repression, and Irish dance suddenly became sexy again. The Irish have always been known for loving to dance. Because most Irish cottages had earth floors up until the late 19th century, dancers used wooden platforms or danced on barrel tops, or even, on occasion, the kitchen table, so that the noise of their feet tapping could serve as a drumbeat to the music. Even today the sound of an Irish dancer is an integral part of the performance.

This fast-moving, fleet-footed style of dancing is known as step dancing and is not to be confused with set dancing. Set dancing consists of four couples dancing in a square, and is essentially the French quadrille, adapted to Irish music and steps. It is easy to pick up, and it is more fun to do it than to watch. Free lessons are often given for visitors before a session, usually held in a pub or community hall.

Certain bars are known for set dancing, including **The Abbey Hotel** (Ballyvourney, County Cork; tel: 026-45324), **The Bridge Bar** (Portmagee, County Kerry; tel: 066-947-7108), **Hayden's Hotel** (Ballinasloe, County Galway; tel: 090-964 2347), **Ostán Loch Altan** (Gortahork, County Donegal; tel: 074-913 5267) and **Vaughan's Barn** (Kilfenora, County Clare; tel: 065-708 8004).

See **www.setdancingnews.net** for other venues. The same website also lists local ceilidh, often in a parish hall, where you will experience a simple, authentically Irish occasion, with singing and set dancing.

The most likely place to find a *Riverdance*-style step dancing show is at a cabaret night *(see box, opposite)*.

Walking the wilderness

Within half an hour of landing at any Irish airport, you can be walking in unspoilt wilderness. The sparsely populated Irish countryside is ideal walking territory, and has recently been enhanced by a network of way-marked routes and looped walks that will please both dedicated and fair-weather walkers.

Although small-scale in world terms, the hills and mountains of Ireland offer a wide range of terrain, from the exposed sandstone peaks of Cork and Kerry to the lush grass of the Glens of Antrim. With the country's highest mountain, Carrauntoohil, reaching only 1,039m (3,414ft), and a temperate climate, this is ideal walking territory.

What Irish peaks lack in height, they make up for in character. Many are topped by a cairn of stones, and often come with a legend or tradition attached. St Patrick's holy mountain, Croagh Patrick in Mayo, is still the venue for a traditional pilgrimage on the last Sunday in July, when many people make the three-hour circuit barefoot. Mount Brandon in Kerry is associated with St Brendan the Navigator, and can be climbed on a traditional pilgrim's path dating to early Christian times. Others, like the Twelve Bens in Connemara, under-pinned by granite, quartz and igne-ous rocks, and the granite Mourne Mountains in County Down, have a strong individual character. South of a line joining Limerick to Dublin, the retreat of glaciers in the Second Ice Age left huge boulders marooned, and created a striated landscape of unusual beauty, dotted with moun-tain lakes and deep corries.

The Mourne Mountains were the inspiraton for C.S. Lewis's *The Chronicles of Narnia*

Vegetation varies from flat black bogs, stretching as far as the eye can see, to the flaming reds of bracken in autumn and bright yellow gorse flow-ers in spring. Abundant wildlife is another attraction of the Irish wilder-ness *(see box, opposite)*.

Walking essentials

Locals have only recently taken to walking for recreation in any great numbers and do not have the long tradition of other countries: the majority of people use no equipment other than a good pair of walking boots, a map and a compass. Strong shoes or boots are essential for off-road walking in Ireland, due to the boggy nature of much of the ground. It is certainly advisable not walk off-road in Ireland in trainers or you'll get wet feet. Be sure to observe this simple rule, and you'll have a great time.

The unpredictable Irish climate, constantly changing due to weather coming in from the Atlantic, makes lightweight rainwear essential: rain is frequent, but it very seldom rains all day. Between April and October, the best time for walking, when the days are longer and the weather mild, you're more likely to have light showers followed by sun and perhaps a rainbow, adding to the beauty of the landscape.

Other than rainwear, nowadays many people stock their backpacks with warm clothing, gloves and hat, maps, compass and guidebook, and snacks such as chocolate or fruit, as well as a warm or hydrating drink, to provide energy to enjoy the walk to the full. A mobile phone is useful in an emergency, but network coverage can be poor in the mountains. You should leave word with someone of where you are going, and your approximate return time.

Carrying an OS map in the Discovery Series, drawn up to 1:50,000 scale, will not only keep you oriented: it will help you to locate ancient monuments, holy wells and

Exploring Clare Glen, one of the many delightful places to go walking

Walking the wilderness

Irish wildlife

Ireland became an island before Britain did, and this had an effect on its fauna. There are no weasels in Ireland, only the smaller Irish stoat. Neither, famously, are there any snakes. The Irish hare is not the English type, but a larger relative of the Scottish highland animal. Eagles have recently been reintroduced, with limited success, and the egret now inhabits southern areas. Deer roam free in Killarney National Park (dawn is a good time to see them) and elsewhere in Kerry you will encounter herds of wild goats. In Connemara wild ponies feed on seaweed as well as grass. Foxes are often seen, and seals bask on the western and southern coasts. There are no dangerous animals, but some visitors are disconcerted by the Irish habit of letting dogs run free. They are usually harmless: a stout stick is a good deterrent.

castles. You will also find on these maps scores of names that have come down from the mythological past or more recent days, tucked away into the crevices and foothills, such as Crotty's Rock, the Colleen Bawn Cottage and, at the summit of Slieve Guliion in south Armagh, Calliagh Berra's Lake. According to the legend, any man who swims in the lake comes out visibly aged.

Visitors are frequently surprised at how empty the country is, especially in the more remote walking areas along the southwest, west and northern coasts. On a typical day's walk you will probably meet more sheep than people and pass no shops or pubs.

Way-marked long-distance routes

There are now 43 way-marked trails in Ireland, offering over 3,000km (1,860 miles) of walking routes suitable for all ages and abilities: see **www.irishtrails.ie** for information. They are signposted with yellow arrows and a walking figure to guide you. However, you will still need a map of the trail (available locally) and an OS map, as the Irish system of way-marking is not totally consistent: signs can get covered by vegetation, or knocked down.

The network ranges from leisurely towpath strolls beside canals and rivers, walks along scenic coastal stretches, to circuits of high mountainous peninsulas. The Western Way, the Wicklow Way, the Beara Way and the Dingle Way are among the most scenic.

Looped walks

About 120 shorter, looped walks taking between 45 minutes and 4–5 hours have been set up around the country, usually starting and finishing at a (free) car park. The **Lighthouse Loop** at the Sheep's Head Peninsula on Bantry Bay, a two-hour walk along rough grassy paths classified as 'hard', is nevertheless one of the most popular. A less challenging option is the **Jenkinstown Wood Walled Garden Loop** in County Kilkenny, a one-hour walk classed as 'easy'. Some of these walks are in Ireland's National Parks. Walking maps and information can be downloaded before setting out at **www.discoverireland.ie/walking**.

The lighthouse on the Sheep's Head Peninsula, Co. Cork

Elevated view of the Poison Glen Donegal

Recommended walks

All Irish walks have something special to offer, but some are more special than others. Here is a selection of the cream of the crop:

The Atlantic is never out of sight on the five-hour **Burren Coastal Walk** (County Clare), which takes you along a stunning stretch of coastline from Black Head to Doolin. It features a variety of terrain including limestone pavement, beaches, grass and sand dunes, all offering pleasant walking amongst the grey stone walls and rocks.

The 8km (5-mile) route to the top of **Diamond Hill** (County Galway) starts from the visitor centre in **Connemara National Park**. From the cairn on the cone-shaped summit at 442m (1,460ft) there is a breathtaking view of islands, bays, beaches, loughs and mountains.

The **Brandy Pad** route in County Down follows an old smuggler's path across the northern section of the Mourne Mountains for 11km (7 miles). It is not overly strenuous, but you are still rewarded with spectacular views across Ulster's highest mountain range.

Errigal Mountain (County Donegal) is a favourite with many. Start from Dunlewy at the car park on the R521. After crossing heathery slopes you will reach firmer footing as it turns into a relatively easy walk through rocks and loose stone to the top, for a view that takes in a large area of the northwest of Ireland.

The **Slieve Bloom Way** (Counties Laois and Offaly) is a 70km (43-mile) route that makes a circuit of an isolated range of mountains in central Ireland and takes two days. There are panoramic views from the tracks through bogland and low hills, much wildlife, and the climbs are not too strenuous.

Walking holidays

Get ahead of the pack by booking a specialised holiday, guided by local experts. **Connemara Safari Walking Holidays** (tel: 096-952 1071; www.walkingconnemara.com) offer a five-day 'Walking and Island Hopping Tour' of the west coast of Ireland, starting in Clifden. Small groups are led by archaeologist Gerry McCloskey.

A week-long walking tour with **Croagh Patrick Walking Tours** (tel: 098-26090) is based in the Clew Bay Hotel, Westport, and visits Clare Island, Croagh Patrick, Kylemore Abbey and Connemara.

Wilderness Walking Tours (tel: 094-954 6089; www.conghostelwilder nesswalkingtours.com), based at Cong Hostel, County Mayo, is a budget option for two- or three-day weekends with guided walks.

Heart of Burren Walks (tel: 065-682 7707; www.heartofburrenwalks):

author and guide Tony Kirby takes walks out almost daily, ranging from gentle strolls to challenging hill walks. He is an expert on The Burren's limestone landscape and unique history. Walking weekends

Sticks for sale, intended to help pilgrims climb Croaghpatrick Mountain

STICKS

PURCHASE €2.00

Wild horses can be seen near Clifden, Connemara

(May–Sept) are based at the historic Old Ground Hotel, Ennis.

Walking and Talking in Ireland (tel: 074-915 9366; www.walktalk ireland.com) is a Donegal-based company offering guided walking holidays in Donegal and Antrim.

Wonderful Ireland (tel: 087-761 3344; www.wakingholiday.ie) offers walking holidays along the Wicklow Way, the Dingle Way and the Kerry Way, with baggage transfer and accommodation in carefully chosen guesthouses.

When a walk becomes a festival

Walking festivals generally take place at weekends, and are usually mounted to attract visitors to the area to benefit local businesses. In turn, the visitors benefit from discovering interesting new routes and learning about them first-hand from enthusiastic locals. Walking festivals usually make a small charge for walks led by local guides, who talk about heritage sites, archaeology and geology, as well as the wild flowers and birdlife. The social side of the festival centres on free pub entertainment, providing a good way to make new friends.

There are more than 30 walking festivals across the year (see www. discoverireland.com), including the **Ballyhoura International Walking Festival** in the Ballyhoura and Galtee Mountains on the Cork–Tipperary border, the **Castlebar International Four Days Walks** in County Mayo, and the **Strolls in the Sperrins Festival** in mid-Ulster, which will introduce you to a sprawling, sparsely populated mountain range.

The Irish pub

The 'Irish pub' has conquered the world, and in its original habitat the pub continues to be the hub of the community's social life, whether in the city or the country. Many pubs have modernised, but there are still traditional gems to be discovered, where time seems to have stood still.

The Irish pub is one of the nation's most famous exports – along with that beloved Irish stout, Guinness. There are more than 1,000 'traditional' Irish pubs overseas, from Durty Nellie's in Amsterdam to Finnegan's in Abu Dhabi, and indeed, brewers set up companies to export the Irish pub concept, supplying standard models complete with (fake) decor. But for the genuine experience, you still need to make your way to the Emerald Isle.

In Ireland, decor is usually a random result of years of tradition, rather than interior designers. A real Irish pub is not just a place to go for a drink: it is a social institution, where the banter among patrons is as much a part of the experience as the drink. This is the famous Irish 'craic', the party atmosphere that builds when people meet not just to drink, but to gossip and interact with each other, and visitors should be prepared to join in if the occasion arises. But pubs can also be quiet places, where you can read a book or newspaper in peace.

Until the 1960s, pubs were predominantly a male bastion, with wooden floors sprinkled with sawdust (to absorb any spills) and hard benches or tall stools for the few who chose to sit. The small bar area

Enjoying Irish coffee and a hot cider in a Galway pub

was often supplemented by snugs, areas where people could drink privately, which vary from a tiny two-person space to a large, screened-off table. Traditionally snugs were used by priests, policemen and women, who did not want to cause gossip by being seen in a pub. Snugs were also places of business, where confidential deals could be discussed without giving rise to gossip.

Guinness barrels stacked outside the Doheny & Nesbitt's pub in Dublin

Many pubs modernised in the late 1960s by creating a lounge bar, a smart, carpeted area with upholstered seats, aimed at making women more comfortable. Today, pubs are largely privately owned, often by a family, and most welcome accompanied children until 7pm. Pubs, especially in rural Ireland, are often the only meeting point in the community, and serve as informal information points, where you will hear all about what is on in the area, from sports to entertainment.

The smoking ban, drink-driving laws and the high tax on alcohol have forced about 1,500 pubs out of business, but that still leaves about 7,500 of them, with over 800 in Dublin alone. Those that survive often offer tempting bar food, coffee from an espresso machine and big-screen sports TV.

City pubs

Dublin is the place to seek out classic old wooden bars, the decor untouched down the years, with creamy pints of stout giving an acrid whiff to the air. They have a well-lived-in look, decked out in brass and mahogany with antique mirrors proclaiming the merits of whiskeys long since gone. **Neary's** (1 Chatham Street; tel: 01-677 7371), has an ornate Victorian interior and is frequented by actors from the nearby Gaiety Theatre. **Doheny & Nesbitt's** (5 Lower Baggot Street; tel: 01-676 2945; www.dohenyandnesbitts. com) has some fine wooden snugs, and is known for political gossip. **O'Donoghue's** (15 Merrion Row; tel: 01-676 2807; www.odonoghues.ie), was where the Dubliners first played, and is still good for impromptu music sessions. The **Stag's Head** (1 Dame Court; tel: 01-679 3701) is famed for its Victorian interior with mosaic floor and marble bar.

Belfast is also richly endowed with traditional pubs, but the most visited and perhaps iconic remains the **Crown Liquor Saloon** (46 Great Victoria Street; tel: 028-9024 9476; www.nationaltrust.org.uk), a large hostelry with a dazzling Victorian interior, in which every possible surface is embossed, etched, panelled, carved or polished.

Smaller cities all have at least one pub frequented by local artists, writers and musicians. Galway's **Tigh Neachtain** (Cross Street, Galway; tel: 091-568 820) is a good example, with its old-fashioned painted wood interior and tiny snugs. Cork's equivalent would be **The Corner House** (7 Coburg Street; tel: 021-450 0655), while the wood-panelled **Hargadon's** (O'Connell Street; tel: 071-915 3709; www.hargadons.com) is the HQ of Sligo's Boho/artistic crowd.

Country pubs

Small-town pubs have an unpredictable charm, often not opening until late afternoon. **O Loclainn's** (Ballyvaughan, County Clare), a carefully preserved country pub, opens at 9pm as the owner farms during the day. **MacCarthy's Bar** (Castletownbere, County Cork; tel: 027-70014; *see box, opposite*) doubles as a busy grocery store. **Dick Mack's** (Dingle, County Kerry; tel: 066-915 1960; www.dickmacks.homestead.com) was once a cobbler's, and still sells leather goods as well as pints.

Scenic pubs

For some pubs, location is a large part of the attraction. A glass of Guinness and a plate of oysters with brown soda bread outside **Moran's of the Weir** (Kilcolgan, County Galway; tel: 091-796 113; www.moransoystercottage.com), watching the swans gliding on the weir, is an unforgettable experience.

Many Irish quays have bars on them, including the **Bulman Bar** (Kinsale, County Cork; tel: 021-477 2131), where locals gather on long summer evenings to drink outside and watch the sun set. **Sean's Bar** (Main Street, Athlone, County Westmeath; tel: 090-649 2358), reputedly the oldest boozer in Britain or Ireland, has direct access for boaters on the River Shannon through its garden and back bar. The **Dunraven Arms** (Main Street, Adare, County Limerick; tel: 061-605 900;

A traditional serving hatch at Dick Mack's

www.dunravenhotel.com), originally a coaching inn, is now a luxury hotel, but has retained its old-fashioned bar, and added a conservatory that overlooks a pretty rose garden, the perfect place for a light lunch.

Unmissable traditional pubs

For when only a quintessential Irish pub will do, there are several that really stand out. **P.J. O'Hare's Anchor Bar** (Carlingford, County Louth; tel: 042-937 3106) has been in the family for 150 years and is decorated with pub mirrors and curios. On sunny Sunday afternoons the yard becomes a dance area. **Morrissey's** (Main Street, Abbeyleix, County Laois; tel: 0502-31281) opened as a grocery in 1775 and is now solely a pub, with the air of a venerable institution. **Nancy's** (Front Street, Ardara, County Donegal; tel: 074-954 1187) is a tiny bar, now in the seventh generation of family ownership. Seafood is a speciality and music is played.

Traditional pubs are often the best places to catch performances of Irish music and dancing *(see p.39)*. Sessions can happen at any time of day in places like **Matt Molloy's** *(see p.41)*; its

The immortalised MacCarthy's Bar in Castletownbere

owner plays with the Chieftains, one of Ireland's leading bands. Even in the middle of the afternoon, a music session can suddenly take over. Another musically-minded place is **Anderson's Thatch Pub** (Elphin Road, Carrick-on-Shannon, County Rosommon; tel: 087-228 3288; www.andersonpub. com), which dates back to 1760, and has an owner who plays 11 instruments. Music sessions are scheduled for Wednesdays and Saturdays.

McCarthy's Bar

Many are the visitors of Irish descent who delight in posing for a picture outside a pub bearing their name: O'Neill or O'Donovan, McGann or MacNamara. The English travel writer and comedian Pete McCarthy based his book *McCarthy's Bar* (2000), on a simple rule, 'Never Pass a Bar That Has Your Name On It.' Born in Warrington to an Irish mother and an English father, McCarthy's erratic progress around Ireland, following his own rule, led him to Castletownbere and a welcoming family-run bar-grocery with his name on (ignoring a slight spelling discrepancy), that still supplies the fishing port's trawlers with their shopping. As well as an entertaining read, his story is an increasingly nostalgic record of the Irish country pub in its prime.

Literary Ireland

Whether in the theatre or in the street, in parliament or in the pub, the Irish are renowned for having the gift of the gab. No wonder, then, that this small island punches well above its weight when it comes to literary talent, which has included James Joyce, Oscar Wilde, W.B. Yeats, Samuel Beckett and George Bernard Shaw.

The Irish love telling stories, as you will quickly discover, and many people are very good at it. This is probably one of the reasons that Irish writers are so popular all over the world. Before the age of mass literacy, travelling storytellers – *seannachie* (pronounced shan-ah-key) – entertained in homes and pubs, with high-spirited impromptu performances. This oral tradition lies behind the good-natured banter of Irish stand-up comedians and broadcasters, many of whom gain huge popularity in the UK and further afield.

In Celtic society, the poet was greatly esteemed for his wisdom and learning, and poets still hold a special place in Irish society. The Irish language survived despite invasions by the Vikings and Normans, and the arrival of English and Scottish settlers. In the mid-19th century, English became the language of commerce and modernity, and was taught in the National School system, inaugurated in 1831. The effects of the 1845–9 great famine and the mass emigration which followed contributed to a dramatic fall in Irish language-speakers.

However, as Ireland established its independence in the 20th century, interest in the native language increased. It is compulsory in schools, and around 15 percent of the

Dublin has many great bookshops

population have reasonably fluent Irish. The everyday use of Irish is fostered in areas along the western seaboard, known as Gaeltacht, including Dingle, the Aran Islands and parts of Connemara and Donegal, and it is the main language of about 92,000 people.

A legacy of the Irish-speaking past remains in the subtly different way that the Irish use the English language, under the influence of Irish language constructions, a linguistic phenomenon known as Hiberno-

English. There are two main strands that characterise this – the persistence in everyday speech of words now obsolete in standard English, and syntax influenced by characteristics of the Irish language. For instance, there is no word for 'yes' or 'no' in Irish, so questions are often answered with affirmative verbs, such as 'I am', 'I have' or 'I have not'.

If you travel on public transport, you will see how much Irish people enjoy reading. Moreover, you will discover that many of them write poetry or fiction. These shared literary ambitions perhaps explain why while successful writers are greatly admired, nobody is overawed by them. The most famous are always spoken of by first name only: Seamus, for Seamus Heaney, Ireland's most recent Nobel Laureate, Neil for filmmaker and writer Neil Jordan, and Roddy for Roddy Doyle, chronicler of contemporary working-class Dublin.

Dublin writers

When Dublin was designated the fourth Unesco City of Literature, in recognition of both its literary past

Your guides on the Dublin Literary Pub Crawl

and the vibrant contemporary scene, Dubliners took it in their stride, as being only right and proper. After all, Ireland produced four 20th-century winners of the Nobel Prize for literature: George Bernard Shaw (1856–1950), W.B. Yeats (1865–39), Samuel Beckett (1906–1989) and Seamus Heaney (b. 1939). Shaw and Beckett were born in Dublin (though

Literary Ireland

Literary pub crawl

The **Dublin Literary Pub Crawl** (starting at the Duke Pub, Duke Street; www.dublinpubcrawl.com; 087-263 0270; Apr–Oct daily, 7.30pm; Nov–Mar, Thur–Sun, 7.30pm) is a lively and accessible piece of street theatre: a pair of actors leads a small group around a half-mile circuit adjacent to Trinity College, visiting four pubs along the way, while entertaining the audience with anecdotes and quotes from Dublin's famous writers.

No prior knowledge of Irish writing is needed, but by the end of the tour you will want to read at least some of the books by the authors mentioned, who include Oscar Wilde, J.P. Donleavy, James Joyce, Sean O'Casey and Brendan Behan. About 20 minutes is spent in each pub, and there is finger food at the second stop: as well as introducing a bevy of writers, the tour also gives a great insight into Dublin pub culture past and present.

they lived, respectively, in London and Paris), while Yeats and Heaney both adopted Dublin as their home.

Discover more about these and other Irish writers with Dublin connections including Sean O'Casey, Brendan Behan and Flann O'Brien at the **Dublin Writers' Museum** (Parnell Square; tel: 01-872 2077; www.writersmuseum.com; Mon–Sat 10am–5pm, until 6pm June–Aug, Sun 11am–5pm; charge).

Trinity College

Because **Trinity College** was the only university in Ireland up until the mid-19th century, many Irish writers studied there, including Jonathan Swift (1667–1745), satirist and author of *Gulliver's Travels* (he was also Dean of St Patrick's Cathedral, Dublin, where he is buried). Oscar Wilde was a promising boxer during his time at Trinity, while Samuel Beckett was on the cricket team. Walk through the cobbled quadrangle and observe today's students hurrying to and from lectures, or sunbathing on the grass outside the Berkeley Library, a modern building named for another illustrious alumnus, the philosopher George Berkeley (1685–1753). There is nearly always a queue for the **Long Room** (tel: 01-896 1171; www.tcd.ie/library; Mon–Sat 9.30am–5pm Oct–May, Sun noon–4.30pm, June–Sept, Sun 9.30am–4.30pm; charge) where the Book of Kells, one of the most beautifully illuminated manuscripts in the world, is displayed.

James Joyce and Bloomsday

The action of James Joyce's great modernist novel *Ulysses* (1922) takes place in Dublin on 16 June 1904, and follows the characters' journeys around the city, in a rough parallel to the voyage of Homer's *Odyssey*. Joyce's intermingling of fact and fiction is the subject of displays at the **James Joyce Centre** (35 North Great George's Street; tel: 01-878 8547; www.jamesjoyce.ie; Mon–Sat 10am–5pm; charge) in a fine Georgian house.

Whether they have read Joyce's novel or not, Dubliners celebrate 16 June, known as 'Bloomsday', after the novel's main character, Leopold Bloom, in great style. Edwardian costume is worn by many, as they re-enact scenes from the novel in the actual places described in the book. The best way to take part is to join one of the organised walks: see **www.jamesjoyce.ie** for details.

In costume for Bloomsday at the James Joyce statue off O'Connell Street

Dublin theatre

A night at the theatre while in Dublin could be the highlight of your visit. The National Theatre performs in Dublin's **Abbey Theatre** (www.abbey theatre.ie), a modernist concrete building dating from 1966. But the interesting repertoire and high standard of performance compensate for the plain surroundings, while seats are affordable and usually bookable at short notice. The **Gate Theatre** (tel: 01-874 4045; www.gatetheatre. ie) occupies a classic 18th-century building near Parnell Square, and has a high reputation for adventurous productions, chiefly of contemporary plays, including the works of Samuel Beckett, Harold Pinter and Brian Friel.

The Gate Theatre is known for its creative productions of modern plays

The poet Yeats

Although William Butler Yeats (1865–1939) had a home in Dublin, he is more closely associated with Sligo, his mother's birthplace, whose geography features prominently in his early poems, most famously *The Lake Isle of Innisfree*. Sligo hosts the **Yeats International Summer School** annually in August (www.yeats-sligo.com),

Ireland's top five bookshops

- **Hodges Figgis**, 56–58 Dawson Street, Dublin 2; tel: 01-677 4754; www.waterstones.com. The original Hodges Figgis is mentioned in Joyce's *Ulysses*; it is now the only branch of Waterstones in Dublin, an impressive modern shop with four floors, stocking over 60,000 titles.

- **The Gutter Bookshop**, Cow's Lane, Temple Bar, Dublin; tel: 01-679 9206; www.gutterbookshop.com. Award-winning independent bookshop in trendy Temple Bar, inspired by Oscar Wilde's remark: 'We are all in the gutter, but some of us are looking at the stars.'

- **Charlie Byrne's**, Middle Street, Galway; tel: 091-561 766; www.charliebyrne. com. With a stock of over 50,000 new, used, second-hand and remaindered books, many at give-away prices, few leave empty-handed.

- **Keohane's**, Castle Street, Sligo; tel: 071-914 2597; www.keohanesbookshop. com. Michael Keohane and his staff are all avid readers, and claim to stock 'good books rather than bestsellers'.

- **Bookfinders Café**, 47 University Road, Belfast; tel: 028-9032 8269. Features a good selection of second-hand books, and also serves food and wine.

which attracts academics and students from all over the world. If you have a serious interest in poetry, it will be a treat. A sign-posted Yeats Drive around Lough Gill near Sligo passes Innisfree, and other locations named in the poems. His grave, with its startling inscription 'Cast a cold eye on life, on death; Horseman, pass by,' is beside Drumcliff Church near Sligo.

Yeats married at 52, and ever the romantic, converted a ruined castle for his 25-year old bride, Georgie Hyde-Lees. **Thoor Ballylee** (Gort, County Galway; tel: 091-631 436; June–Sept Mon–Sat 9.30am–5pm; charge) is a Norman tower house situated beside a peaceful river deep in the Galway countryside. It still contains the traditional cottage-style furniture designed by the poet, and a visit brings the poet and his work vividly to life.

The Irish language tradition

One of the last bastions of the Irish language was An Bhlascaoid Mhóir (the Great Blasket), an island near Dún Chaoin, Dingle. An Irish-speaking community of fishermen and farmers lived there until 1953. The islanders were great storytellers and

made a lasting contribution to Irish literature. *The Islandman* by Tomás Ó Crohan (1937) describes a hard way of life virtually unchanged for centuries. Today you can take the 20-minute ferry to the **Great Blasket** (Easter–Sept; tel: 086-335 3805; www.blasket islands.ie), visit the largely ruined village and walk the narrow paths that encircle the rocky island, absorbing a

The status of local son Yeats in Sligo town

Books for sale at a stall in Temple Bar, Dublin

peaceful ambience seldom found in modern times. **Ionad An Bhlascaoid Mhóir** (The Great Blasket Centre; tel: 066-915 6444; www.heritageireland.ie; Apr–Oct daily 10am–6pm; charge) on the mainland has interesting exhibits about the islanders.

Literary festivals

Readings and literary festivals are relaxed events in Ireland, where nobody pulls rank, and everybody waits their turn to order a drink. They provide a great way to meet people with a common interest.

Listowel Writers' Week (www.writersweek.ie) features week-long literary workshops, in which established writers share their skills, poetry and short story competitions, and big-name readings. It is held annually in late May, and is known for its friendliness. Also in Listowel, the **Kerry Writers' Museum** (tel: 068-22212; www. kerrywritersmuseum.com; charge) celebrates Kerry writers, including John B. Keane, whose play *The Field* was subsequently filmed, and Maurice Walsh, who wrote the story on which director John Ford based *The Quiet Man*.

Cúirt International Festival of Literature (www.cuirt.ie) takes over Galway's compact historic centre in mid-April for an intensive week of readings, performance and public interviews with Irish and international writers. It's a great place to make friends.

Belfast Festival at Queen's (www. belfastfestival.com), held annually in mid-October, always has a strong literary programme, given the close connection between Queen's and the new generation of Irish poets, including Michael Longley, Paul Muldoon and Seamus Heaney. Also at Queen's, check out free literary events year-round at the **Seamus Heaney Centre** (www.qub.ac.uk/heaneycentre).

PLACES

Dublin – *p.64* The southeast – *p.96* County Cork – *p.112*
The southwest – *p.128* Limerick and the Shannon – *p.150*

The west – Galway and Mayo – *p.170* **Inland Ireland** – *p.188*
The northwest – *p.202* **Belfast** – *p.218* **Northern Ireland** – *p.234*

Getting your bearings

Situated on the western extremity of Europe, the island of Ireland is 486km (301 miles) long and 275km (171 miles) wide. Northern Ireland, in the northeast corner, is part of the United Kingdom; its capital is Belfast and its currency is the British pound. The rest of the island consists of the 32 counties of the Republic of Ireland, which has Dublin as its capital and the euro as its currency. The island consists of a low-lying central plain and a discontinuous border of coastal mountains. In Celtic times, Ireland was divided into four provinces: Ulster (north), Leinster (east), Munster (south) and Connaught (west).

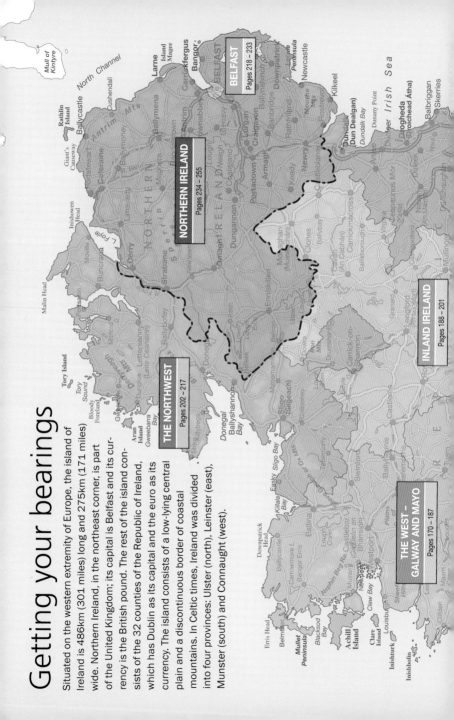

BELFAST
Pages 218 – 233

NORTHERN IRELAND
Pages 234 – 255

THE NORTHWEST
Pages 202 – 217

INLAND IRELAND
Pages 188 – 201

THE WEST – GALWAY AND MAYO
Pages 170 – 187

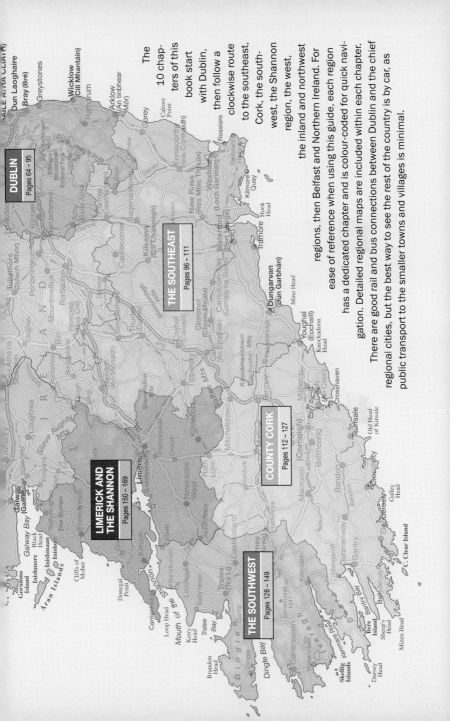

The 10 chapters of this book start with Dublin, then follow a clockwise route to the southeast, Cork, the southwest, the Shannon region, the west, the inland and northwest regions, then Belfast and Northern Ireland. For ease of reference when using this guide, each region has a dedicated chapter and is colour-coded for quick navigation. Detailed regional maps are included within each chapter. There are good rail and bus connections between Dublin and the chief regional cities, but the best way to see the rest of the country is by car, as public transport to the smaller towns and villages is minimal.

DUBLIN
Pages 64 – 95

THE SOUTHEAST
Pages 96 – 111

COUNTY CORK
Pages 112 – 127

THE SOUTHWEST
Pages 128 – 149

LIMERICK AND THE SHANNON
Pages 150 – 169

 # Dublin

With its vibrant mix of traditional pubs, fashionable bars, elegant Georgian architecture, cool shops and a colourful cultural scene to rival any European capital, Dublin bubbles with an infectious energy. The vivacity of its citizens and the hospitality they show to visitors have made this lively city on the Liffey one of Europe's most popular destinations.

Dublin

Population: 1.1 million (Great Dublin area 1.7 million)

Local dialling code: 01

Local tourist office: Dublin Tourism Centre, St Andrew's Church, Suffolk Street; 01-605 7700; **www.visit dublin.ie**

Main police station: Phoenix Park; tel: 01-666 0000

Main post office: General Post Office, O'Connell Street

Main hospital: Mater Misericordiae University Hospital, Eccles Street; tel: 01-803 2000; **www.mater.ie**

Media: *The Evening Herald*; **www. herald.ie**. For full entertainment listings pick up a copy of the monthly *Totally Dublin*, or consult it online at **www.totallydublin.ie**

The Irish capital is full of life, from the café-packed side streets around Grafton Street to the African and Asian stores that rub shoulders with traditional street traders on Moore Street. Culturally, the city is famed throughout the world for its rich theatre, literature, art and music, which is no surprise considering that some of Europe's most famous artists, writers and musicians – including Francis Bacon, James Joyce, W.B. Yeats, Brendan Behan and, of course, U2 – hail from here.

As a city, Dublin means different things to different people. For some it's an inspirational centre of historic treasures, from ancient Viking sites to the grand Georgian townhouses that give the city its grace and beauty. For others, it is a city of talkers, its pubs overflowing with Guinness and a distinctive atmosphere that makes locals believe Dublin pubs are the best in the world.

South of the Liffey: Georgian Dublin

Dublin is divided by the River Liffey, which flows through its centre, creating two distinct Dublins, according to its natives: the affluent and fashionable 'southside', and the more commercial, traditionally working-class 'northside'. Northsiders see themselves as authentic 'Dubs', while the better-off, more bourgeois southsiders 'wouldn't be seen dead on the northside? Like all generalisations, there are numerous exceptions, but even the casual visitor will notice a different character to the shops and pubs on either side of the river.

College Green

College Green contains two of Dublin's most impressive and historic buildings: the Bank of Ireland and Trinity College. With its curving, columnar, windowless facade, the building occupied by the **Bank of Ireland** ❶ (tel: 01-661 5933; www.visitdublin.com; Mon–Fri 10am–4pm, Thur until 5pm; free; guided tours Tue 10.30am, 11.30am and 1.45pm) was begun in 1729 to house the Irish parliament, whose builders could not have foreseen how brief its age of glory would be. The bank moved in when parliament was

View of Trinity College courtyard

abolished by the Act of Union in 1801 *(see p.281)*. The statue of Henry Grattan, the parliament's greatest orator, stands in the middle of College Green, in mid-gesture, apparently delivering one of his ringing speeches. The tradition was continued when Barack Obama addressed the Irish nation from the steps of the bank in 2011, after visiting his 'Irish roots' in County Offaly.

Trinity College

Founded by Queen Elizabeth I in 1592, **Trinity College** ❷ is a timeless enclave of calm and scholarship in the middle of this bustling city. For centuries it was an exclusively Protestant institution. The restriction on Catholic students was lifted in 1873, but it is only since 1970 that Catholics have attended in substantial numbers. Today, students of TCD, as it is known, lead informative college tours (mid-May–Sept, every 40 minutes from 10.15am; charge) from a desk at the front arch of the college. Most of Trinity's buildings date from the 18th century. The entrance is flanked by statues

Dublin

Georgian doorway on Merrion Square

Dublin

Botanic Gardens, Glasnevin Cemetery ↑

0 — 200 m
0 — 200 yds

Tram Line and Station

N

St Brendan's Hospital

St Brendan's Hospital

Prussia

Aughrim Street

Manor Street

Stoneybatter

North Circular Road

Ross Street

Oxmantown Road

Ben Edar Rd

Halliday Rd

Harold Rd

Ivar Street

Manor Place

Mount Temple Rd

Sitric Road

Arc-High Rd

Kirwan Street

Grangegorman Upper

Grangegorman Lower

King's Inns

Constitution Hill

Church St Upper

Coleraine St

North

Brunswick Street North

King Street

Bow Street

Bereton St

Greek St

Mary's

O'Devaney Gardens

Aberdeen St

Infirmary Road

Montpelier Gardens

Arbour Hill

Place

Queen Street

Blackhall

Hendrick Street

Smithfield

The Chimney 36

Old Jameson Distillery 35

St Michan's

May Lane

Four Courts Chancery

Dublin Criminal Courts Complex

Montpelier Hill

National Museum of Decorative Arts & History (Collins Barracks) 37

Incorporated Law Society

Parkgate Street

Benburb Street

Museum

Smithfield

St Paul
Arran Quay

Hammond Lane

Four Courts 34

Inns Quay

Chancery Pl

Winetavern

Phoenix Park

Wolfe Tone Quay

Ellis Quay

Heuston

St John's Road West

Heuston Station

St John's Road West

Victoria Quay

Usher's Island

Island Street

Usher's Quay

Liffey

Usher's Island

Island Street

Merchants Quay

Brazen Head

Franciscan Church

St Augustine Street

Bridge Street

Cook Street

Dublinia & The Viking World

High St

Irish Museum of Modern Art

LUAS Tram (Red Line)

Steevens's Lane

Guinness Brewery (St James's Gate Brewery)

Military Road

Bow Lane West

St Patrick's Tower

Watling Street

Bonham Street

Bridgefoot Street

Usher

Oliver Bond Street

John Street West

Cornmarket

St Audoen

An Taisce (Tailors' Hall)

Iveagh Market

Back Lane

Nicholas St

National College of Art and Design

Thomas Street West

St Catherine

Crane St

Hanbury Lane

St Augustine and St John

Francis Street

Meath Street

Kilmainham Gaol

James's Street

St Lwr

James's

Basin Street Upper

St James's

Robert Street

Rainsford Street

Guinness Storehouse 21

Bellevue

Bond St

Newport St

Pim St

Marrowbone Lane

Earl St South

Meath Place

Pimlico

Swift's Alley

St Nicholas of Myra

John Dillon St

St Patrick's Cathedral

Convent

St James's Hospital

Fatima

Our Lady's Rd

Summer St South

John Street South

Ardee St

The Coombe

Carman's Hall

Dean St

Patrick

Rialto

St James's Walk

Lourdes Rd

Rosary Rd

Cork Street

Brown Street South

Newmarket

Ward's Hill

Mill Street

Chamber St

Fumbally La

New Street South

New Row South

Rialto Street

St Anthony's Rd

Reuben Street

Dolphin's Barn Street

Cameron St

O'Thomas Rd

O'Curry Road

Susan Ter

Donore Avenue

Clarence Mangan Road

Malpas St

Blackpitts

Clanbrassil Street Lower

Daniel St

South Circular Road

Reuben Ave

Donore Rd

O'Donovan Road

DOLPHIN'S BARN

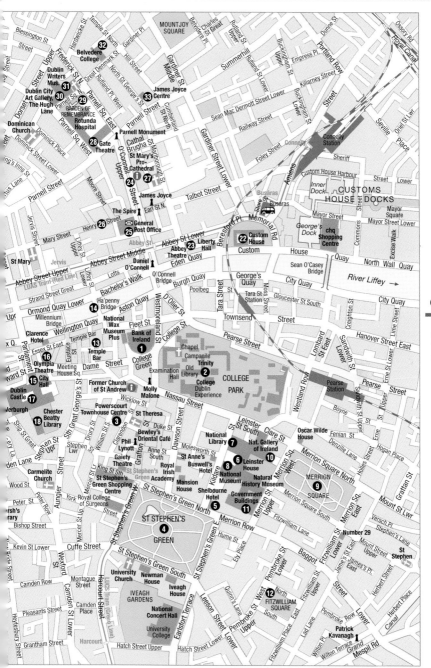

Dublin

Airport: Dublin International Airport; tel: 01-814 1111; **www.dublinairport.com**; 12km (7½ miles) north of the city. Transport to the city centre: Dublin Bus Airlink: every 10 minutes, Mon–Sat 5.45am–11.30pm, Sun 7.30am–11.30pm; **www.dublinbus.ie**; €6 single, €10 return. Taxi: 30 minutes; about €25

 Ferries: Dublin Ferry Port; tel: 01-887 6000; **www.dublinport.ie**; close to the city centre with frequent bus connections. Dun Laoghaire Ferry Port; tel: 01-280 1018; **www.dharbour.ie**; 12km (7 miles) south of the city centre; has frequent light rail connections (DART)

 Trains: Trains from Cork and Kerry arrive into Heuston Station, 3km (2 miles) west of the city centre, with frequent bus and tram connections. Trains from Belfast, Sligo and Rosslare terminate at Connolly Station, which has bus, DART and tram connections. Dublin Area Rapid Transport (DART) is operated by Irish Rail; tel: 01-836 6222; **www.irishrail.ie**

 Buses: Bus, DART and LUAS tickets can be bought from most newsagents, and at the stations for DART and LUAS. You can also pay on board buses. One-, three- or seven-day travel cards for bus and LUAS offer the best value, and include the hop-on-hop-off service connecting the main visitor attractions. Buses are operated by Dublin Bus (Bus Átha Cliath), O'Connell Street; tel: 01-873 4222; **www.dublinbus.ie**. Exact change is required on board; no notes accepted. Within the city centre the fare is 50 cents; from Heuston Station to the centre is €1.20. Express services arrive at the central bus station, Busáras, Store Street (behind the Custom House)

 Trams: The Dublin LUAS tram system connects the outer suburbs to the city centre, and links Heuston Station with Busáras. In Ireland tel: 1800-300 604; **www.luas.ie**

 Bicycles: Dublin Bikes can be hired and returned to 44 stations around the city. A three-day ticket costs €2. See **www.dublinbikes.ie**

 Car-hire companies: Renting a car in Dublin is expensive, the traffic system is complicated and congested, and parking is pricey. Try, therefore, only to hire a car when leaving the city for the rest of Ireland. Shop around for the best deals at **www.carhireireland.com** (online only). Budget: in Ireland tel: 1850-575 767; **www.budget.com**

 Taxis: Taxis can be hired at taxi ranks, but at peak times book by phone. Eight Twenty Cabs; tel: 01-820 2020; **www.8202020.ie**

of two of Trinity's many famous alumni, the historian and statesman Edmund Burke (1729–97) and the writer Oliver Goldsmith (1728–74). The porch inside the main gate leads to a spacious, cobbled quadrangle dominated by a campanile, some 30m (100ft) high.

The greatest treasures are in the vaulted Long Room of the **Old Library** (tel: 01-896 2320; www.tcd.ie; Mon–Sat 9.30am–5pm, Sun 9.30am–4.30pm, Oct–Apr Sun noon–4.30pm; charge), where double-decker shelving holds thousands of books published before 1800. In the adjacent

Busker on Grafton Street

Colonnades Gallery, queues of tourists reverently wait for a look at the Book of Kells. This magnificently ornate 9th-century manuscript copy of the Gospels in Latin forms the greatest expression of the flowering of Irish culture between the 7th and 9th centuries, the era of 'the land of saints and scholars.'

Grafton Street

Grafton Street, just outside Trinity's main gate, is the southside's principal shopping thoroughfare, a pedestrianised street teeming with people. Buskers entertain passers-by on their way to the famous Brown Thomas department store and other shopping emporiums. Follow Johnston's Court, a narrow alley on the right, for the stunning **Powerscourt Townhouse Centre ❸** (South William Street; tel: 01-679 700 059) – three storeys of stylish shops and cafés in a mansion built in 1774 for Viscount Powerscourt.

St Stephen's Green

St Stephen's Green ❹ is a relaxing refuge with delightful gardens and ducks on the lake. During the 18th century the square was made up entirely of elegant townhouses. Some survive to this day, though unfortunately there has also been some insensitive modern development.

On the Green's south side at Nos 85 and 86 are two exceptionally grand Georgian houses. **Newman House** (tel: 01-475 7255; www.visitdublin. com; June–Aug Tue–Fri, guided tours at 2pm, 3pm and 4pm; charge) was once the Catholic University of Ireland, where James Joyce, Flann O'Brien and Gerard Manley Hopkins worked or studied; note its generous Georgian proportions, and its fine interior plasterwork. **Iveagh House** nearby was once home to the Guinness family, and is now the Department of Foreign Affairs.

A landmark on the Green's northside is **The Shelbourne Hotel ❺** (tel: 01-676 6471; www.marriott.co.uk; *see p.89*). Built in 1824, the hotel has been an intrinsic part of Dublin's social life ever since reopening in 2007 after a major refurbishment. It's a grand, elegant spot, which attracts well-heeled Dubliners to its bars and restaurants.

Dublin pubs

Dublin has about 800 pubs, and some of the most characterful are between St Stephen's Green and Dame Street (*see also p.51*).

- **Davy Byrne's**, 21 Duke Street; tel: 01-671 1298; more a cocktail bar than a traditional pub, but still proud of its walk-on role in *Ulysses*; it serves excellent pub grub.
- **Horseshoe Bar**, The Shelbourne Hotel, 27 St Stephen's Green; tel: 01-676 6471; this intimate semicircular bar is a favourite haunt of politicians, barristers and other power-brokers.
- **Kehoe's**, 9 South Anne Street; tel: 01-677 8312; tiny corner pub with snugs and an ornate wooden interior.
- **Long Hall Pub**, 51 South Great George's Street; tel: 01-475 1590; cavernous Victorian interior said to be unchanged for 100 years. The real thing. Good pints and sandwiches.

Kildare Street

On the north side of St Stephen's Green, Kildare Street leads to the 18th-century **Leinster House** ⑥, home of the Dáil Eireann, the Irish parliament. It is flanked by two nearly symmetrical edifices: the National Library and National Museum.

Apart from more than 500,000 books, the **National Library** ⑦ (tel: 01-603 0200; www.nli.ie; exhibition area Mon–Wed 9.30am–9pm, Thur–Fri 9.30am–5pm, Sat 9.30am–4.30pm; free) has an extensive collection of old newspapers and periodicals, a genealogy centre and temporary exhibitions. The reading room, in a large rotunda, is well worth a look.

The treasures in the **National Museum** ⑧ (tel: 01-677 7828; www.

The National Musem is housed within the Collins Barracks, named after Michael Collins

Inside the National Gallery of Ireland

O'Connell at No. 58; W.B. Yeats at No. 52; the Duke of Wellington was born at No. 24 Upper Merrion Street. The lush gardens in the square are open to the public and are used for festivals in the summer.

The **National Gallery of Ireland** ⑩ (tel: 01-661 5133; www.national gallery.ie; Mon–Sat 9.30am–5.30pm, Thur until 8.30pm, Sun noon–5.30pm, guided tours Sat 2pm, Sun 1pm and 2pm; free, charge for exhibitions) has two entrances: the original one at Merrion Square West, and a new one on Clare Street. By the old entrance is a statue of George Bernard Shaw, who said he owed his education to the gallery and left it a third of his estate: this income increased enormously when his play *Pygmalion* was reincarnated as the musical *My Fair Lady*.

In the gallery, some 2,000 works of art are on display. Many are by grand masters, and the collection is generally considered one of the finest in Europe. Look out for the work of Jack B. Yeats, brother of the famous poet. The new Millennium Wing houses temporary exhibitions, the gallery shop and a self-service restaurant.

Passing the **Natural History Museum** (closed for refurbishment) are the imposing gates of **Government Buildings** ⑪ (tel: 01-662 4888; www. taoiseach.gov.ie; tours Sat 10.30am–3.30pm; tickets available that morning from National Gallery; free), which house the office of the Taoiseach (Prime Minister) and the Cabinet room, both recently restored to their original Georgian splendour.

museum.ie; Tue–Sat 10am–5pm, Sun 2–5pm; free) are one of Dublin's highlights, with exhibits dating from prehistory through the early Christian period and the Vikings to the independence struggle. Don't miss the 8th-century Ardagh Chalice, the delicate Tara Brooch from the same era or the 12th-century Shrine of St Patrick's Bell.

Merrion Square

Merrion Square ⑨ is one of Dublin's finest remnants of Georgian splendour. Laid out in 1762, the square has had many distinguished inhabitants: Sir William and Lady 'Speranza' Wilde, surgeon and poetess, and parents of Oscar, lived at No. 1; Daniel

This walk travels through the heart of Dublin's fashionable southside, with its green spaces, wide streets and impressive Georgian architecture. The streets have been laid out in such a way that on clear days you can even get sightlines to the Dublin Mountains to the south.

A short stroll south down bustling **Grafton Street** takes you to leafy **St Stephen's Green**. At the corner, cross over the road and head through the **Dublin Fusiliers' Arch** (1904) to enter the green, which was laid out in 1880. Walking around the green in an anti-clockwise direction, you will see statues of Irish patriot Robert Emmet, the writers W.B. Yeats and James Joyce, the Three Fates, and Wolfe Tone, the leader of the 1798 Wexford Rebellion.

A statue of James Joyce, one of several on St Stephen's Green

Behind the monument is a touching memorial to those who died in the Great Famine of 1845–9.

On a sunny day, picnic provisions can be bought from the **Unicorn Food Emporium** on Merrion Row (see p.92).

Leaving St Stephen's Green by the northeastern gate, turn right to find Merrion Row. On the left-hand side is a surprising site: the tiny Huguenot cemetery, constructed in 1693. Tucked in next to the imposing **Shelbourne Hotel**, the cemetery is usually locked, but you can peer through the railings to see the gravestones of the descendants of the Huguenots, French Protestants who had fled persecution in France. A list of the 239 surnames of those who are buried here can be seen on the wall plaque to the left; this mentions the Becquett family, ancestors of the playwright Samuel Beckett.

At the end of Merrion Row, turn left onto Upper Merrion Street, home to **Restaurant Patrick Guilbaud** (see

Tips

- Distance: 2km (1¼ miles)
- Time: Two hours
- Start: St Stephen's Green
- End: Oscar Wilde House
- Many city-centre buses pass close to the starting point for the walk, which is also the terminus for the LUAS Green Line (tram). The nearest DART station is Pearse Street. Alternatively, from north of the Liffey, St Stephen's Green is a 10-minute walk from the Abbey Street LUAS Red Line (tram) stop.

p.92), one of Dublin's most exclusive restaurants. Continuing along Upper Merrion Street, you will see the imposing **Government Buildings**, housing the office of the Prime Minister (Taoiseach), on your left. They were built in 1911 as the Royal College of Science, and the Irish government occupied the northern wing in 1922. The next building on your left is the Natural History section of the **National Museum of Ireland**. This neoclassical structure was completed in 1856.

Upper Merrion Street takes you straight to **Merrion Square**, the most famous of Dublin's Georgian squares, laid out between 1762 and 1764. It is worth taking the time to walk anticlockwise around the streets that line the square. Beginning at Merrion Square South, the houses progress in descending numerical order: look out for the old residences of W.B. Yeats (Nos 82 and 52), the playwright Sheridan le Fanu (No.

Georgian door-knocker, Merrion Square

70) and Daniel O'Connell (No. 52).

For a glimpse of what life was like in Georgian times, you can visit **29 Lower Fitzwilliam Street** at the southeastern corner of the square. The house has been restored with period furnishings that reflect the lifestyle of a middle-class family in the late 18th century.

Oscar Wilde House, on the northwestern corner at No. 1, was the first building to be built here. Wilde, born in 1855, lived here for the first 23 years of his life.

Georgian Dublin walk

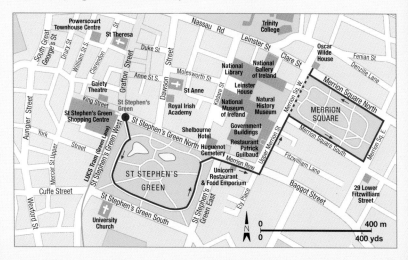

Fitzwilliam Square ⓬ is the city's smallest, latest (1825) and best-preserved Georgian square. To see what the interiors were like in its heyday, visit **Number 29** (tel: 01-702 6165; www. esb.ie/numbertwentynine; Tue–Sat 10am–5pm, Sun noon–5pm; charge).

Temple Bar

Known as **Temple Bar ⓭**, the network of small cobbled streets between Dame Street and the river quays has undergone a remarkable renaissance to become Dublin's 'Left Bank'. Full of studios, galleries, vintage clothing and music stores, specialist bookshops, pubs, clubs, cultural centres, restaurants and craft shops, this area is buzzing. The streets are thronged with tourists in the summer, and on Saturday nights the main street feels like a Disneyland of Irishness. The area's renewal created two new public squares: **Temple Bar Square**, a meeting point for shoppers, and **Meeting House Square**, a cultural centre and performance space, which still draws the locals for its excellent Saturday farmers' market, as well as its outdoor cinema events.

Just off Temple Bar Square, Merchant's Arch – a favourite spot for buskers – leads to the river quay and the **Ha'penny Bridge ⓮** (1816), named for the toll once charged for crossing it. This cast-iron pedestrian bridge across the Liffey is a handy short cut between Temple Bar and the shopping area to the north.

Continue along Essex Street across Capel Street into the Old City section of Temple Bar, less frequented by tourists. Here you will find retro design shops, and the excellent **Gutter Bookshop** (*see p.57*). **Cow's Lane**, a pedestrian street, has a market every Saturday combining designer clothes and artisan food.

The bustling Temple Bar area is peppered with bars, art galleries, boutiques and clubs

Ha'penny Bridge takes its name from the toll once charged to cross it

uncovered recently by archaeologists. Dublin's number one attraction, the Guinness tour, features a different kind of national heritage.

Dame Street

City Hall ⓰ (tel: 01-222 2204; www.dublincity.ie; Mon–Sat 10am–5.15pm, Sun 2–5pm; charge) was designed in 1769 as the Royal Exchange, and served as a prison for rebels, a military depot and a corn exchange, before being taken over by the Corporation of Dublin in 1852. The entrance rotunda has a splendid illuminated dome. The exhibition 'The Story of the Capital' is housed in the vaults.

The ornate Victorian canopied entrance of the **Olympia Theatre ⓰** marks the modest frontage of Dublin's largest theatre; its programme mixes plays, musicals, comedy and rock concerts.

Set on a hill above the original Viking settlement, just behind City Hall, is **Dublin Castle ⓱** (tel: 01-645 8813; www.dublincastle.ie;

Central Dublin

Once Dublin's medieval city centre, today the area is rich in historic heritage, from the opulent State Apartments of Dublin Castle to Dublin's two cathedrals and Viking artefacts

Culture trail

When Temple Bar was redeveloped, several important new cultural institutions were established there in high-spec new buildings. They have helped to revitalise the Irish arts scene.

- The **Ark** (Eustace Street; tel: 01-660 7108; www.ark.ie), is a cultural centre set up for children.
- The **Gallery of Photography** (Meeting House Square; tel: 01-671 4654; www.galleryofphotography.ie) shows both Irish and international work.
- The **Irish Film Institute** (Eustace Street; tel: 01-679 5744; www.ifi.ie), is an arthouse cinema with a book/DVD shop, café/restaurant, bar and film archive.
- The **Temple Bar Gallery & Studios** (5 Temple Bar; tel: 01-671 0073; www.tempbargallery.com) hosts exhibitions of cutting-edge contemporary art.

Mon–Sat 10am–4.45pm, Sun and public holidays 2–4.45pm; guided tours; charge). Originally built between 1208 and 1220, it was the symbol of English rule in Ireland for almost eight centuries. The building as it now stands is mainly 18th-century. Over the years it has served as a seat of government, a prison, a courthouse, and occasionally as a fortress under siege. Most impressive are the lavishly furnished State Apartments (viewed by guided tour only). The splendid St Patrick's Hall is probably the grandest room in Ireland. It was used by the British for various state functions and since 1938 has been the scene of the inauguration of Irish presidents.

To the castle's rear, the Clock Tower accommodates the **Chester Beatty Library** ⓲ (tel: 01-407 0750; www.cbl.ie; Oct–Apr Tue–Fri 10am–5pm, May–Sept Mon–Fri 10am–5pm, Sat 11am–5pm all year, Sun 1–5pm all year; free), with a fine collection of Chinese, Japanese, Persian, Indian and Middle Eastern manuscripts, paintings and ornaments.

The cathedrals

Dublin has two noteworthy cathedrals, and although it is the capital of a predominantly Catholic country, both belong to the Protestant Church of Ireland. **St Patrick's Cathedral** ⓳ (tel: 01-453 9472; www.stpatrickscathedral.ie; Mar–Oct daily 9am–5.30pm, Nov–Feb Mon–Sat 9am–5pm, Sun 9am–3pm; charge) is dedicated to Ireland's national saint. It is said that St Patrick himself baptised 5th-century converts at a well on this very site. This church was consecrated in 1192, but the present structure dates mostly from the 13th and 14th centuries. The cathedral is known for its association with Jonathan Swift, author of

Dublin's first castle dated from the 13th century, but the current building is mostly 18th-century

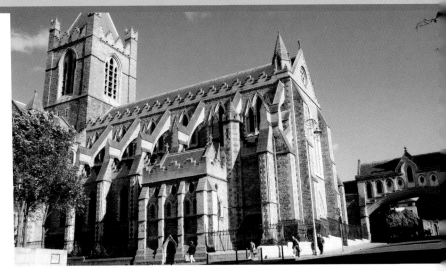

The Gothic Revival-style Christ Church Cathedral

Gulliver's Travels, who was Dean from 1713 until his death in 1745. Many Swiftian relics can be seen in the north transept; a simple brass plate in the floor marks his grave.

A short walk away, **Christ Church Cathedral** ⑳ (tel: 01-677 8099; www. cccdub.ie; daily 9am–6pm in summer, 9.45am–5 or 6pm in winter; charge) is the older of the two, dating from 1038. Largely rebuilt in Gothic Revival style in the 1870s, it still contains Romanesque as well as Early English and fine neo-Gothic elements. The crypt, now displaying Christ Church's valuable treasures, dates from the 12th century, when the cathedral was expanded by Strongbow *(see p.279)*, whose remains are believed by some to lie buried here.

To delve more deeply into Irish history, take the covered bridge linking the cathedral with the Synod Hall. Here, **Dublinia & The Viking World** (tel: 01-679 4611; www.

dublinia.ie; daily 10am–5pm, last admission 4.15pm Apr–Sept, 4pm Oct–Mar; charge) gives an insight into the medieval world of Dublin

---

Dublin Castle gardens

Outside the Chester Beatty Library in Lower Castle Yard is a large circular lawn, inset with curving brick paths and surrounded by benches, known as the Dub Linn Garden. It's a favourite spot for office workers to take a break in summer, and it's a safe area for children to run around and let off steam. It is believed to be the site of the 'Black Pool' (Dub Linn) that gave the Viking city its name. There's also access to a roof garden here: take the lift to the third floor of the Chester Beatty Library (free), and enjoy great views over Dublin. No food or drink is allowed: the garden's sole purpose is to provide an oasis of peace in the city centre. Opening times are as for Dublin Castle *(see p.76)*.

through interactive displays and reconstructions. From the top of the 60m (200ft) St Michael's Tower, you can enjoy wonderful panoramic views of the city.

Guinness heritage

Another important part of the national heritage is enshrined just a short walk away. **Guinness's Brewery** is the biggest in Europe, and churns out 2½ million pints of its celebrated black stout every day. The **Guinness Storehouse** ❷ (tel: 01-408 4800; www.guinness-storehouse.com; daily 9.30am–5pm, July–Aug 9.30am–7pm; charge) provides an exhibition on the making of the world's most famous stout. The building also houses the Gravity Bar, the highest bar in Dublin, with a spectacular panoramic view of the city. The admission ticket entitles you to a complimentary pint in the rooftop bar; it's probably the best pint of Guinness you'll ever have, since it hasn't had to travel far.

North of the Liffey

O'Connell Street is the backbone of Dublin's northside, linking O'Connell Bridge to Parnell Square, the epicentre of the original Georgian Dublin, where the houses are bigger and older than on the southside. A hundred years ago these were tenement slums, where families lived one to a room, as depicted in the plays of Sean O'Casey. Among the area's most famous residents was the novelist James Joyce, author of *Ulysses*.

Custom House and Eden Quays

A prominent landmark of Dublin's north bank is **Custom House** ❷ (tel: 01-888 2538; wwwlvisitdulbin. com; mid-Mar–Oct Mon–Fri 10am–12.30pm, Sat–Sun 2–5pm, Nov–mid-Mar Wed–Fri 10am–12.30pm, Sun 2–5pm; free), one of the masterpieces of James Gandon, the greatest architect of 18th-century Dublin. The visitor centre traces the building's history,

The gates of the Guinness Brewery

Pedestrians and traffic compete for space on O'Connell Street

and the life of James Gandon. The gleaming new building just downstream is the **Irish Financial Services Centre** (known as the IFSC), built in the late 1980s. This area was developed into Dublin's financial district during the boom years.

Nearby is the **Abbey Theatre** ㉓ (www.abbeytheatre.ie), the home of Ireland's National Theatre. The present building, completed in 1966, replaces an earlier one that was destroyed by fire. The Abbey, founded in 1904 by W.B. Yeats and Lady Gregory, played a vital role in Ireland's cultural renaissance around the turn of the 19th century, and earned a worldwide reputation through the great works of John Millington Synge and Sean O'Casey, and for its players' naturalistic acting style.

O'Connell Street

The once elegant **O'Connell Street** ㉔ is not what it was, blighted by fast-food joints, amusement arcades and ugly modern buildings. Some improvements have been made, but there's still a way to go. Its focal point is the imposing **General Post Office** ㉕ (tel: 01-872 8888; www.anpost.ie; Mon–Sat 8am–8pm, Sun 10.30am–6pm; free), built in 1815. During the 1916 Uprising, this became the rebels' headquarters, from where they proclaimed the republic (*see p.282*). The GPO's pillars are still bear the pockmarks of bullets. Artefacts in its main concourse recall its dramatic past. Reaching to the sky nearby is **The Spire**, an aspirational and strangely beautiful 120m (390ft) stainless-steel pillar, erected in 2003.

Henry Street ㉖ is the northside's main shopping street. Its tributary, Moore Street, is filled with the hubbub of fruit and vegetable stalls, ethnic food outlets and hair and beauty stores that cater to Dublin's burgeoning immigrant population. The traditional stall-holders are famed for razor-sharp Dublin wit.

Close by is **St Mary's Pro-Cathedral**  (Marlborough Street; tel: 01-874 5441; www.procathedral. ie; free), the city's main Catholic church. It was built between 1816 and 1825 in a classical style. Its famous Palestrina Choir sing a Latin Mass at 11am every Sunday. Many Irish tenors started their singing career here, including Count John McCormack (1884–1945).

Parnell Square

At the north end of O'Connell Street are the late 18th-century **Rotunda Rooms**, now an occasional music venue. The **Rotunda Hospital,** Europe's first maternity hospital, was financed by concerts in the Rooms. The **Gate Theatre** (tel: 01-874 4045; www.gate-theatre.ie) was founded in 1928; its most recent successes have been separate seasons of the work of Samuel Beckett and Harold Pinter. Nearby is the **Garden of Remembrance**, which commemorates those who died in Ireland's struggle for independence from British rule; Queen Elizabeth II, accompanied by President Mary MacAleese, laid a wreath here in a significant gesture of reconciliation on her state visit in 2011.

The nucleus of the **Dublin City Art Gallery, The Hugh Lane** (tel: 01-222 5550; www.hughlane.ie; Tue–Thur 10am–6pm, Fri–Sat 10am–5pm, Sun 11am–5pm; free) is formed by the mainly Impressionist collection of Sir Hugh Lane, who died when the *Lusitania* was torpedoed in 1915. In 1998, a team of archaeologists painstakingly dismantled the London studio of Dublin-born artist Francis Bacon and reconstructed it here.

The **Dublin Writers Museum** (tel: 01-872 2077; www.writers museum.com; Mon–Sat 10am–5pm,

The neoclassical Four Courts, the Republic's main courthouse

Deer in Phoenix Park *(see p.82)*

Dublin

June–Aug until 6pm, Sun 11am–5pm; charge) displays photographs, paintings, busts, letters, manuscripts, first editions and other memorabilia relating to celebrated writers such as Swift, Shaw, Yeats, O'Casey, Joyce, Beckett and Behan.

North Great George's Street

Just off Parnell Square East is **Belvedere College ㉜**, occupying a fine 18th-century mansion. The college has been run by the Jesuit order since 1841. James Joyce, an ex-pupil, described its atmosphere in *A Portrait of the Artist as a Young Man*. In North Great George's Street, many grand Georgian houses have been saved from decrepitude. No. 35, a beautifully restored late 18th-century townhouse, is the **James Joyce Centre ㉝** (tel: 01-878 8547; www.jamesjoyce. ie; Tue–Sat 10am–5pm; charge). Its

exhibition features photographs and storyboards about Joyce's family and the many houses they inhabited.

The northside quays

A companion piece to the Custom House on the north quays is the magnificent domed **Four Courts ㉞**, another Gandon masterpiece. The lantern-dome is fronted by a six-columned Corinthian portico flanked by two wings enclosing courtyards. It was seriously damaged by prolonged shelling during the 1922 civil war, but is now fully restored.

St Michan's Church ㉟ (tel: 01-872 4154; Mar–Oct Mon–Fri 10am–12.45pm, 2–4.45pm, Sat 10am–12.45pm, Nov–Mar Mon–Fri 12.30–3.30pm, Sat 10am–12.45pm; charge for crypt tours) was founded in 1095, but has been rebuilt several times since. The main attraction here is the crypt, where wooden coffins and mummies can be seen in a remarkable state of preservation.

Across the road, the **Old Jameson Distillery** ❸ (tel: 01-807 2355; www.jamesonwhiskey.com; daily 9am–5.15pm, charge) is located within the warehouse of the 1791-built whiskey factory. The guided tours always conclude with a tasting. A small lane leads from here to **Smithfield village**. Its distinctive architecture includes the distillery's 53m (175ft) chimney built in 1895 and now serving as a viewing platform, accessible by glass lift, giving panoramic views (closed for maintenance at the time of writing).

The **National Museum of Decorative Arts and History** ❸ (tel: 01-677 7444; www.museum.ie; Tue–Sat 10am–5pm, Sun 2–5pm; free)

occupies an elegant former barracks that dates from the early 18th century. It displays a dazzling collection of Irish silver, glassware, furniture and other decorative arts.

Phoenix Park ❸, the southern boundary of which extends west on the Liffey's north bank for about 3 miles (5km), is over five times as big as London's Hyde Park. It accommodates the President's residence; the Wellington Monument, an obelisk erected after Waterloo; and **Dublin Zoo** (tel: 01-677 1425; www.dublinzoo.ie), well known for the breeding of lions.

West and north of city centre

Kilmainham is a traditional working-class area, now partly gentrified, with two famous landmarks, the Royal Hospital, built for army pensioners

A tempting sign at the Old Jameson Distillery

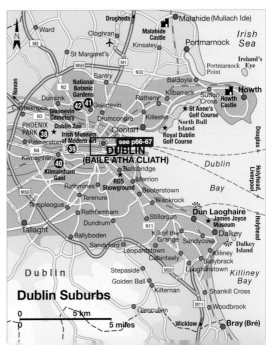

Dublin Suburbs

The Irish Museum of Modern Art, in the grand setting of the former Royal Hospital

charge for special exhibitions), which is arranged around the large central square, formerly a parade ground. Nearby, the forbidding **Kilmainham Gaol** ⑩ (tel: 01-453 5984; Apr–Sept daily 9.30am–6pm, Oct–Mar Mon–Sat 9.30am–5.30pm, Sun 10am–6pm; charge) has been carefully restored. Many heroes of Irish nationalism were imprisoned or died here. The central cell block has exhibits from Ireland's stormy history, which can be a moving experience.

Glasnevin

The main attraction in Glasnevin (buses 13 and 19 from O'Connell Street) is the beautiful **National Botanic Gardens** ⑪ (tel: 01-804 0300; www.botanicgardens.ie; daily, Mon–Fri 9am–5pm, winter until 4.30pm, Sat–Sun 10am–6pm, winter until 4.30pm; free). The magnificent Victorian curvilinear glasshouses have been fully restored. Nearby **Glasnevin Cemetery** ⑫ (tel: 01-830 1133; www.glasnevintrust.ie) is the Republic's national burying ground, and contains the remains of Daniel O'Connell, Eamon DeValera, Michael Collins, Brendan Behan and many other famous historical figures.

South of Dublin – County Wicklow

Wicklow, to the south of Dublin, is a county of contrasts, with rugged highlands and sheltered river valleys with lush vegetation that have given it the nickname 'the garden of

but now Ireland's Museum of Modern Art, and Kilmainham Gaol, which evokes vivid memories of the struggle for independence. An easy bus ride from O'Connell Street to Glasnevin will take you to one of Dublin's older Victorian suburbs, and its Botanic Gardens.

Kilmainham

In Kilmainham, a stone tower gate guards the grounds of the Royal Hospital, founded by Charles II (1680–4) as a home for army pensioners. Today it houses the **Irish Museum of Modern Art** ㊴ (tel: 01-612 9900; www.imma.ie; Tue–Sat 10am– 5.30pm, Wed 10.30am–5.30pm, Sun noon–5.30pm; free,

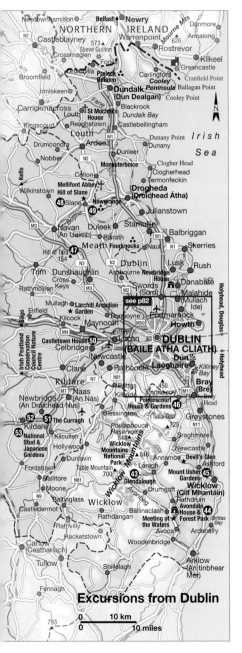

Excursions from Dublin

0 — 10 km
0 — 10 miles

Ireland. The beautifully sited monastic remains at Glendalough and the enormous Powerscourt Estate are the main attractions.

Glendalough

Drive across the bleakly beautiful Wicklow Gap to **Glendalough 43** (tel: 0404-45325; Nov–Feb daily 9.30am–5pm, Mar–Oct until 6pm; guided tours; charge). Here, in the spectacular steep-sided valley between two lakes, St Kevin founded a monastic settlement in the 6th century. The ruins date from the 11th and 12th centuries.

Vale of Avoca

Beyond the gently wooded Vale of Clara near Rathdrum is **Avondale 44** (tel: 0404-46111; mid-Mar–Oct daily 11am–6pm, house closed Mon in Apr, Sept and Oct, except bank holidays; charge). The Georgian home of the great Irish politician Charles Stewart Parnell (1846–91) is now a museum devoted to his memory and is surrounded by hundreds of acres of forest park.

The picturesque village of **Avoca**, with its multicoloured houses and working weaving mill, is further south. It gained new fame as the locaion for the 1990s BBC series *Ballykissangel*. Also at this end of the county is **Brittas Bay**, with its sandy dunes, beloved of Irish holidaymakers.

Mount Usher Gardens and Powerscourt House

Returning to Dublin, the splended **Mount Usher Gardens 45** (www.mountushergardens.ie; Mar–Oct only), are a must for tree-lovers.

The thundering Powerscourt Waterfall

Boyne Valley. To see these properly requires a full day trip.

The Hill of Tara

County Meath was the terrain of the pagan High Kings of Ireland. The ancient seat of the rulers was the **Hill of Tara** ❼ (tel: 046-902 5903; access all year, guided tours late May–mid-Sept; charge), situated 44km (28 miles) from Dublin. The limestone ridge commands fittingly regal views over Ireland's central plain, framed by distant mountain ranges. Ring forts, ruins and a standing stone mark the place that was the island's spiritual and cultural capital for millennia.

The Boyne Valley

Slane ❽, the prettiest village in the Boyne Valley, is a beautiful 18th-century estate village. The central crossroads contains a quartet of identical, three-storey, limestone Georgian

Heading north again, **Powerscourt House and Gardens** ❻ (tel: 01-204 6000; www.powerscourt.ie; daily 9.30am–5.30pm, dusk in winter; charge) feature an imposing 18th-century stately home, with magnificent Italianate landscaped grounds and a backdrop of mountain scenery, all on a grand scale. In the grounds are upmarket shops, a garden centre and a restaurant. **Powerscourt Waterfall** is the tallest waterfall in Ireland, cascading 121m (398 ft).

North of Dublin – County Meath

The countryside north of County Dublin is rich in antiquities, with well-preserved pre-Christian monuments, as well as later monastic sites. For most visitors, the major attraction is the megalithic passage graves in the

---

Avoca Handweavers

Stop for a visit to **Avoca Handweavers** (Old Mill, Main Street; tel: 0402-35105; www.avoca.ie). Ireland's oldest working mill has been producing linen since 1723 and today is known for mohair and lambswool in lovely jewel colours. Rugs, bed linen, clothing and accessories are sold in the mill shop and in Avoca shops throughout Ireland. Their cafés are known for tempting home-baked items, including scones and scrumptious cakes. There are also home-made soups and sandwiches. If you enjoy what's on offer, you can buy an Avoca cookbook.

houses, gazing implacably at each other across the square. The Gothic Revival **Slane Castle** (tel: 041-988 4400; www.slanecastle.ie; Sun–Thur May–Aug; castle by guided tour only; charge) is an annual venue for monster rock concerts.

Less than 1.5km (1 mile) north of the village is the windswept **Hill of Slane** where, in 433, St Patrick lit a Paschal fire to celebrate the arrival of Christianity in Ireland. The hill contains the ruins of a 16th-century Franciscan friary, and has good views of the surrounding countryside.

Newgrange

Newgrange ➋ is a Unesco World Heritage site, one of Europe's most important prehistoric clusters. Access to the burial mounds at Newgrange and Knowth is solely by tour from the **Brú na Bóinne Visitor Centre** (tel: 041-988 0300; Nov–Jan 9.30am–5pm, Feb–Apr and Oct 9.30am–5.30pm, May and mid-Sept–end Sept 9am–6.30pm, June–mid-Sept 9am–7pm; charge). Dowth may be visited separately and viewed from the outside. Newgrange is the only monument where access is allowed to the interior passage and chamber – the latter is aligned so that the rising sun sends in a shaft of light at the winter solstice (entry to the chamber for that occasion is by lottery). Built around 3200 BC, Newgrange is several hundred years older than the Pyramids, and 1,000 years older than Stonehenge. The sites are busy in summer. Go early in the day, or visit by guided tour bus from Dublin, to guarantee entry to the mound.

West of Dublin – County Kildare

Kildare, once known for its stud farms and lush green pastures, is now

The World Heritage site of Newgrange, with its prehistoric burial mounds

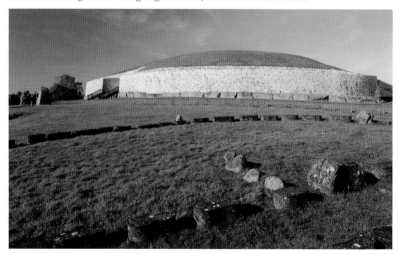

The National Stud is home to some of Ireland's finest thoroughbreds

also a dormitory county for Dublin. Quiet country towns and villages have sprouted apartment and housing developments. Despite all this, the county still breeds some of the best horses in the world, and preserves some very grand houses too.

County Kildare

Castletown House ❺⓿ (tel: 01-628 8252; www.castletownhouse.ie; mid-Mar–Oct; charge) in **Celbridge** stands at the end of a long avenue of trees. Ireland's largest Palladian country house was built for the speaker of the Irish House of Commons, William Conolly, in 1722. The oustandingly grand, palace-like mansion was rescued from imminent dereliction by the newly founded Irish Georgian Society, and first opened to the public in 1967. It is now in the care of the state.

Kildare Town

County Kildare is Ireland's capital of horse racing, and the **Curragh ❺❶**, a broad plain encompassing about 31 sq km (12 sq miles), is used for grazing and gallops. In the middle of this vast plain, bisected by the N7 and the Dublin–Cork railway line, is the **Curragh Racecourse**, where the Irish Derby is held every June.

On the edge of the Curragh, the town of **Kildare ❺❷** is notable for its cathedral associated with St Brigid. The 33m (108ft) Round Tower beside the cathedral belongs to a 12th-century monastery. You can climb to the top for excellent views of the surrounding countryside.

The **National Stud and Horse Museum ❺❸** (tel: 045-521 617; www.irish-national-stud.ie; Mar–Oct; charge), is a state-owned institution where top-class breeding stallions are stabled. Visit in spring and early summer if possible to see the foals. Admission includes entry to the immaculate Japanese Gardens created by the stud's founders in the early 20th century. Once a bog, it is now a world of tidy shrubs and trees with a lotus pond and teahouse.

ACCOMMODATION

Dublin offers a wide range of accommodation, from safe, well-run budget hostels to five-star hotels, rich in history, or ablaze with bling. Hotels cluster in the central areas north and south of the Liffey, within walking distance of most visitor attractions. If you value peace and quiet and a good night's sleep, head for Ballsbridge, the leafy embassy district, a short bus ride or 20 minutes' walk from the centre.

South of the Liffey: Georgian Dublin

Aberdeen Lodge
55 Park Avenue, Ballsbridge
Tel: 01-283 8155
www.halpinsprivatehotels.com
A large, three-storey Victorian house in elegant Ballsbridge, with spacious bedrooms, all beautifully furnished, and free parking. Good bus and DART connections to centre. **€€€**

Bewley's Hotel Ballsbridge
Merrion Road
Tel: 01-668 1111
www.bewleyshotels.com
A large, excellent-value hotel occupying a converted 19th-century Masonic building next to the RDS Arena. Over 300 rooms are offered at a flat per-room rate. The hotel has a lively lounge bar and a good restaurant. **€**

The fashionable Clarence Hotel

Buswell's Hotel
23–27 Molesworth Street
Tel: 01-614 6500
www.buswells.ie
These Georgian townhouses have been used as a hotel since the 1920s. It is a popular haunt for politicians because of its proximity to Leinster House. **€€€**

Central Hotel
1–5 Exchequer Street
Tel: 01–679 7302
www.centralhotel.ie
Has more character than some of Dublin's bigger, pricier places, with the first-floor Library Bar a popular spot with literary types. Situated close to Grafton Street. **€**

The Clarence Hotel
6–8 Wellington Quay
Tel: 01-407 0800
www.theclarence.ie
City-centre, riverside location, backing onto Temple Bar. The Art Deco interior has been lovingly restored by new owners (who include U2). A hip clientele are drawn in by great cocktails and a first-class restaurant. **€€€**

The Dylan Hotel
Eastmoreland Place
Tel: 01-660 3000
www.dylan.ie
This redbrick Victorian hotel, between the city centre and Ballsbridge, has been given a boutique makeover, with candle and champagne extravaganzas in the lobby and bar, and bedside speakers for your iPod. **€€€€**

Four Seasons
Simmonscourt Road, Ballsbridge
Tel: 01-665 4000
www.fourseasons.com/dublin
This vast and very swanky hotel is situated near the RDS horse show grounds. Stylish and spacious, it boasts two bars – traditional or ultra modern – as well as a classic restaurant, Seasons. €€€€€

Harcourt Hotel
60 Harcourt Street
Tel: 01-478 3677
www.harcourthotel.ie
The Harcourt occupies a Georgian house, just off St Stephen's Green. Rooms are small, and can be noisy as the hotel has its own nightclub. For the location and ambience, on the other hand, it's good value. €

The Merrion
Upper Merrion Street
Tel: 01-603 0600
www.themerrion.com
A stunning hotel, converted from four Georgian townhouses, with individually designed rooms and suites, and beautiful bathrooms. The Merrion is so discreet that you could be forgiven for missing it; there's no hotel sign, just a small brass plaque. €€€€€

Number 31
31 Lesson Close
Tel: 01-676 5011
www.number31.ie
Combining a classic Georgian townhouse with a modernist mews, this beautiful hotel is situated close to Fitzwilliam Square. It is famous for its excellent breakfasts and unique 'sunken lounge'. €€€€

Sandymount Hotel
Herbert Road, Lansdowne Road, Ballsbridge
Tel: 01-614 2000
www.sandymounthotel.ie
The Sandymount is a 168-room hotel cobbled together from eight interconnected Victorian houses near Lansdowne Road stadium. Rooms are simply but smartly furnished in a sleek modern style, and the

The gracious Shelbourne Hotel

hotel benefits from a restaurant, bar, terrace and gardens. €€

The Shelbourne Hotel
St Stephen's Green
Tel: 01-663 4500
www.theshelbourne.ie
This grand old institution has competition as Dublin's finest hotel these days, but it still boasts a historic aura that's hard to beat, with a liveried doorman and the best address in town. Room 112 is known as the The Constitution Room, as the Irish Constitution was drafted there in 1922. €€€€€

La Stampa
35 Dawson Street
Tel: 01-677 4444
www.lastampa.ie
This luxurious boutique hotel benefits from an excellent location near Grafton Street. The flamboyant decor has an Asian theme. Underneath is the ever-popular Balzac Brasserie. Prices rise at weekends. €€–€€€

The Westbury Hotel
Grafton Street
Tel: 01-679 1122
www.doylecollection.com
Consistently rated one of the most popular hotels in Dublin, The Westbury Hotel prides itself on its level of luxury, its city-centre location and its excellent restaurant. Book online for large savings. €€€€€

Listings

Central Dublin: medieval and Viking Dublin

Kinlay House
2–12 Lower Edward Street
Tel: 01-679 6644
www.kinlayhouse.ie
This popular hostel is situated close to Christ Church Cathedral, backing onto Temple Bar. It offers singles, doubles, 4–6-bedded rooms and dorms. €

Jurys Inn Christchurch
Christchurch Place
Tel: 01-454 0000
www.jurysinn.com
Pleasantly located on a hill overlooking the cathedral, this modern hotel is part of a no-frills budget chain that is popular with Irish families. €

North of the Liffey

Charles Stewart Parnell Guesthouse
5–6 Parnell Square
Tel: 01-878 0350
www.charlesstewart.ie
This lovely Georgian house is located right on Parnell Square, near a bus stop to the airport. The rooms are simply decorated but well maintained; staff are helpful and enthusiastic. €

Gresham Hotel
23 O'Connell Street
Tel: 01-874 6881
www.gresham-hotels.com
This landmark Victorian hotel was once the last word in elegance, but has faded somewhat, along with its O'Connell Street location. All the same, it still offers a warm Dublin welcome, as well as large, comfortable rooms. €€€

Hotel Isaacs
Store Street
Tel: 01-813 4700
www.isaacs.ie
This efficiently run and friendly place is situated close to Connolly Station (rail) and Busáras (central bus station). €€

Hotel St George
7 Parnell Square
Tel: 01-874 5611
www.thecastlehotelgroup.com
A large Georgian townhouse, smartly done out in traditional style for a real 'old Dublin' feel. O'Connell Street and the airport bus are just a step away. Ask for an interior room overlooking the garden if you like quiet. €€

The Morrison
Lower Ormond Quay
Tel: 01-887 2400
www.morrisonhotel.ie
With its contemporary styling, the Morrison vies with the Clarence *(see p.88)* for the title of most media-hip hotel in town. It also benefits from a central location on the Liffey, and offers good value for money. €€€

South of Dublin: County Wicklow

Woodenbridge Hotel
Vale of Avoca, Arklow
Tel: 0402-35573
www.bestwestern.ie
Although it has seen better days, this hotel is a bargain for County Wicklow, with bright, spacious rooms, a decent breakfast and lovely views over the Vale of Avoca. €

North of Dublin: County Meath

The Millhouse
Slane
Tel: 041-982 0723
www.themillhouse.ie
This Georgian country house by the River Slane is an 11-bedroom boutique hotel with dramatically styled rooms. €€€€

West of Dublin: County Kildare

Barberstown Castle
Straffan
Tel: 01-628 8157
www.barberstowncastle.ie
This country house hotel 30 minutes from the airport is a good base for Dublin's outskirts. The bedrooms are large and luxurious; the bar and lobby are lively. €€€€

RESTAURANTS

Dublin has a thriving restaurant scene, with expensive fine dining establishments alongside good-value student haunts. The more fashionable places can be found to the south of the Liffey, around Merrion Square and Grafton Street. For real Dublin character, though, central Dublin and north of the Liffey are the best bets.

Restaurant price categories
Prices are per person for two courses, not including drinks:
€ = below €20
€€ = €20–28
€€€ = €28–38
€€€€ = over €38

South of the Liffey

Bewley's Oriental Café
78–79 Grafton Street
Tel: 01-672 7720
www.bewleys.com
Bewley's is part of the city's cultural heritage – a large, old-world café with fine stained-glass windows. It's a handy place for a quick bite, and a favourite spot for afternoon tea. Occasionally, it also hosts lunchtime theatre entertainments. **€**

Cornucopia
19 Wicklow Street
Tel: 01-677 7583
www.cornucopia.ie
Wholesome, home-style vegetarian cooking, organic food and wine with yeast-free, dairy-, gluten- and wheat-free options: it's a great place for breakfast or lunch, and its generous portions have gone down well with generations of hungry students. **€**

Dunne & Crescenzi
14–16 South Frederick Street
Tel: 01-677 3815
www.dunne&crescenzi.com
Billed as an authentic 'enoteca Italiana', this restaurant and deli near Grafton Street is renowned for its simple food and good wine. **€€**

Elephant & Castle
18 Temple Bar
Tel: 01-679 3121
www.elephantandcastle.ie
A cousin of the New York deli of the same name, this is a much-loved café serving familiar American food – char-grilled burgers, steaks, etc. Sunday brunch is popular, and the large windows overlooking Temple Bar are good for people-watching. **€**

Ely Winebar
22 Ely Place, St Stephen's Green
Tel: 01-676 8986
www.elywinebar.ie
Experience the elegance of old Dublin at this wine bar-cum-restaurant in a classic Georgian house near the Shelbourne Hotel. Organic meat and veg from the family farm are served with a wide selection of wines – about 70 are available by the glass. **€€€**

Fallon & Byrne
11–17 Exchequer Street
Tel: 01-472 1010
www.fallon&byrne.com
This large former telephone exchange building is now organic central: on the ground floor is a deli, in the cosy cellar is a wine bar, and on the top floor there's a large, light-filled brasserie which offers a menu of predominantly French cuisine. **€€**

Dublin's stylish Ely Winebar

Pearl Brasserie
20 Upper Merrion Street
tel: 01-661 3572
www.pearl-brasserie.com
Cool contemporary basement brasserie in fashionable location. The traditional French cuisine is based on the freshest Irish produce. **€€€€**

Restaurant Patrick Guilbaud
21 Upper Merrion Street
Tel: 01-676 4192
www.restaurantpatrickguilbaud.ie
Probably the most expensive restaurant in Dublin, and also one of the best. It is renowned for its excellent French cooking and the impeccable presentation of its dishes. Well worth exceeding your budget for a once-in-a-lifetime experience. **€€€€**

The Tea Room at The Clarence Hotel
6 Wellington Quay, Dublin 2
Tel: 01-407 0800
Landmark Art Deco restaurant attached to a celebrity hotel *(see p.88)*. In order to weather the economic downturn, the menus have been adapted so that you can now enjoy superb cooking at keen prices. **€–€€**

Unicorn Café, Restaurant and Food Emporium
12b Merrion Court, Merrion Row
Tel: 01-662 4757
www.unicronrestaurant.com
The Food Emporium offers takeaway food that includes gourmet sandwiches, 'designer' salads and smoothies. The restaurant is an old Dublin favourite – a lively, sometimes noisy spot, offering antipasti and Italian dishes. **€–€€**

Yamamori Noodles
71–72 South Great George's Street
Tel: 01-475 5001
www.yamamorinoodles.ie
This busy Japanese restaurant has basic decor and is perennially popular with students. It serves freshly prepared noodles, sushi and ramen. Try the seafood hotpot or the good-value daily bento-box specials. **€**

Central Dublin
Burdock's
2 Werburgh Street
Tel: 01-454 0306
www.burdocks.ie
The best place in Dublin to sample traditional fish and chips is takeaway only. Fresh haddock or cod is the best bet, while battered sausages are a Dublin favourite. There's an almost permanent queue outside for their near-perfect chips. **€**

Lord Edward
23 Christchurch Place
Tel: 01-454 2420
www.lordedward.ie
Situated near Christ Church Cathedral and Dublin Castle, this long-established seafood restaurant resides above a bar of the same name, and is famed for its authentic Dublin atmosphere. The seafood is served in the old style, with rich creamy sauces, and their Irish stew is also highly recommended. **€€€**

North of the Liffey
101 Talbot
101 Talbot Street
Tel: 01-874 5011
www.101talbot.ie
This small upstairs restaurant is a favourite with theatregoers heading to the Abbey Theatre, just round the corner *(see pp.79, 94)*. The menu exhibits Mediterranean and Eastern influences, and the dishes are prepared with good-quality ingredients. The arty clientele give the place a buzzing atmosphere. **€€**

The entrance to Chapter One

Chapter One
18–19 Parnell Square
Tel: 01-873 2266
www.chapteronerestaurant.com
Special-occasion restaurant in the basement of a large Georgian house, renowned for its fine modern Irish cooking and elegant atmosphere. Lunch or the pre-theatre menu offers the best value for money. €€€€

The Winding Stair
40 Lower Ormond Quay
Tel: 01-872 7320
www.winding-stair.com
Once a famous second-hand bookshop, this riverside spot overlooking the Ha'penny Bridge is now a characterful, book-lined restaurant serving traditional Irish dishes cooked in a contemporary style. Unique Dublin atmosphere. €€

West and north of city centre
Andersons Food Hall & Cafe
3 The Rise, Glasnevin
Tel: 01-797 9004
www.andersons.ie
Stylish delicatessen, wine shop and café situated near the Botanic Gardens. Andersons offers an excellent selection of Irish and continental charcuterie and cheeses for picnics, as well as sit-down meals at little marble-topped tables. Here, you can sample the hot dishes of the day, chosen from the blackboard. €

South of Dublin: County Wicklow
Roundwood Inn
Roundwood
Tel: 01-281 8107
www.visitwicklow.ie
Classic 17th-century village inn, en route to Glendalough, serving Irish-German fusion cuisine, with an emphasis on locally sourced meat and fish. Dishes include crab bisque, Wicklow trout, suckling pig and, in winter, roasted stuffed goose. €€€

North of Dublin: County Meath
The Station House Hotel
Kilmessan
Tel: 046-902 5239
www.thestationhousehotel.com
A former railway station has been converted into a family-run hotel. Choose between The Signal Restaurant, with formal white napery, or the casual dining in the bar. Great Sunday lunch, and children are always welcome. €€

West of Dublin: County Kildare
The Ballymore Inn
Ballymore Eustace
Tel: 045-864 747
www.ballymoreinn.com
This traditional country pub has a high reputation, so book ahead for weekends. The dining room and 'back bar' offer local artisan produce and organic meat. €€–€€€

NIGHTLIFE AND ENTERTAINMENT

Dublin swings, and you never have to go far to find a party, with drinkers spilling out of the pubs onto the pavements on warm summer evenings. All late-night venues are fully licensed. See the *Evening Herald* for full listings of what's on. For more venues see www.visitdublin.com and click on 'See & Do'.

Nightlife
The Button Factory
Curved Street, Temple Bar
Tel: 01-670 9202
www.buttonfactory.ie
Live music venue with top DJs and hot acts.

The Gaiety Theatre
South King Street
Tel: 01-677 1717
This theatre opens to the after-hours crowd, with live music on one floor, DJs on another, and beer and conversation on a third.

Ri-Ra
Dame Court, Exchequer Street
Tel: 01-677 4835
One of Dublin's most popular places for the younger crowd.

Tripod
Old Harcourt Street Station
Tel: 01-478 0166
Huge club with a capacity of 1,300 and great sound and light systems. Hosts international DJs and live acts.

Gay-friendly venues
For more venues see www.gaydublin.com.

The George
89 South Great George's Street
Tel: 01-478 2983
The George is probably the city's most popular gay club.

Theatre
Tickets can often be bought on the day for that evening's performance, and are usually priced at about €30 or less.

Abbey Theatre
Lower Abbey Street
Tel: 01-878 7222
www.abbeytheatre.ie
Ireland's national theatre.

Gaiety Theatre
South King Street
Tel: 01-677 1717
www.gaietytheatre.com

Smoking is banned indoors, so pavements outside pubs are often lively

Opera, ballet, pantomime, variety concerts and drama in a fine Victorian building.

Gate Theatre
1 Cavendish Row, Parnell Square
Tel: 01-874 4045
www.gate-theatre.ie
Avant-garde theatre by Irish and international playwrights.

Olympia Theatre
72 Dame Street
Tel: 01-679 3323
Once a Victorian music hall, but now a theatre as well as a venue for live bands.

Project Arts Centre
39 East Essex Street
Tel: 01-881 9613
www.projectartscentre.ie
Cutting-edge music and performance.

TOURS

Dublin's compact centre lends itself perfectly to walking tours. Meanwhile, the attractions around Dublin can be visited by bus on day trips. Dublin Tourism Centre is the best place to get information and book tours.

Walking tours
Dublin Tourism Centre
Suffolk Street
Tel: 01-605 7700

www.visitdublin.com
The website has free podcast audioguides to Dublin. Pick up a booklet at the centre, and follow the Rock 'n' Stroll trail to visit sites

associated with U2, Westlife, Bob Geldof, the Dubliners and other local stars. Alternatively, you could also book a literary tour or traditional music pub crawl, or choose from one of eight historic walks of Dublin city centre. All walks are available daily Apr–Oct, and on a less frequent basis in the off season.

Bus tours
Bus Éireann
Tel: 01-836 6111
www.buseireann.ie

Gray Line Tours
Tel: 01-670 8822
www.grayline.com
Both companies offer a range of one-hour city tours, half-day tours that include the outer suburbs, and day trips to Glendalough

and County Wicklow, the Boyne Valley, and County Kildare.

Dublin Bus
Tel: 01-703 3028
www.dublinsighteeing.ie
A Freedom of Dublin bus pass for one or three days is a good buy, giving access to all city bus services as well as the hop-on-hop-off bus tour that passes all major attractions. Dublin Bus also operates day tours to the coast north and south of Dublin.

Viking Splash Tour
Tel: 01-707 6000
www.vikingsplash.ie
For a change from the usual bus tour around the city, try this military amphibious vehicle – it's always a great hit with kids.

FESTIVALS AND EVENTS

Dublin's festival calendar provides plenty of free entertainment and some wonderful opportunities to sample the best of international culture.

March
St Patrick's Festival
Tel: 01-676 3205
www.stpatricksfestival.ie
A four-day festival of film, music, comedy and family events. The festivities culminate in Ireland's biggest parade.

June
Street Performance World Championships
Tel: 01-639 4859
www.spwc.ie
Street performers from all over the world compete in Merrion Square for the title of world champion.

August
Dublin Horse Show
Tel: 01-240 7213
www.dublinhorseshow.com
For many, this is still the social highlight of the year: five days of horse-related events,

including international show jumping, and a best dressed competition on Ladies' Day.

September–October
Dublin Theatre Festival
Tel: 01-677 8439
www.dublintheatrefestival.com
Over two weeks of the finest Irish and international theatre.

Raising a glass in classic Irish style

The southeast

Over the whole year, Ireland's southeast enjoys up to an hour more sunshine a day than other parts of the country, making its long, sandy coast a favourite holiday destination. The places in this chapter can be visited en route from Dublin to the South – take either the coastal route via Waterford city or head inland via Kilkenny and the Rock of Cashel, ending with an optional scenic detour into the Blackwater Valley.

Waterford

Population: 45,650

Local dialling code: 051

Local tourist office: Merchant's Quay; tel: 051-875 823; www. waterfordtourism.org

Main police station: Ballybricken; tel: 051-874 888

Main post office: 12 Broad Street

Main hospital: Waterford Regional Hospital, Dunmore Road; tel: 051-848 000

Airports: Waterford Airport, Airport Road; tel: 051-846 000;

www.waterfordairport.ie

Trains: Plunkett Station, Terminus Street; tel: 051-873 401; www.irishrail.ie

Buses: Bus Éireann, Merchant's Quay; tel: 051-879 000; www.buseireann.ie

Car-hire companies: Car Hire Ireland; no tel – book only online; www.carhireireland.com

Taxi companies: Rapid Cabs, Olympia Court, Parnell Street; tel: 051-858 585; www.rapidcabs.com

The 'sunny southeast', as it is popularly known, has one obvious advantage over the rest of Ireland: good weather. With almost double the annual quota of sunshine that other regions receive, it has long been favoured as a holiday destination by the Irish themselves, and many Dubliners have holiday homes here.

The region bears a distinct geographical contrast to the rest of the country, with undulating plains intersected by meandering river valleys producing fertile agricultural land. Its towns and cities have long and interesting histories: Cashel was the seat of the kings of Munster, while Wexford and Waterford were founded by Viking invaders.

Counties Wexford and Waterford

Long sandy beaches, rocky bays and low cliffs are features of these counties' scenic shorelines, lined with pleasant and picturesque towns that grew up around the sea.

County Wexford

Wexford is about an hour and a half's drive from Dublin, south of County Wicklow. **Gorey ❶**, the first town you reach entering County Wexford coming from the northeast along the coast, has a more genteel ambience than Arklow (in County Wicklow). It is not actually on the sea, but nevertheless is chiefly a holiday resort. Its seaside cottages are found by turning left in Gorey onto the R742, a pleasant alternative route to Wexford further south.

The R742 passes **Curracloe Strand ❷**, 11km (7 miles) northeast of Wexford harbour, which stood in for the Normandy Beaches in the 1998 war film *Saving Private Ryan*. The totally unspoilt strand is backed by dunes, and stretches for some 10km (6 miles).

Wexford harbour

The harbour and its mud flats attract a variety of ducks, geese and swans.

The next main town due south along the coast is **Wexford ❸**, is a small, easily explored place, consisting of a

Wexford hosts an opera festival each October, and its new opera house was built in 2008

Wexford Opera House

The huge modern building that dominates Wexford's centre is the Wexford Opera House, which was completed in 2008 at a cost of €33 million. It replaced the much-loved Theatre Royal, built in 1830, and has 769 seats, making it 4.5 times bigger than the old theatre. Its walnut-lined interior does, however, feature horseshoe-shaped balconies similar to those of its predecessor. The reason that this small town has such a large opera house is the two-week long Wexford Festival Opera (www.wexfordopera.com), an annual event that produces full-scale productions of three little-known operas every year in late October (see p.110). In addition, there is a packed calendar of recitals, orchestral performances and other events. The festival celebrated its 60th anniversary in 2011.

The southeast

strip of quays parallel to the waterfront, with a network of smaller streets parallel to the quays. Walking tours leave from the Tourist Information Office (*see p.110*), visiting the town's highlights, including the Westgate Tower, the only remaining one of five fortified gateways in the Norman town walls. Other attractions in the town include its old-fashioned shops and pubs and the **Wexford Festival Opera** (*see box, p.97*), each October.

The **Irish National Heritage Park** (tel: 053-912 0733; www.inhp. com; daily, Mar–Oct 9.30am–6.30pm, Nov–Feb 9.30am–5.30pm; charge), at Ferrycarrig, 5km (3 miles) northwest of Wexford, is an open-air museum on the banks of the River Slaney. A couple of hours among its life-size replicas of typical dwelling places – including a prehistoric homestead, a *crannog* (lake

dwelling), an early Christian fortified farm, a monastery and a Norman castle – should do wonders for your knowledge of Irish history and architecture, from Stone Age man in 6000BC up to the 12th-century Norman settlements.

County Waterford

The main road travels to Waterford via New Ross, but for a more scenic alternative route go via **Kilmore Quay ❹**, a quaint little fishing village of whitewashed cottages and friendly pubs built between the dunes and a stone harbour wall. It looks out to the uninhabited **Saltee Islands**, which are one of Ireland's most important bird sanctuaries.

Heading west, the R736/R733 leads to the **Hook Head Peninsula** (and its lighthouse), which forms the east side of Waterford harbour. Beyond Arthurstown is **Ballyhack**, a pretty waterside

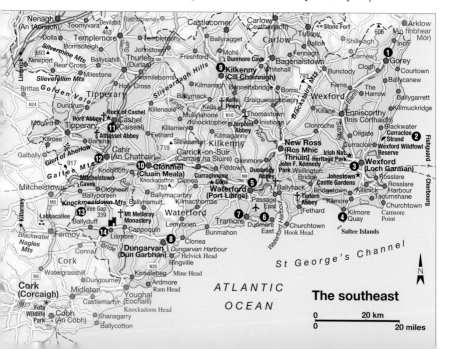

The southeast

0   20 km

0   20 miles

12th-century Viking jewellery. At the eastern extremity of the quays stands **Reginald's Tower** (tel: 051-304 220; June–Sept daily 10am–6pm, Easter–May and Oct daily 10am–5pm, Nov–Easter Wed–Sun 10am–5pm; charge), the city's most venerable building. The walls of this giant circular fortification, 3m (10ft) thick and about 24m (80ft) tall, have survived many sieges since first being erected in 1003. Municipal mementoes, including Waterford's important collection of medieval charters, are preserved inside.

Among the other attractions in Waterford are the Garter Lane Arts Centre, a lively venue in a converted townhouse; the Mall, an elegant Georgian street starting at the Quay; Christ Church Cathedral, the only neoclassical Georgian cathedral in Ireland; and Waterford City Hall, built in the 1780s

village on the estuary of the River Barrow and dominated **by Ballyhack Castle** (tel: 051-389 468; mid-June–mid-Sept daily; charge), a 16th-century tower house. From Ballyhack it's a five-minute car-ferry ride across the estuary to the Waterford side.

Waterford ❺ is a port 29km (18 miles) from the open sea, and was at its busiest in the 18th century. From the far side of the River Suir, its long quayside presents a pretty image. Walking tours leave daily from the Tourist Office on Merchants Quay *(see p.110)*. In the same building is the **Waterford Museum of Treasures** (tel: 051-304 500; June–Aug Mon–Sat 9am–6pm, Sun 11am–6pm, Sept–May Mon–Sat 10am–5pm, Sun 11am–5pm; charge). Its display of original artefacts includes

Conquerors

Ireland was never conquered by the Romans, and the introduction of Christianity in the 5th century was a peaceful process. The first hostile invaders were the Vikings during the 9th century. They founded Ireland's first towns, including Wexford (*Waesfjord* in Old Norse) and Waterford (*Vadrefjord*). The Normans, who landed at Waterford from Wales in 1169, intermarried with Irish nobles and were quickly assimilated. Strongbow, a Norman conqueror, married Aoife (or Eve), daughter of the Irish chief Dermot MacMurrough, at Waterford's Reginald's Tower in 1170.

and with notable features including the magnificent Waterford crystal chandelier in the Council Chamber.

And, on the subject of chandeliers, opposite City Hall, **The Waterford Crystal Experience** (The Mall; tel: 051-351 936; www.waterfordvisitor centre.com; charge) celebrates the city's long glass-making tradition, which dates back to 1783. (It used to be possible to tour the Waterford Wedgwood factory, but this has not been possible since the firm went into receivership in 2009 and the factory closed.) The 50-minute tour features glass-blowing, cutting and engraving.

The coast road to Dungarvan

The N25 takes a fast inland route from Waterford to Dungarvan. If time allows, however, take the coastal route, leaving Waterford on the R684 for **Dunmore East ❻**. This pretty cliff-side fishing village and holiday resort of thatched cottages is set by the open sea at the head of Waterford harbour. Slightly further west is **Tramore ❼**, a total contrast, with a long, flat, sandy beach, a funfair, caravan parks and other facilities aimed at families. It is also extremely popular with surfers between September and May.

The coast road continues through **Annestown**, **Bunmahon** and **Clonea**, a trio of villages with good beaches. Known as Waterford's Copper Coast, this region was given European Geopark status by Unesco in recognition of its volcanic geology and copper-mining heritage.

Continuing west leads to **Dungarvan ❽**, situated on Dungarvan harbour and backed by wooded hills. The county town of Waterford, it has some lively waterside pubs and a farmers' market on Thursday mornings.

Kilkenny and Tipperary

The historic medieval town of Kilkenny, with its magnificently restored

Demonstrating how Waterford crystal used to be made in Ireland by master craftsmen

Tramore beach is popular with watersports fans

castle, should not be missed. You can linger in the Kilkenny area exploring the pretty riverside villages of the Nore and the Barrow, or continue on towards **Clonmel**, a compact market town on the River Suir. Both options lead to Tipperary, and the spectacular ecclesiastical ruins on the Rock of Cashel. At Cahir, there is a massive castle to visit and quiet woodland walks through the relatively unfrequented Glen of Aherlow.

County Kilkenny

Kilkenny ❾ has a colourful past and present. This was the capital of the old kingdom of Ossory, a small feuding realm in pre-Norman Ireland.

Kilkenny craft trail

Kilkenny – both the city and county – has a high reputation for crafts and is a good place to seek out handmade goods. Kilkenny Castle Yard, formerly the stables of Kilkenny Castle, houses the **Kilkenny Design Centre** (a popular craft shop, selling traditional Irish knitwear, pottery, glass and jewellery), as well as the headquarters of the **Crafts Council of Ireland** and its flagship exhibition space, the **National Craft Gallery**.

The goldsmith **Rudolf Heltzel** (10 Patrick Street, Kilkenny; tel: 056-772 1497; www.heltzel.ie) is internationally renowned

for his modern jewellery. **Jerpoint Glass** (near Mount Juliet Hotel, Thomastown; tel: 056-772 4350; www.jerpointglass.com) produces handmade glass in striking modern designs; you can sometimes watch the glass-blowing at the studio there. **Nicholas Mosse** (Bennettsbridge; tel: 056-772 7505) produces hand-decorated country-style pottery and sells a wide range of country-style gifts at his pottery shop. Pick up a leaflet locally for the Made in Kilkenny Craft Trail (www.madeinkilkenny.ie), which also includes leather goods and a wool mill on its list of hits.

🚗 NORE VALLEY DRIVE

Drive from Kilkenny through picturesque villages on the River Nore to tranquil Jerpoint Abbey deep in the countryside. Finish off on board a famine ship at New Ross in County Wexford.

Head straight out of Kilkenny city from the castle and join the R700, a pretty minor road that follows the River Nore southwards to its estuary.

The stone bridge at **Bennettsbridge**, 6km (3¾ miles) south of Kilkenny, dates from 1285 and is one of the oldest crossings of the River Nore. The road swings right over the bridge, and passes Chesnau Leather Goods, a factory outlet selling fine leather handbags. The shop marks the start of the **Kilkenny Craft Trail**. Pick up a brochure here with details of the other craft-makers on the trail. These include the Nicholas Mosse Pottery and Country Shop, also in Bennettsbridge, which produces hand-

decorated spongeware, and hand-blown glass at **Jerpoint** *(see below)*.

Thomastown, 12km (7 miles) further south, is an attractive village of grey-stone buildings and steep hills that dates from the 13th century. Follow the signs in the village for a 2km (1¼-mile) detour southwest across another narrow stone bridge to **Jerpoint Abbey**. Founded in 1158 by the Cistercians, this is one of the finest monastic ruins in Ireland, consisting of a cloister,

Tips

- Distance: 46km (28½ miles)
- Time: A half-day drive
- Start: Kilkenny City
- End: New Ross
- Kilkenny is 116km (72 miles) southwest of Dublin and approximately 100km (62 miles) west of Arklow. New Ross is 14km (9 miles) northeast of Waterford and 53km (33 miles) west of Rosslare ferryport.

The lush view, looking down from Inistioge towards the River Nore

quadrangle and three-naved church with Romanesque arches set against a peaceful rural backdrop. Walk around the two sides of the cloisters to appreciate their unusual carvings, some of which are like medieval cartoons.

Return to Thomastown and rejoin the R700 south, crossing the Nore again via a long, 12-arched stone bridge, amid sweeping views of a wooded valley, to **Inistioge** (Tighe's Island in Irish, pronounced *Inishteeg*). The village is situated on a bend of the river and has a tree-lined square leading to a tall stone bridge. It's a favourite location for films, which include *Widows' Peak* (1994) with Mia Farrow and Joan Plowright, and *Circle of Friends* (1995) with Minnie Driver and Saffron Burrows.

Follow the road to the left at the Woodstock Arms for the riverfront. A flat grassy area next to the river is a perfect spot for picnicking and has views of the picturesque bridge backed by a line of Georgian houses. One of these is a restaurant, **Footlights** *(see p.109)*.

Continue along the R700 for another 17km (10½ miles), crossing the border into County Wexford at New Ross. The town was built on a steep hill overlooking the River Barrow at a strategically important water crossing. On the river bank you will see the tall masts of the *Dunbrody* **famine ship**, a full-scale replica of a wooden sailing ship built in 1845 to transport emigrants to North America. On board, actors tell the stories of the passengers, who travelled in appalling conditions in this 'coffin ship' in order

The slow pace of life in Inistioge

to escape the Great Famine. It is both entertaining and a sobering reminder of the ordeal suffered by the 2 million and more people who emigrated from Ireland's ports at that time.

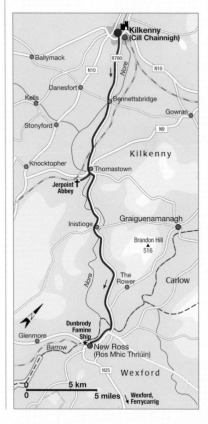

Nore Valley drive

Parliament, which convened here in 1366, passed the notorious but ineffectual Statutes of Kilkenny, with the aim of segregating the Irish from the Anglo-Normans; in those days intermarriage was seen as high treason. In the 17th century an independent Irish parliament met here for several years. Oliver Cromwell took the town for the English in 1650, suffering heavy losses in the process.

St Canice's Cathedral, built during the 13th century, is on the original site of the church that gave the town its name – the Irish *Cill Choinnigh* means St Canice's church. Though Cromwell's rampaging troops badly damaged the building, it has since been restored to an admirable state. Medieval sculptures and monuments abound in this Protestant church. The 6th-century **Round Tower** in the cathedral grounds is the only remnant of St Canice's monastery. You can climb its 167 steps, from where there are astounding views.

Kilkenny Castle (tel: 056-770 4100; guided tours only; daily Mar 9.30am–5pm, Apr–May and Sept 9.30am–5.30pm, June–Aug 9am–5.30pm, Oct–Feb 9.30am–4.30pm; charge for castle; grounds and gallery free), on The Parade in the town centre, was built in the 13th century to replace the primitive fortress erected by Strongbow. The Butler family, one of the great Anglo-Norman dynasties, held the castle until 1935, but today it is owned by the Irish state. The ornate Georgian stableyard across the main road is occupied by the **Kilkenny Design Centre**, which displays local and national crafts and runs workshops.

County Tipperary

From Kilkenny, the N76 leads south to **Clonmel** ⑩, a busy market town with elegant Georgian buildings on the River Suir. The area north and east of the town is known for its apple orchards, and Clonmel is the centre of the Irish cider-making industry.

First built in the 13th century, Kilkenny Castle was remodelled during Victorian times

Cromwell's campaign. **Cormac's Chapel** is a simpler building dating from 1127, before the Norman invasion, with a high, corbelled roof similar to those found in early saints' cells in Glendalough and Dingle. Cormac's Chapel is generally considered one of the greatest achievements of native Irish church architecture.

Incredible though the rock is, it's worth noting that absolutely every tour bus in this part of Ireland stops here. It will greatly enhance your visit if you can avoid the crowds by getting here at lunchtime or late afternoon.

Cahir ⑫ (pronounced *Care*), set on a hill above the River Suir, has a faded charm, due chiefly to the well-proportioned Georgian houses on its Mall and main square. It is known for its antique shops and castle (tel: 052-744 1011; www.heritageireland.ie; charge), a massive limestone fortress from the 12th century set on a rock in the River Suir. Walk up the hill beside the castle to the attractive main square.

The **Glen of Aherlow**, south of Tipperary town, is a quiet country valley between the Galtee Mountains and the Slievenamuck Ridge. The way-marked walks through quiet countryside offer good views across the plain, and pass several corrie lakes and mountain streams as well running through ancient woodlands and hills rich in folklore.

The Vee Gap to Lismore

A 20-minute drive from Cahir south to Clogheen and Lismore brings you to the **Vee Gap** ⑬, a famous beauty spot

105

The southeast

From Clonmel, head 32km (20 miles) northwest to **Cashel** ⑪. A cluster of romantic-looking, turreted buildings stands on a limestone outcrop rising 60m (200ft) above the Tipperary plain. This is the **Rock of Cashel** (tel: 062-61437; www.cashel.ie; daily, mid-Mar–early June 9am–5.30pm, early June–mid-Sept 9am–7pm, mid-Sept–mid-Oct 9am–5.30pm, mid-Oct–mid-Mar 9am–4.30pm; charge). It was probably once a centre of Druidic worship, but by the 4th century AD had become the ceremonial centre of the kings of Munster. St Patrick visited in 450 and baptised King Aengus and his brothers here.

The largest building on the rock, the shell of **St Patrick's Cathedral**, built in the Gothic style, was in use from the 13th to the mid-16th century, when it was desecrated in Oliver

on the Knockmealdown Mountains. Straddling the county borders of Tipperary and Waterford, 'The Vee', which is named after the V-shaped gap in the mountains, offers panoramic views of the Galtee Mountains in the northwest. The vegetation is mainly grass and heather, and woolly sheep roam free. There are a number of lay-bys on this road to stop and take in the views and to access to picnicking spots and way-marked walking trails *(see p.110)*.

Lismore

A short drive downhill from the Vee Gap is the pretty village of **Lismore** ⓮. As you cross the bridge into the village, you will have a dramatic view of **Lismore Castle** (tel: 058-54424; www.lismorecastle.com; gardens and art gallery 17 Mar–mid-Oct; charge), perched on a cliff above the River Blackwater. Built during the mid-18th century, the dramatic structure, which is often described as the most spectacular castle in Ireland, overlooks the Blackwater Valley with views across rolling, wooded hills to the Knockmealdown Mountains beyond.

The castle itself is used as a summer residence by the Duke of Devonshire, and is closed to the public, apart from the West Wing, which has been converted into a contemporary art gallery. The gardens, which feature an 800-year-old yew walk and some fine contemporary sculpture, are open to the public.

Lismore was an important monastic centre from the 7th to the 12th century, which is why it has a cathedral. **St Carthage's**, built in 1633 just off the main street in the North Mall, incorporates parts of an earlier, 9th-century church and is worth a visit for its fine effigies. More information on the village's past can be found at the **Lismore Heritage Centre** (tel: 058-54975; charge), opposite the castle's car park.

Grubb Monument, where Samuel Grubb is buried standing up, with his tomb facing the view he so loved in the Knockmealdown Mountains

ACCOMMODATION

The rolling countryside of the southeast is home to some fine country-house hotels. The coast of the counties of Wexford and Waterford has a range of family-friendly resort hotels, while Tipperary and the Comeragh Mountains offer comfortable accommodation for walkers. Waterford city, Kilkenny and Wexford town, meanwhile, offer a good mix of modern and traditional hotels and guesthouses.

Counties Wexford and Waterford

Arlington Lodge Town House and Restaurant
John's Hill, Waterford
Tel: 051-878 584
www.arlingtonlodge.com
Charming hotel in a former bishop's palace, 10 minutes' walk from the town centre. €€

Cliff House Hotel
Ardmore, Co. Waterford
Tel: 024-878 800
www.thecliffhousehotel.com
Luxury boutique hotel with famed restaurant and stunning cliff-top location. €€€€

Dooley's Hotel
The Quay, Waterford
Tel: 051-873 531
www.dooleys-hotel.ie
Family-run hotel with a lively bar in the centre of town on the River Suir. €€

Dunbrody Country House Hotel
Arthurstown, Hook Peninsula, Co. Wexford
Tel: 051-389 600
www.dunbrodyhouse.com
Set in 8 hectares (20 acres) of parkland, this stylish Georgian manor is now an informal hotel and restaurant run by the award-winning owner-chef and his wife. €€€€

Ferrycarrig Hotel
Ferrycarrig Bridge, near Wexford
Tel: 053-912 0999
www.ferrycarrighotel.ie
Stylish modern hotel in a pleasant setting by Slaney River 5km (3 miles) outside of town, on the Enniscorthy road. €€€

Ferryport House
Rosslare Harbour, Co. Wexford
Tel: 053-913 3933
www.ferryporthouse.com
A modern guesthouse with spacious rooms a stone's throw from the ferryport. €

Foxmount Farm and Country House
Passage East Road, Waterford
Tel: 051-874 308
www.foxmountcountryhouse.com
You can stay in the elegant Georgian mansion on the Kent family's working dairy farm, 10 minutes' drive from Waterford city centre. Attractive gardens and good breakfasts. €€

Hanora's Cottage
Ballymacarbry, Nire Valley, Co. Waterford
Tel: 052-613 6134
www.hanorascottage.com
Hikers in Waterford's Comeragh Mountains appreciate the comfort of this award-winning riverside retreat – and the imaginative home cooking on offer here. €€

Kelly's Resort Hotel
Rosslare Village, Co. Wexford
Tel: 053-913 2114
www.kellys.ie
This beachfront resort hotel was established in 1895, and has been run by the Kelly family ever since. Outstanding sports facilities and fine food. €€€

Listings

St George Guest House

Georges Street, Wexford
Tel: 053-914 3473
www.stgeorgeguesthouse.com
A pleasant, traditional-style guesthouse, three minutes' walk from the town centre. **€**

Counties Kilkenny and Tipperary

Aherlow House Hotel and Lodges

Glen of Aherlow, Co. Tipperary
Tel: 062-56153
www.aherlowhouse.ie
Choose between the main hotel or separate lodges. All are surrounded by pine forest and overlook the Galtee Mountains, and are a good base for walking and climbing. **€€**

Butler House

Patrick Street, Kilkenny
Tel: 056-776 5707
www.butler.ie
Once the dower house of Kilkenny Castle, this town-centre Georgian house has large gardens. It combines period elegance with contemporary design. **€€**

Cashel Palace Hotel

Main Street, Cashel, Co. Tipperary
Tel: 062-62707
www.cashel-palace.ie
A Queen Anne-style bishop's palace converted into a sumptuous hotel. Views of the Rock of Cashel from the back rooms. **€€€**

Hotel Kilkenny

College Road, Kilkenny
Tel: 056-776 2000
www.hotelkilkenny.ie
Modern hotel and leisure complex built around a Georgian house. Pool, Jacuzzi. **€€€**

Kilcoran Lodge

Cahir, Co. Tipperary
Tel: 052-744 1288
www.kilcoranlodgehotel.com
Old-fashioned former hunting lodge in its own grounds with a pool and views over the Knockmealdown Mountains. Self-catering lodges also available. **€€**

Mount Juliet Conrad

Thomastown, Co. Kilkenny
Tel: 056-777 3000
www.mountjuliet.ie
An elegant 18th-century house on an estate with a Jack Nicklaus golf course, equestrian centre and tennis centre. Also has 16 less formal (cheaper end of range) rooms in the separate Hunter's Yard. **€€–€€€€**

Waterside

The Quay, Graiguenamanagh, Co. Kilkenny
Tel: 059-972 4246
www.watersideguesthouse.com
These simple, comfortable rooms above a popular restaurant are in a converted stone-built corn mill overlooking the River Barrow. The quiet village, which is popular with outdoor types, has some old-fashioned pubs. **€**

Zuni Townhouse

26 Patrick Street, Kilkenny
Tel: 056-772 3999
www.zuni.ie
Zuni is a town-centre boutique hotel with minimalist decor and a popular Asian-themed restaurant. Also has parking. **€**

Mount Juliet Conrad, in Thomastown, Co. Kilkenny

RESTAURANTS

A new awareness of the high quality of local produce has led to the showcasing of locally reared meat, fresh fish and locally grown fruit and vegetables. Some of the finest restaurants are in hotels, but they are resolutely informal.

Counties Wexford and Waterford

L'Atmosphere
19 Henrietta Street, Waterford
Tel: 051-858 426
www.restaurant-latmosphere.com
French bistro in an old Georgian townhouse. Offers good value for money. €€

La Dolce Vita
6–7 Trimmer's Lane, Wexford
Tel: 053-917 0806
One of Ireland's favourite Italian restaurants (also a café and deli). Roberto's cooking and menus are enticingly authentic. €–€€

The Granary
Merchants Quay, Waterford
Tel: 051-304 500
The hearty, home-baked fare at the café in the lobby of the Waterford Treasures Museum is a favourite with locals. Sofas add to the informal atmosphere. €

The House
Cliff House Hotel, Ardmore, Co. Waterford
Tel: 024-87820
www.thecliffhousehotel.com
Dutch chef Martijn Kajuiter gives the high-tech treatment to the freshest Irish produce with sensational results. €€€€

O'Brien Chophouse
Main Street, Lismore, Co. Waterford
Tel: 058-53810
www.obrienchophouse.ie
Converted Victorian pub with a pretty garden. Serves robust versions of locally sourced, simply served traditional Irish food. €–€€

The Tannery
10 Quay Street, Dungarvan, Co. Waterford
Tel: 058-45420
www.tannery.ie
This warehouse is the base of Paul Flynn, whose imaginative modern Irish cuisine has won a legion of fans. Also a cookery school. €€€€

Counties Kilkenny and Tipperary

Café Hans
Moor Lane, Cashel
Tel: 062-63660
A nice café in a former chapel below the Rock. Does salads, sarnies and hot daily specials. €

Footlights
The Square, Inistioge, Co. Kilkenny
Tel: 056-775 8724
www.footlights.ie
Child-friendly bistro in a period riverside house. Snacks include ciabattas, salads and pizzas; mains are made with local produce. €

Kilkenny Design Centre
Castle Yard, Kilkenny
Tel: 056-772 2118
www.kilkennydesign.com
A lively first-floor restaurant serving wholesome daily specials such as chicken and broccoli crumble with Lavistown cheese, plus soups, salads and home-baking. €

Langton's House Hotel
69 John Street, Kilkenny
Tel: 056-776 5133
www.langtons.ie
Within Langton's there are several restaurants and bars, but all focus on fresh local food and enticing textures. €–€€

NIGHTLIFE AND ENTERTAINMENT

Most of the nightlife in the area is pub-based, consisting mainly of live music. For listings of music pubs and gay-friendly venues, pick up the free brochure *Whazon? Waterford and Kilkenny* or see www.whazon.com.

Auditorium of Wexford Opera House

Garter Lane Arts Centre
O'Connell Street, Waterford
Tel: 051-877 153
www.garterlane.ie
Arts centre with a lively programme of dance, film, studio-theatre and exhibitions.

Theatre Royal
The Mall, Waterford
Tel: 051-874 900
www.theatreroyal.ie
This Georgian playhouse puts on a lively programme of plays, concerts and comedy.

The Watergate
Parliament Street, Kilkenny
Tel: 056-776 1674
www.watergatetheatre.com
The theatre offers a varied programme of drama, dance and music.

Wexford Arts Centre
Cornmarket, Wexford
Tel: 053-23764
www.wexfordartscentre.ie
Arts centre hosting changing contemporary exhibitions and workshops.

Wexford Opera House
High Street, Wexford
Tel: 053-912 2400
www.wexfordoperahouse.ie
Outside the main festival *(see opposite),* there is a programme of touring theatrical productions, music recitals and concerts.

A ceilidh is held nightly from June to August at Colaiste na Rinne (Ring), an Irish-language school near Dungarvan; tel: 058-46104.

TOURS

The best way to explore the southeast's historic towns is on a guided walk, usually costing €5–7 for an hour. Tours leave daily between mid-March and September, so phone ahead to confirm any held outside those peak months.

Kilkenny Tourist Information Office
Shee Alms House
Tel: 056-776 3955
www.kilkennytourism.ie
Tynan Tours run walks starting at the tourist office: Mon–Sat 10.30am, 12.15pm, 3pm and 4.30pm, Sun 11.15am, 12.30pm.

Waterford Treasures Museum
Merchants Quay

Tel: 051-873 711
Veteran tour guide Jack Burtchaell leads a walking tour daily from the museum at 11.45am and 1.45pm.

Wexford Tourist Information Office
The Crescent
Tel: 053-912 3111
www.discoverireland.ie/places
Tours leave daily at 11am.

SPORTS AND ACTIVITIES

The quiet rural roads and paths of the southeast make it ideal for walking and cycling. Cycling enthusiasts in the area are inspired by the County Waterford-born former professional bicycle racer Sean Kelly (www.theseankellytour.com).

Ballyhoura International Walking Festival
Tel: 063-639 1300
www.ballyhouracountry.com
The Ballyhoura Mountains offer excellent walking on gentle slopes.

Easy Wheeling Cycling Tours
Tramore, Co. Waterford
Tel: 051-390 706
www.discoverireland/southeast
Basic bike hire and guided cycling tours.

Glen of Aherlow
Tel: 062-56331

www.aherlow.com
Tipperary's walkers share their knowledge of the Galtee Mountains at a festival each June.

Kilkenny Cycling Tours
Castlecomer Road, Kilkenny
Tel: 086-895 4961
www.kilkennycyclingtours.com
Bike hire and guided city and rural tours.

Nire Valley – Comeragh Mountains
www.nirevalley.com
Discover one of Ireland's best, but lesser-known, walking regions in County Waterford.

FESTIVALS AND EVENTS

The southeast hosts two of Ireland's biggest arts events, the Kilkenny Arts Festival and the Wexford Festival Opera.

April

Kilkenny Rhythm and Roots Festival
www.kilkennyroots.com
In late April: four days of the best in Americana and Roots music across town.

Waterford Festival of Food
Dungarvan
www.waterfordfestivaloffood.com
A mid-April weekend showcasing the area's artisan food producers and eateries.

June

The Cat Laughs Comedy Festival
Kilkenny City
www.thecatlaughs.com
World-class comedy festival with Irish and international performers.

The Happy Valley Festival
Thomastown, Co. Kilkenny
www.happyvalleyfestival.com

Around the June bank holiday: a week of music, theatre and visual arts. Family fun.

Lismore Music Festival
www.lismoremusicfestival.com
June bank holiday music and opera festival.

August

Kilkenny Arts Festival
www.kilkennyarts.ie
Ten days of music, dance, theatre, film, etc.

SPRAOI Festival
Waterford City
www.spraoi.com
Bank-holiday weekend: free, family-friendly street-theatre and world-music festival.

October

Wexford Festival Opera
www.wexfordopera.com
Eleven days of opera, concerts and recitals.

County Cork

Ireland's largest county features gently rolling farmland, rugged, stony peninsulas and delightful bays, all within easy driving distance of Ireland's second city. Enclosed by steep hills, Cork city has all the facilities of a major commercial centre, plus bags of atmosphere. Its narrow lanes, half-hidden flights of steps and unexpected plazas lend themselves to both lazy strolls and more structured sightseeing.

Cork city

Population: 123,000

Local dialling code: 021

Local tourist office: Cork Tourism, 35 Grand Parade; tel: 021-425 5100; www.discoverireland.ie/southwest

Main police station: Bridewell; tel: 021-494 3330

Main post office: GPO, Oliver Plunkett Street

Main hospital: Cork University Hospital, Wilton; tel: 021-454 6400

Media: *Irish Examiner* (national daily), *Evening Echo* (evening paper)

Airports: Cork Airport; tel: 021-431 3131; www.corkairport.com. Skylink (tel: 021-432 1020; www.skylinkcork.com) operates a shuttle service between Cork Airport and city-centre hotels from 5.20am to midnight. Tickets cost €5 each way and can be purchased online or on board. Skylink also connects Cork with Shannon Airport. **Bus Éireann** (tel: 021-450 8188; www.buseireann.ie) has a bus link between Cork Airport and Cork City Bus Station about every 30 minutes, costing €3.40 one way. Tickets can be bought on board

Trains: Kent Station; Lower Glanmire Road; tel: 021-836 6222; www.irishrail.ie

Buses: Cork Bus Station; Parnell Place; tel: 021-450 8188; www.buseaireann.ie

Car-hire companies: Cork Airport Car Rentals; tel: 1850-206 088; Car Hire Ireland; no tel – book online only; www.carhireireland.com

Taxi companies: Cork Taxi Co-Op; tel: 021-477 2222; www.corktaxi.ie

Ireland's biggest and most southerly county offers an attractive combination of sea and hill scenery, interspersed with lively small towns and villages, especially along its long indented coast. Because of the Gulf Stream, parts of the southwest coast are frost-free-year round, and have lush, subtropical vegetation, with massive rhododendrons and azaleas from mid-April to May. An added bonus is the high quality of County Cork's natural produce – farmhouse cheeses made from the milk of sleek cows grazing the fertile green meadows, locally reared beef, pork and lamb, and freshly caught fish. Local honey, home-grown potatoes, salads and vegetables (increasingly organic) will impress with their flavour and freshness. These are sold locally in specialist food shops and at farmers' markets, and feature on restaurant menus, giving the area a high reputation among food-lovers.

The vibrant hub of the southwest, Cork city has long divested itself of its sleepy second-city status, with multinationals (including Apple, which has its European headquarters here) creating jobs, a thriving student community and a significant population from European Union states such as Poland, Hungary and Lithuania adding a multicultural feel. The result is a cosmopolitan city bristling with

Beara Peninsula, Co. Cork *(see p.122)*

fashionable bars and restaurants, live music venues and festivals.

Cork city

The historic centre of **Cork ❶** is built on an island created by two channels of the River Lee. Easily walked in a day, it is ideal for leisurely sightseeing, shopping and idle strolling.

The centre

The main office for **Cork Tourism** (tel: 021-425 5100; www.discoverire land.ie/southwest) on **Grand Parade ❹** offers free maps of the city centre. From here, across the south channel of the River Lee, you can see the spires of **St Fin Barre's Cathedral ❸** (tel: 021-496 3387; www.cathedral. cork.anglican.org; Oct–Mar Mon–Sat 10am–12.45pm, 2–5pm, Sun 12.30am–5pm, Apr–Sept Mon–Sat 9.30am–5.30pm, Sun 12.30–5pm), named after the city's patron saint, who founded a monastic school here around AD650. Both the Gothic Revival-style cathedral and the bridge across the Lee are built of white limestone.

Back on the north side of the river is another of the city's showpieces,

The neo-Gothic St Fin Barre's Cathedral

the sprawling **Princes Street Market** 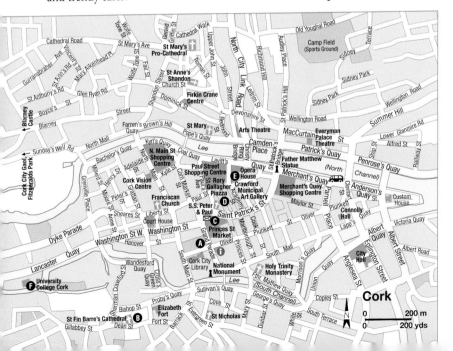 (Mon–Sat 9am–5pm), also known as the English Market. This elaborate warren between Grand Parade and St Patrick's Street, framed by ornate Victorian cast iron, shelters around 150 stalls selling food from artisan, often organic wares and continental delicatessen produce to traditional fishmongery and butchery.

Follow Grand Parade into the graceful curve of **St Patrick's Street**, Cork's main shopping street. On the left-hand side, an alleyway leads to the **Rory Gallagher Piazza** ⏺, a pedestrian square that is popular with buskers, and named after the Cork-born rock and blues guitarist who died in 1995. This area is the closest Cork gets to an arty 'Left Bank', with a cluster of fashion and vintage clothing boutiques and trendy cafés.

Turn right onto Paul Street for the **Crawford Municipal Art Gallery** ⏺ (tel: 021-490 7855; www.crawford artgallery.com; Mon–Sat 10am–5pm, Thur until 8pm; free). Most major 20th-century Irish artists are represented in its collection, alongside topographical paintings of Cork in its 18th- and 19th-century prime.

West of the city centre

A 10-minute walk west from Grand Parade along Washington Street leads to **University College Cork** ⏺. The Visitor Centre (tel: 021-490 3000; www.ucc.ie; free) is located in the north side of the 19th-century Tudor-Gothic style **Quadrangle**, adjacent to a display of ancient Ogham Stones – rock tablets named after the ancient language in which they are engraved. The **Honan Chapel**, a Hiberno-

University College Cork's main 'Quad'

which the castle is so famous. Kinsale, half an hour's drive to the south, is a historic town famed for its harbour, restaurants and craft shops.

Fota Island

The road from Cork to Cobh passes the walls of the 315-hectare (780-acre) Fota Estate, where **Fota Wildlife Park** ❷ (tel: 021-481 2678; www.fotawild life.ie; Mon–Sat 10am–4.30pm, Sun 11am–4.30pm; charge) aims to breed species that are under threat in the wild. Giraffes, zebras, ostriches, oryx and antelopes roam freely on the grass, monkeys swing through trees on islands in the lake, while kangaroos, wallabies, lemurs and peacocks have complete freedom within the park. Fota is the world's leading breeder of cheetahs, one of the few animal species here that is caged.

Beside the Wildlife Park, **Fota House** (tel: 021-481 5543; www.fota house.com; gardens daily 9am–6pm,

Romanesque chapel dating from 1916, showcases Celtic Revival-style arts and crafts. The campus has several other notable buildings, such as the **Lewis Glucksman Gallery** (tel: 021-490 1844; www.glucksman.org; Tue–Sat 10am–5pm, Sun 1–5pm; free), an award-winning art gallery with its top floor among the treetops.

Around Cork city

These excursions from Cork city can be made by public transport (see p.127) or by car. Fota Island and Cobh offer great harbour views and are good trips to make with children.

All first-time visitors should try to visit the magnificent Blarney Castle, whether or not they kiss the stone for

---

Cork's ups and downs

The northern bank of the River Lee rises steeply from the river, and local wits like to joke that this is the origin of the distinctly 'up-and-down' Cork accent. The sing-song qualities of the local accent can prove baffling to the visitor, especially when combined with the speed of delivery, generally recognised as the fastest in the country. You will hear fine examples of its distinctve lilt on Patrick Street in the afternoons, when veteran newspaper sellers hawk the *Evening Echo* with loud cries of 'Eeeeeko!'.

free; house Apr–Oct Mon–Sat 10am–5pm, Sun 11am–5pm, Nov–Mar, phone ahead; charge) is a modest 18th-century neoclassical shooting lodge, the interior of which has been partially renovated. **Fota Arboretum** (free) has a wonderful collection of mature trees, many of which were introduced from Asia, Australia and the Americas during the 19th century.

Cobh

Attractively located on a steep slope, **Cobh ❸** (pronounced *Cove*) has a Victorian-style promenade and panoramic views of Cork harbour. It is popular with visitors for its maritime history as the first – and last – European port of call for transatlantic shipping. Between 1848 and 1950, around 2.5 million adults and children emigrated via this port. Their transport ranged from convict transport and the 'coffin ships' of the famine years *(see p.103)*, all overcrowded and unseaworthy, to the luxury of the White Star and Cunard liners. Cobh was also the last port of call for the *Titanic* in 1912.

The old railway station is now the **Cobh Heritage Centre** (tel: 021-481 3591; www.cobhheritage.com; daily 9.30am–5.30pm; free). The history of emigration from Cobh is covered in **The Queenstown Story** (charge), an imaginative audiovisual exhibition. Allow at least an hour to see this.

Other attractions include the large, Gothic Revival-style **St Colman's Cathedral**, built in granite between 1868 and 1915. From its parapet you can see Roches Point, which marks the harbour entrance and the sea beyond.

Blarney

A visit to **Blarney Castle ❹** (tel: 021-438 5252; www.blarneycastle. ie; daily 9am–sundown, Sun until 5.30pm in summer; charge) makes a

Colourful houses in Cobh, an easy excursion from Cork city

Blarney Castle Tower

Kinsale

About 29km (18 miles) south of Cork, steep green hills shelter the seaport of **Kinsale** ❺, with a large, virtually landlocked harbour. The town is renowned for its restaurants, which are among the best in south-west Ireland. Other highlights in the town include the Market Square's Old Courthouse, which dates from 1600 and now houses the **Kinsale Regional Museum** (tel: 021-477 7930; http://homepage.eircom.net/~kinsalemuseum; Sat 10am–5pm, Sun 2–5pm; charge). Exhibits include mementoes of the *Lusitania*, sunk in 1915 by a German submarine, some 23km (14 miles) off the coast.

Also of interest nearby is the 12th-century **St Multose Church**, located on Church Street and, on Cork Street, the 16th-century restored **Desmond Castle**, which houses a **wine museum** (tel: 021-477 4855; www.winegeese.ie; Apr–mid-Oct daily 10am–6pm; charge).

Finally, **Charles Fort** (tel: 021-477 2263; daily, mid-Mar–Oct 10am–6pm, Nov–mid-Mar 10am–5pm; charge), on the east side of Kinsale harbour, is a star-shaped fortress built in 1677. Alongside the edifice there is a pleasant footpath, which runs along the sea for about 1.5km (1 mile).

West Cork

Until the 1980s, the west of County Cork was a rather run-down agricultural backwater, decimated by emigration. But its natural beauty has since been discovered, which in turn has led

pleasant half-day outing from Cork. The castle, a formidable keep built in the mid-15th century, is surrounded by well-tended gardens, two rivers, a 'Druid' grotto and parkland with an attractive lake.

Kissing the **Blarney Stone**, a slab set high up in the wall below just the castle's battlements, is supposed to bestow the gift of eloquence. Those who wish to romance the stone have to ascend the castle's many steps to the rooftop, then lean backwards by the battlements (there are iron bars to hold onto – asking someone to hold you by the waist is also recommended), before finally landing a smacker onto the legendary surface. There is no charge for this odd ritual, but many people are so happy to survive it that they pay €10 at the exit for a souvenir photograph.

🚗 BANTRY BAY DRIVE

Take a leisurely drive around the Sheep's Head, Cork's smallest peninsula, with sea views of sheltered Dunmanus Bay, and the wide expanse of Bantry Bay, backed by mountain ranges.

The Sheep's Head Peninsula is a skinny finger of land dividing Dunmanus Bay from its bigger neighbour, Bantry Bay. Inhabited since megalithic times, it is now home to a number of small farms with big sea views.

At the top of Dunmanus Bay is the village of **Durrus**, where the road from the Mizen Head meets the one from the Sheep's Head. A good point for a pitstop here is **The Sheep's Head Bar and Restaurant** (tel: 027-62822). As you drive west along the sheltered inlet, past **St James' Church of Ireland** (1792), you can see the Mizen Head across the bay.

The **Air India Memorial**, about 12km (7½ miles) west of Durrus, is a peaceful waterside garden commemorating the 392 people who died on 23 June 1985, when an Air India flight was destroyed by a bomb. Many of the bodies came ashore near here. Every year there is a memorial ceremony, and the sun hits the sundial in the garden at the exact moment of the explosion.

Park in **Ahakista** on the bend beyond the Ahakista Bar. Follow the signpost

Tips
• Distance: 67km (42 miles)
• Time: A half-day
• Start: Durrus
• End: Bantry Bay
• A car is essential for this tour, which is really only worth doing in good visibility. Bantry is approximately 2km (1¼ miles) from the Kilnaruane Pillar Stone.

Dunmanus Bay and the hills of the Sheep's Head Peninsula

for the Old Kilcrohane Road and walk up it about 10m/yds to a sign for the **Rossnacaheragh Stone Circle**. A flagstone path climbs uphill to a raised site with a small circle of megalithic stones. The view from the site is superb.

Now return to your car and follow the main road for about 10km (6 miles) to the tiny village of **Kilcrohane**; in summer there is a choice of restaurants open here, making it a good option for a break.

Thrill-seekers may want to push on for another 12km (7½ miles) to the **Sheep's Head Lighthouse**, where there is rugged scenery, a car park and a café, but the main tour takes the **Goat's Path** for 19km (12 miles) to Bantry. (Note that if you dislike driving along narrow roads with unfenced, sheer drops, you can return to Bantry via Durrus instead.)

The Goat's Path crosses to the northwest coast of the peninsula, past two viewing points. Here, on this more exposed shore, are stark cliffs, and the fuchsia hedges and orange montbretia that characterised the south coast are replaced by ling, heather and gorse. There are no villages here, just a few widely scattered houses, built into sheltered spots between the hills.

Where the road joins the N71, turn left for Bantry, then immediately right at the West Lodge Hotel to the **Kilnaruane Pillar Stone**. The stone is indicated by a green-and-white fingerpost, and accessed by a galvanised gate. The Pillar Stone, which you only see as you reach the top of the field, is an early Christian pillar around 1.5m (5ft)

Boats in Bantry Bay

119

high, dating from the 9th century, and carved with figurative and interlaced panels. Finally, turn northwest for a breathtaking view of Bantry Bay , which is 34km (21 miles) long by 6.5km (4 miles) wide, and Whiddy Island, which currently has around 17 inhabitants and is linked by ferry with the mainland.

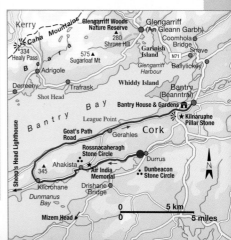

to regeneration. Today, the area is home to a thriving community, and the pretty, brightly painted houses that characterise its villages, plus the high-quality craftwares, artisan food and excellent restaurants available here, have placed it firmly back on the tourist map.

Clonakilty area

Arriving at **Clonakilty** ❻, take the by-pass and park to explore the colourful and compact town centre on foot. Look out for **Emmet Square**, lined by tall Georgian houses, and the **Post Office**, in a small 19th-century church on Bridge Street.

Just outside Clonakilty is the birthplace of local hero **Michael Collins**, who played an important role in the founding of the Irish state *(see p.282)*.

Travelling west, the road crosses a wide inlet at **Rosscarbery** ❼, an

important monastic centre from the 6th to the 12th century. Highlights include the small Protestant Cathedral (1612), which has been attractively renovated, and the pretty village square, set on a hill above the main road and with craft shops and several bars and cafés.

Just beyond Rosscarbery, turn left onto the R597 Glandore road leading to the **Drombeg Stone Circle** (free), one of the most complete and most impressively situated of the region's early Iron Age remains.

Skibbereen area

In summer, **Glandore** ❽, a tiny village built on the south-facing slope of a protected harbour, teems with wealthy visitors and their yachts. This lovely spot is known locally as Millionaire's Row. On the opposite

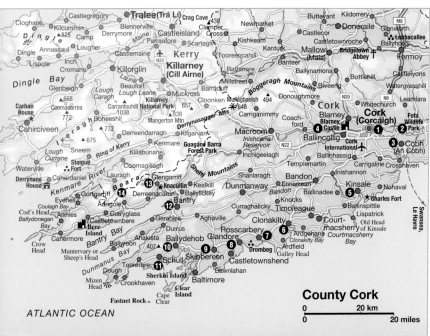

County Cork

0   20 km

0   20 miles

ATLANTIC OCEAN

Food is serious business in this part of Cork

Heritage Centre (tel: 028-40900; www.skibbheritage.com; mid-May–mid-Sept daily 10am–6pm, rest of year Tue–Sat; charge) makes a fine attempt at explaining the causes of the 1845–7 Great Famine, which took the lives of over 10,000 people in the area.

South of Skibbereen, if visibility allows, look southwards for the lighthouse on **Fastnet Rock**, the most southerly point of Ireland, some 23km (14 miles) away.

Back on the mainland, **Ballydehob** ⑩ is a lively village, with pretty, brightly painted houses – a popular retreat for city folk seeking a quieter way of life. Continue on towards Schull. In good weather you will see **Mt Gabriel** (407m/1,335ft) on your right. While Ballydehob has a reputation for being arty, **Schull** ⑪ is the heart of fashionable west Cork, a summer resort for wealthy Dubliners.

side of Glandore harbour is the small fishing village of **Union Hall**, where brightly painted trawlers moor at Keelbeg Pier.

Castletownshend, signposted from Union Hall, may be the prettiest village in west Cork, but it is also the least typical. Wander along its two streets, noting its large, well-designed three- and four-storey houses, many of which are built in stone and in the neoclassical style. These belonged to 'planter' families – Protestant English ex-soldiers, who were given lands in the area in the late 17th century.

The main place along the coast is **Skibbereen** ⑨, a historically bourgeois market town built in the 19th and early 20th centuries. On Upper Bridge Street, the **Skibbereen**

Lighthouse visit

If you like lighthouses, take a detour 14.5km (9 miles) from Schull to the **Mizen Head**, mainland Ireland's southernmost tip, where wild Atlantic waves pound the rocks even in the calmest weather. The **Mizen Head Visitor Centre** (tel: 028-35115; www.mizenhead.net; mid-Mar–Oct daily 10.30am–5.30pm, Nov–mid-Mar Sat–Sun 11am–4pm; charge) is located in the lighthouse keeper's house on an island at the tip of the peninsula. To reach it, you must go over a concrete suspension bridge, while the waves swirl around below – an invigorating crossing.

Bantry Bay

Bantry Bay, one of the big attractions of Southwest Ireland, is around 34km (21 miles) long and 6.5km (4 miles) wide. The town of **Bantry** ⑫ is nestled in a magnificent setting at the top of the bay. Beside it, looking out to sea and set in subtropical gardens, is **Bantry House** (tel: 027-50047; www.bantryhouse.com; Mar–Oct daily 10am–6pm; charge), a stately home with a fine collection of antiques including Aubusson carpets, Gobelin tapestries, Russian icons, Chinese lacquer and French and Irish 18th-century furniture.

Beyond Bantry Bay the road climbs into open, more rugged country, offering ever-changing views across the bay. **Glengarriff** ⑬, a wooded glen with a sheltered harbour warmed by the Gulf Stream, has an especially mild climate. The village is teeming with craft shops, serving coaches en route to Killarney to the north, but **Ilnacullin Gardens** (tel: 027-63040; www.heritageireland.ie; Apr–Sept Mon–Sat 10am–6.30pm, Sun 1–6pm, June–Aug Sun from 11am; charge, separate ferry charge), on Garinish Island, five minutes offshore, are well worth a visit. The flora comes from five continents, and the centrepiece is a stunning walled Italian garden, surrounding a pool, its straight architectural lines contrasting with the ruggedness of the distant mountains that frame it.

The north side of Bantry Bay is formed by the **Beara Peninsula** ⑭, which stretches for about 48km (30 miles) southwest from Glengarriff. The southern part of the peninsula is in County Cork, while the north is in Kerry, with the Caha and Slieve Miskish mountains running down its centre. The road around the Beara, the Ring of Beara, makes a less busy alternative to the Ring of Kerry *(see box p.131)*.

Cod's Head, between Urhan and Allihies, on the Ring of Beara tourist route

ACCOMMODATION

Cork city and its surrounding county offer lots of places to stay in all price ranges. Several new hotels were successfully established during the boom years, but the majority of places in both the city and county are carefully converted old buildings dating mainly from the 19th century.

Cork city

Ambassador Hotel
Military Hill, St Lukes
Tel: 021-453 9000
www.ambassadorhotelcork.ie
An imposing Victorian building has been converted into a stylish hilltop hotel with great views of the city and harbour. €€

Clarion Hotel
Lapp's Quay
Tel: 021-422 4900
www.clarionhotelcorkcity.com
The Clarion is housed in a large six-storey modern building with a central atrium and has chic boutique hotel-style bedrooms. The bar serves Asian food. €€

Garnish House
Western Road
Tel: 021-427 5111
www.garnish.ie
Sample real Irish hospitality at this Victorian guesthouse near the university. €

Hayfield Manor Hotel
Perrott Avenue, College Road
Tel: 021-484 5900
www.hayfieldmanor.ie
This modern luxury hotel is built in the country-house style on landscaped grounds near University College. A haven of tranquillity five minutes' drive from the centre. €€€€€

Around Cork city

Ballymaloe House
Shangarry, Midleton
Tel: 021-465 2531
www.ballymaloe.ie

One of Ireland's leading country-house hotels, Ballymaloe is a stylishly decorated Georgian house surrounded by the family farm. Renowned for its restaurant, which pioneered the imaginative use of fresh local produce. Children welcome. €€€€

Blarney Castle Hotel
Tel: 021-438 5116
www.blarneycastlehotel.com
Simple accommodation in a friendly family-run hotel on the village green. €€

Friar's Lodge
Friar Street, Kinsale
Tel: 021-477 3445
www.friars-lodge.com
Comfortable, modernised Georgian town-house with large rooms. Excellent value. €€

Pier House
Pier Road
Tel: 021-477 4169
www.pierhousekinsale.com
Family-run guesthouse overlooking the harbour. Children welcome. €

Trident Hotel
Pier Head, Kinsale
Tel: 021-477 2301
www.tridenthotel.com
Modern hotel adjacent to the town pier, with sea views from all rooms. Lively bar. €€€

West Cork

Dzogchen Beara Retreat Centre
Garranes, Allihies
Tel: 027-73032
www.dzogchenbeara.org

Buddhist centre on a remote cliff top offers dormitory accommodation in the farmhouse, and self-catering cottages. Book ahead. €

The Glen Country House
Kilbrittain
Tel: 023-884 9862
www.glencountryhouse.com
Homely, creeper-clad Victorian farmhouse house deep in the Cork countryside. €€

Hillcrest House
Ahakista, Bantry
Tel: 027-67045
www.ahakista.com

Simple rooms in a traditional farmhouse on the Sheep's Head, near Dunmanus Bay. €

The Maritime Hotel
The Quay, Bantry
Tel: 027-54700
www.themaritime.ie
Large modern hotel with spacious rooms, some with kitchens. Has an indoor pool. €€€

Seaview House Hotel
Ballylickey, Bantry
Tel: 027-50073
 www.seaviewhousehotel.com
Old-fashioned hotel in wooded grounds. €€€

RESTAURANTS

Cork has always been renowned for good meat and fresh fish, and is also a leader in the revival of artisan foods, most notably farmhouse cheeses and smoked fish. The region boasts many small restaurants of character, especially in Kinsale and west Cork, and many of the restaurants within hotels are also highly rated.

Restaurant price categories
Prices are per person for two courses, not including drinks:

€ = below €20
€€ = €20–28
€€€ = €28–38
€€€€ = over €38

Cork city
Café Paradiso
16 Lancaster Quay, Western Road
Tel: 021-427 4973
www.cafeparadiso.ie
Legendary vegetarian restaurant. Friendly service in an ever-crowded space. €€€

Farmgate Café
English Market, Cork
Tel: 021-427 8134
www.farmgate.ie
In the gallery of Cork's food market, this café serves great-quality dishes at good prices. €

Greenes
48 MacCurtain Street
Tel: 021-450 0011
www.greenesrestaurant.com
French cuisine is served in a minimalist interior overlooking a natural waterfall. €€€

Isaacs Restaurant
48 MacCurtain Street
Tel: 021-450 3805
www.isaacsrestaurant.ie
This place is an informal, bustling brasserie in a converted warehouse. Does good vegetarian options. €€

Around Cork city
Blairs Inn
Cloghroe, Blarney
Tel: 021-438 1470
Blairsinn.ie
Riverside country pub serving Irish meat, seafood, game and vegetarian dishes. €€

Fishy Fishy
Crowley's Pier, Kinsale
021-470 0415
www.fishyfishy.ie
Fish Fishy's owner-chef Martin Shanahan is

renowned for his catch-of-the-day dish at this excellent seafood restaurant. €€–€€€

Gilbert's Restaurant
Pearse Square, Cobh
Tel: 021-481 1300
www.gilbertsincobh.com
Stylish brasserie located on the town's

central square. €€–€€€

La Jolie Brise
Baltimore
Tel: 028-20600
A Breton-Irish family offers a menu of pizzas, fresh fish, grills and *moules frites*. €

NIGHTLIFE AND ENTERTAINMENT

Outside Cork city, most entertainment is pub-based, and it's plentiful in summer. To check what is on at the cinema, consult www.entertainment.ie, buy the *Evening Echo* or pick up a free copy of the entertainment listing magazine *Whazon?* or its accompanying website, www.whazon.com/cork.

Pubs

An Spailpín Fánach
South Main Street, Cork
Tel: 021-427 7949
Cork's best bet for live traditional music.

The Blue Haven
Pearse Street, Kinsale
Tel: 021-477 2209
www.bluehavencollection.com
Free live music in the lounge bar most nights.

Bushes Bar
Baltimore
Tel: 028 882 0125
www.bushesbar.com
Local traditional players often gather here.

Corner House
7 Coburg Street, Cork
Tel: 021-450 0655
A friendly local pub with live music from Wednesday to Sunday.

De Barra
Pearse Street, Clonakilty
Tel: 028-883 3381
www.debarra.ie
Hosts live music, from folk-rock to traditional.

Hackett's
Main Street, Schull

Tel: 028-28625
Old pub with frequent music sessions.

Loafers
26 Douglas Street, Cork
Tel: 021-431 1612
Gay bar with a beer garden. Has DJ sets on Fridays and Saturdays.

Reardens
26 Washington Street, Cork
Tel: 021-427 1969
A busy student bar; live music most nights.

The Sin É
Coburg Street, Cork
Tel: 021-450 2266

Traditional Irish music at An Spailpín Fánach

Live traditional music on Friday, Sunday and Tuesday evenings.

The Spaniard
Scilly, Kinsale
Tel: 021-477 2436
Live traditional music on Wednesdays from 9.30pm, and on summer weekends.

Theatre
Cork Opera House

Lavitt's Quay, Cork
Tel: 021-427 0022
www.corkoperahouse.ie
Cork's main venue for theatre and opera.

Everyman Palace
MacCurtain Street, Cork
Tel: 021-450 1673
www.everymanpalace.com
This ornate Victorian theatre hosts touring and local productions, comedy and variety.

SPORTS AND ACTIVITIES

County Cork, with its rocky peninsulas and indented sea coast, is the ideal place to enjoy the outdoors, whether on land or at sea.

Angling
Kinsale Angling
Tel: 021-477 4946
www.kinsaleangling.com
Day trips for deep-sea anglers. Also organises whale-watching and diving.

Cycling
Roycroft Cycles
Town Car Park, Skibbereen
Tel: 028 21235
www.skibbereen.ie
A wide range of bikes for hire.

Skibbereen Cycle Hub
Tel: 028-21766
www.discoverireland.ie/things-to-do
Skibbereen has three challenging cycling routes on quiet back roads.

Walking
Beara Way
St Peter's Church, Castletownbere
Tel: 027-70054
www.bearatourism.com
The local tourist office helps plan walking tours.

Sheep's Head Way
Bantry
Tel: 027-61052

www.thesheepshead.com
Way-marked route with great views of Bantry Bay. Also several shorter looped walks.

Watersports
G'town Surf School
Kinsale
Tel: 087-876 8549
www.surfgtown.com
Surf lessons and equipment hire; particularly good for beginners.

Heir Island Sailing
Heir Island, Skibbereen
Tel: 028-038 511
www.heirislandsailingschool.com
Sailing and kayaking in sheltered waters.

Sailing boats around Kinsale

TOURS

Visitors to Cork can use a combination of public transport and organised tours to see the sights and explore the countryside.

Walking tours

Cork Historic Walking Tours
Tel: 085-100 7300
www.walkcork.ie
Book in advance for walking tours of the city.

Titanic Trail
Cobh
Tel: 021-481 5211
www.titanictrail.com
Ninety-minute walking tour of Cobh departs daily from the Commodore Hotel at 11am.

Bus tours and day trips

Bus Éireann
Parnell Square, Cork
Tel: 021-450 8188
www.buseireann.ie
Tour the city and travel to Blarney in an open-top bus.

Michael Collins Centre
Clonakilty
Tel: 023-884 6107
www.michaelcollinscentre.com
Small visitor centre offers a guided tour of sites associated with Collins in your own car.

Boat trips

Whale Watch With Colin Barnes
Union Hall, Skibbereen
Tel: 028-36789
www.whalewatchwithcolinbarnes.com
See whales, porpoises, dolphins and seals.

FESTIVALS AND EVENTS

Cork is known as Ireland's festival city, and has a packed calendar of events bringing a party atmosphere to the streets.

March

Cork St Patrick's Day Festival
www.corkstpatricksfestival.ie
Centred on 17 March, the city enjoys four days of music and street events.

April

Cork International Choral Festival
www.corkchoral.ie
A city-wide programme of concerts.

May

Baltimore Fiddle Festival
www.fiddlefair.com
Small festival with a big reputation.

June

Cork Midsummer Festival
www.midsummer.com
A prestigious 16-day arts festival.

July

Kinsale Arts Week
www.kinsaleartsweek.com
Concerts in Charles Fort are a highlight.

August

Cobh Peoples Regatta
www.cobhpeoplesregatta.com
One of Europe's oldest regattas.

October

Cork Film Festival
www.corkfilmfest.org
Week-long Irish and international programme.

Kinsale Gourmet Festival
www.kinsalerestaurants.com/autumn.php
Taste some great dishes at this thriving seaside resort with so many restaurants that it holds an annual eating festival.

The southwest

Most people who visit the southwest are here for the outdoors and the scenery. The lakes of Killarney are spectacular, while the Ring of Kerry offers a variety of seascapes and great golfing. The Dingle Peninsula is rich in prehistoric and early Christian remains, with rugged coastal scenery. In contrast, the town of Dingle is a lively spot, known for good food and traditional music.

Killarney

Population: 13,500

Local dialling code: 064

Local tourist office: Discover Ireland Centre, Beech Road; tel: 064-663 1633; www.killarney.ie

Main police station: New Road; tel: 064-663 1222

Main post office: New Street; tel: 064-663 1461

Main hospital: Kerry General Hospital, Rathass, Tralee; tel: 066-718 4000. For medical care in Killarney, contact Southdoc, Park Road Shopping Village; tel: 1850-335 999

Airport: Kerry Airport, Farranfore; tel: 066-976 4644; www.kerry airport.com. On the Tralee Road (N22), 18km (11 miles) north of Killarney, it has daily flights from London, Dublin and Frankfurt. Bus Éireann operates a regular service between the airport and Killarney (around €5); a 20-minute taxi ride to Killarney costs approximately €25

Train/Bus station: Killarney Bus and Train Station; East Avenue Road; bus: Bus Éireann; tel: 064-63011; www.buseireann.ie; train: Irish Rail; tel: 064-663 1067; www.irishrail.ie

Car-hire companies: Car Hire Ireland; no tel – reserve only online; www.carhireireland.com; Budget, International Hotel, Kenmare Place, Killarney; tel: 064-663 4341; www.budget.ie

Taxi companies: Killarney Cabs; tel: 064-663 7444

This is a spectacular part of the world, with deep-blue lakes, steep, heathery mountains, a coastline characterised by slate and sandstone cliffs, long sandy beaches and rocky inlets, and offshore islands with abundant wildlife.

Bring strong walking shoes and waterproof jackets. The further west you go, the more likely you are to encounter rain, as the clouds come in from the Atlantic, but it is seldom continuous heavy rain, and the showery weather typical of Killarney and Dingle often alternates with sunshine, creating some beautiful light effects, including gorgeous rainbows.

Killarney

Killarney ❶ is a good base from which to explore the area. It may be the most commercialised part of the southwest, but it is still possible to avoid the crowds and enjoy its lakes and hills. The romantic scenery of boulder-strewn, heather-clad mountains, deep-blue lakes dotted with wooded islands, and wild woodland has been preserved within a large national park. Killarney's nascent tourism industry was given a great boost by Queen Victoria's visit in 1861; parts of the national park are still traffic-free areas, where you can either walk, travel by boat or go on horseback or in a jaunting car (open horse-drawn carriage), designed in the 19th century for the express purpose of sightseeing.

Killarney National Park is one of six national parks in Ireland

Entertainment in Killarney

Killarney National Park

Arriving from Kenmare *(see p.137)*, you may decide to stop on the N71 and climb the path beside the **Torc Waterfall** ❹ to enjoy the view. An attractive contrast to the wilderness of Torc can be found across the road in **Muckross Park** ❺, a neatly trimmed lakeside area with gravel paths that forms the nucleus of the Killarney National Park. This is a car-free zone, and it is a good place to sample one of Killarney's famous jaunting cars. The drivers ('jarveys') are traditionally great talkers.

Built during the 19th century in the Elizabethan style, **Muckross House** ❻ (tel: 064-663 1440; www.heritage ireland.com; daily 9am–5.30pm, July and Aug until 7pm; charge for the house, gardens free) is worth a visit for its period rooms and outstanding formal gardens.

The **Visitor Centre** next door has leaflets on the national park's walking trails and other information. **Muckross Traditional Farms** (hours as Muckross House, but mid-Mar–Apr, Sat–Sun and holidays 1–6pm; charge) is a walking trail of approximately

The southwest

2km (1¼ miles), visiting three working farms of the pre-electric era, complete with Kerry cows and a pair of Irish wolfhounds. You can enjoy an informative chat with the costumed 'farmers' and their 'wives', who are highly knowledgable about the area and the old-style farms.

Located near old copper mines on a peninsula of Lower Lake, **Ross Castle** ❶ (tel: 064-663 5851; www.killarney.ie/history; daily 9.30am–5.30pm, July and Aug until 6.30pm; charge) is a 14th-century castle keep that has been fully restored and furnished. You can hire a rowing boat here, and take a picnic over to **Innisfallen Island** about a mile offshore, or take the covered launch (*see p.148–9*). The wooded island has the remains of an abbey that was founded around AD600 and is famous for the *Annals of Innisfallen*, a chronicle of world and Irish history written in this remote and beautiful spot up to 1320 by a succession of monastic scribes.

Consider taking an organised half-day coach, horse and boat trip through the **Gap of Dunloe** ❺, a narrow mountain pass formed by glacial action (*see p.148–9*). The organised trip has the advantage of allowing you to travel through the Gap from **Kate Kearney's Cottage** ❻ (an historic, rather touristy bar and restaurant) on foot or horseback and then go back to town by boat without having to retrieve your car. The Gap itself is an unpaved path that stretches for 6.5km (4 miles) between the **Macgillicuddy's Reeks** and the **Purple Mountain**, which gets its name from the heather that covers it in the autumn.

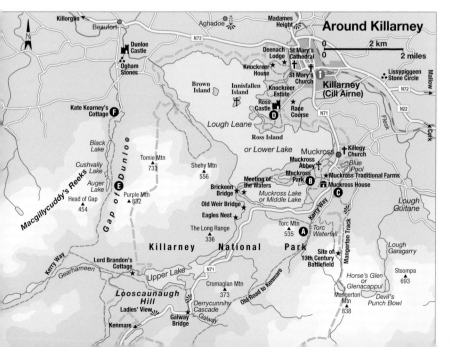

The lush, green Ring of Kerry

There is no motor traffic, but in summer there is a constant stream of ponies, jaunting cars and pedestrians. The scenery is first-rate, with a chain of five small lakes beside the road, and massive glacial boulders, but don't expect solitude, as it's a popular tourist route.

The Ring of Kerry

The **Ring of Kerry** is a scenic drive, justifiably famous for its combination of lush subtropical vegetation and rugged seascapes. You can drive the 180km (112-mile) route in under four hours, but it's best to allow a full day to allow for making several stops. In July and August the narrow two-lane road can be clogged by a slow procession of tour buses, vans and cars. If you would prefer to avoid the crowds, do the Ring of Beara (*see box*) instead, or go straight to Dingle.

North coast road

Towards the coast, **Killorglin ➋** is a busy village with a strategic position on the road between Killarney and Dingle. Its focal point is now a modern square at the top of the town, a product of recent redevelopment. It is famous for Puck Fair – Ireland's oldest festival, dating back to pagan times – on 10–12

The Ring of Beara

The **Ring of Beara** is less well known than its neighbour to the north, the Ring of Kerry, yet it also offers impressive scenery. It is a favourite haunt of walkers, cyclists, bird watchers and outdoor types. Although the drive covers only about 110km (68 miles), much of it is on narrow, winding roads, so allow a full day to complete it. The route goes via Castletownbere, a busy working port, through the villages of Allihies and Eyeries, both characterised by colourful cottages set between sea and hills. The Allihies Copper Mine Museum (tel: 027-73218; www.acmm.ie; daily Apr–Oct 10am–5pm; charge) expands on the local mining tradition. The road between the two villages is one of the highlights of the Ring of Beara. Travel on Kenmare via Derreen Gardens, which were planted 100 years ago beside Kilmakilloge harbour, a sheltered inlet on the south shore of the Kenmare River.

Killorglin, an attractive village near the Dingle Peninsula

August (*see p.134–5*). On the first day a mountain goat is crowned King Puck, garlanded with ribbon and installed overlooking the town on a tall throne, where it stays until the evening of the third day. There are various explanations of its origin, but nowadays it is chiefly a drinking and horse-trading festival, and can get rowdy.

A short drive south on the road to Glenbeigh, then inland slightly, leads to **Caragh Lake ❸**, a delightful, sheltered spot, popular with game anglers. The lake's shore is discreetly dotted with luxury hotels and holiday homes, mostly dating from the 19th century.

Glenbeigh ❹ is a good touring base, being convenient for both the sea and the hills. Nearby **Rossbeigh** is a 5km (3-mile) long sandy beach facing west over Dingle Bay, and backed by dunes. There are good walks here in Glenbeigh Woods.

Cahersiveen ❺ (pronounced Cah-her-sigh-*veen*) is the chief market town for the Iveragh Peninsula. Don't miss the visitor centre, **The Barracks** (tel: 066-947 2777; www.theold barracks.com; June–Sept Mon–Fri 10am–4.30pm, Sat 11.30–4.30pm, Sun 1–5pm; charge), a community-led initiative occupying an exotic-looking white-turreted building. The centre houses an amusing and informative series of exhibitions. Follow the sign outside The Barracks to the pier. The prettiest part of Cahersiveen is its backside, which overlooks the wide estuary of the River Ferta and the green hills beyond.

The head of the peninsula

Look out for signs to the Valentia Island car ferry, around 5km (3 miles) west of Cahersiveen. This lands you in Knightstown at the eastern tip of **Valentia Island ❻**, a sleepy place with a couple of bars. Its relative lack of traffic and wonderful sea views make Valentia a good destination for walkers; maps are available locally; don't miss the Tetrapod footprints made by a precursor of the dinosaur near the Slate Quarry. Valentia is connected to the mainland by a causeway at **Portmagee.**

Around 12km (8 miles) south of Valentia Island are the Skellig Islands. From Valentia's visitor centre, the **Skellig Experience** (tel: 066-947 6306; www.skelligexperience.com; Mar–Nov daily 10am–6pm, July and Aug until 7pm, Oct–Nov until 5pm; charge) takes you for a boat trip (*see p.148–9*) to the islands. (Boats also run from Portmagee, back on the mainland.) Bear in mind that most of the boats are open (more expensive ones are covered), the water can be rough, and bad weather leads to cancellations, sometimes for days on end.

The larger of the two Skellig islands is **Skellig Michael** ❼ (*see p.37*), which was inhabited by monks from the 7th until the 12th century. It rises in a cone shape to a double peak 217m (712ft) high. A flight of over 500 steps lead to the monastery, built of dry stone with no mortar. It has had major restoration work to enable it to cope with the number of visitors. Enthusiastic guides, all trained archaeologists, live on the island from June to August to supervise visitors and tell the island's history.

Back on the mainland, if the weather is good, take the scenic road from Portmagee to Waterville through Ballynahow, along an impressive arc of coast and mountains with the best views so far of the Skelligs. Rejoin the main ring road just before **Waterville** ❽, a popular base for golfers, who come here for the famous links courses, and anglers who have a choice of deep-sea fishing in Ballinskelligs Bay or angling on Lough Currane, about 0.8km (½ mile) inland.

The next stretch of road is one of the most scenic in this area, winding along the edge of **Ballinskelligs**

A causeway at Portmagee links Valentia Island with the mainland

★ HORSE TRADING

Killorglin's Puck Fair, held in early August, is not just a festive occasion with free concerts, fireworks and extended pub opening hours. It is the one of a number of fairs at which horses and donkeys are traded in the open air, as they have been since time immemorial. The buyers and sellers, with their arcane traditions, give a colourful glimpse into an older, fast-vanishing Ireland.

The traditions of Puck Fair are proudly upheld by the natives of Killorglin, a small town on the Ring of Kerry in southwest Ireland. It is held annually on the 10, 11 and 12 August, and is attended by thousands of people, all in festive, party mood.

The horse trading and animal dealing (goats, donkeys, puppies and poultry) are held in a field on the outskirts of town from 7am, while street traders selling novelties and food line the town itself. On the evening of the first day, a procession assembles at the bridge. A large billy goat, captured from the wild, his horns decorated with ribbons and rosettes, is carried in triumph on a lorry through the streets to a raised platform on the town square. Here 'King Puck', as he is called, is enthroned for the next two days, presiding over the merriment, and generously fed and watered.

It has been suggested that the Puck tradition has pagan origins, and the goat is a symbol of fertility like Pan, the goatee-bearded Greek god of the wild,

The animal trading takes place outside town, while the other festivities occur in Killorglin itself

nature and shepherding. Another tradition argues that Puck commemorates an occasion during Oliver Cromwell's sacking of the countryside in the first half of the 17th century, when stampeding goats gave warning of the approach of English forces.

The horse and cattle traders, many – but not all – of whom belong to Ireland's travelling community, are accompanied by a retinue of street traders, who follow the fair circuit, from Spancil Hill in County Clare on 23 June, Buttevant in north Cork on 12 July, to Ballinsaloe in County Galway in early October, a serious equestrian event worth a mean €8.5m to the local economy, and Maam Cross Fair in Connemara on the last Tuesday in October, held along the main road.

The majority of animals are not the famous Irish throughbred horses, but are general-purpose 'coloured' (piebald or skewbald) ponies and horses, that can pull a plough or pony and trap, and also make good riding horses (see p.28).

The actual dealing has its own rituals. The buyer hovers in the vicinity of a particular horse, in such a way that the seller understands that he is interested. An offer is made, and by tradition refused, and the seller then declares his price, which the buyer finds outrageous. At this point, a broker appears to bring the two parties to an agreement with much dramatic gesturing. When the sale is finally made, the seller returns some 'luck money' to the buyer, usually around 5 percent of the price.

Inspecting one of the horses' teeth to determine his age

A highlight of Killorglin's festival is the crowning of a wild goat as King Puck

The Liberator

Daniel O'Connell (1775–1847), popularly known as 'the Liberator', was born in Cahirciveen and adopted by an uncle from whom he inherited the estate at Derrynane. A lawyer and excellent orator, he dominated Irish politics in the early 19th century. Educated in France (as many wealthy Catholics were at that time), he was responsible for the Catholic

Emancipation Act of 1829, allowing Catholic and Dissenters to vote, enter the professions and own land. O'Connell was famed for his huge appetite and physical stamina. He killed a man in a duel in his youth and was known to be a womaniser, but this only seemed to endear him to the people. Nearly all Irish towns and villages now have an O'Connell Street.

Bay through rocky coastline backed by rugged green hills. **Derrynane House** (tel: 066-947 5113; www.heritageireland.com; May–Nov daily 10.30am–6pm, Oct and Nov Wed–Sun 10.30am–5pm; charge) is 1.5km (1 mile) beyond **Caherdaniel ❾**. The house belonged to the statesman Daniel O'Connell (*see box, above*). The 130 hectares (320 acres) of woods

surrounding the house (year-round; free) have pleasant walks and access to an attractive sandy beach.

South coast road

Heading along the coast road, you'll reach **Castlecove**, a small, friendly place with lovely sandy beaches. A narrow lane beyond the church climbs 3km (1¾ miles) to **Staigue**

The southwest

Fort. This is a well-preserved example of a prehistoric stone fortress, dating from 1500BC. A series of steps in the walls lead to a platform with good sea views. A small donation is requested by the landowner.

Further along the coast road, beneath a semicircle of low mountains, is **Sneem** ⑩. The village is untypical in that it's laid out in the English style around a green. It's pretty, but some of its charm has been lost following over-intensive development of holiday homes. Turn your back on these and walk down the road beside the Blue Bull (signposted 'Pier'), past an attractive communal garden for about 300m/yds. Looking back through the reeds, you can appreciate Sneem's sheltered setting.

In fact, Sneem marks the start of the most sheltered part of the Ring of Kerry's coast. Here you will see lush, subtropical growth – wild

The fine sandy beach at Castlecove

rhododendrons, azaleas, camellias and bamboo – evidence of the benign effect of the Gulf Stream. The N70 continues past Parknasilla, a large hotel resort with pleasant walks in its wooded waterside grounds, on to **Kenmare** ⑪, an attractive town laid out in a triangle in the early 19th century

The southwest

The village of Sneem is attractively set between the hills and the sea

by local landowner Lord Landsdowne. Today it has a lively restaurant scene and interesting boutiques, and is a good place to stop for a break.

The Dingle Peninsula

The Dingle Peninsula is like a long, dramatic finger, pointing some 48km (30 miles) into the Atlantic Ocean. On the south shore, amid rocky coves, a sandbar grows into an arc of beach that juts more than halfway across the bay. The weather can make or break a visit to **Dingle** (now signposted as An Daingean by government decree). If the sea mist is down, consider postponing your trip. From the base to the tip of the peninsula all the hamlets are Irish-speaking parts of the Gaeltacht, where the traditional language is in everyday use. It is regarded by Irish people as one of the strongholds of the old traditions.

Dingle town

On the south coast of the peninsula is **Inch Strand** ⓬, where 6.5km (4 miles) of sand form a bar across the bay. It's a good place to stretch the legs.

Further west along the south coast is the small fishing port of **Dingle** ⓭, the most westerly town in Europe. It has a population of about 1,500, which can treble in summer. It is a delightful mix of cosmopolitan and local – farmers still come to town on their tractors. Since 1985, a wild bottle-nosed dolphin, Fungie, has been entertaining visitors with his playful antics, and a bronze statue of him was recently erected on the pier.

The town has some excellent restaurants and lively music pubs. A triangular 10-minute walk from the pier area, up Green Street (the best place for craft shops), down Main Street and back along the Mall to the pier takes

A statue of Fungie the dolphin honours the mammal, a regular visitor to Dingle's waters

The Slea Head promontory sits at the most westerly part of the Dingle Peninsula

you past the majority of the shops, pubs and restaurants.

Children will enjoy a visit to **Ocean World** (The Wood; tel: 066-915 2111; www.dingle-oceanworld.ie; daily 10am–6pm; charge), which has over 1,000 species of marine life, a touch tank and an overhead tunnel tank.

Slea Head Drive

Continuing west on the R559 leads through harsh farming country, where old stone walls are overrun with shrubs and divide skimpy parcels of land into fields. Between **Ventry ⑭** and **Slea Head ⑮** there are over 400 *clocháns* ('beehive' huts; *see box*). The farmers charge you a nominal sum to visit them. Built dramatically on the cliff's edge, **Dunbeg Fort** (tel: 066-915 9755; Easter–Apr daily 9.30am–7pm; charge), just beyond Ventry, is an Iron Age promontory fort dating from *c*.AD800, with a massive stone rampart and a souterrain to allow its defenders to escape. The adjacent Visitor Centre

is also worth a visit, as are the *clocháns* a few minutes' drive further on. The road then climbs westwards around Eagle Mountain to the Slea Head **promontory** and has impressive panoramas.

139

The southwest

Dingle archaeology

Clocháns (beehive huts) abound in the Slea Head area and are also found on Skellig Michael *(see p.133)*. The earliest of these small conical huts of unmortared stone date from the 5th to the 8th century and were used by hermit monks. Others were built in the past 100 years to house farm implements – there is little timber in these parts, so it is cheaper to build with stone. **Gallarus Oratory** to the north of Slea Head is an extraordinary little building of unmortared dry stone, which probably dates from the 8th century. It is designed in the shape of an inverted boat, with a self-supporting corbelled roof, a door at the west and a window in the east wall. It remains as dry and solid as the day it was built, and is dark inside.

The group of seven rocky islands offshore at this point are the **Blasket Islands**. The largest of them, the **Great Blasket**, is about 6.5km (4 miles) long and 1.5km (¾ mile) wide, and was inhabited until 1953. The islanders were great storytellers and have made a lasting contribution to Irish literature. **The Great Blasket Centre** (tel: 066-915 6444; www.heritageireland. ie; daily 10am–6pm, Jul and Aug until 7pm; charge) tells their story using old records and photographs.

Back on the peninsula, below Mount Eagle, is **Dunquin** ⓰, a scattered village. Stop at Dunquin Pier, once the islanders' landing point, and walk down the steep, concrete path. Boats go to the island regularly in summer *(see p.148–9)*. The crossing takes 20 minutes, but, until a long-promised new pier is built, landing is by transfer to dinghy, so you must be agile.

Tralee and North Kerry

In spite of its fame in song, Tralee is a rather unremarkable town. North Kerry is flat and featureless compared to the splendours of south Kerry, but its coast has some lovely beaches, there's golf at Ballybunion, and Listowel is famous for its races and literary heritage.

Tralee

Tralee ⓱ is the county town of Kerry, but while it may seem like a booming metropolis after a few days in Dingle, overall it is somewhat impersonal, with a newly built town centre. The exception to this is in August, when the whole town parties for a week during the **Rose of Tralee Festival**, a beauty pageant and celebration of local culture; it then adjourns to the adjacent Ballybeggan racecourse for a six-day race meeting *(see p.149)*.

Traditional drummers in Tralee

Ballybunion Golf Club – former US president Bill Clinton's favourite links course

The town's most attractive area comprises the **Town Park** and **Denny Street**, with its elegantly proportioned Georgian houses. At the top of Denny Street is the **Kerry County Museum** (tel: 066-712 7777; www.kerrycounty museum.ie; June–Aug daily 9.30am–5.30pm, Sept–May Tue–Sat only; charge), which documents the history of life in this part of Ireland.

North Kerry

The country to the north of Tralee is the flatter, more sheltered part of Kerry. **Ardfert**  is a small village with the impressive ruins of a large 12th-century cathedral (tel: 066-713 4711; www. heritageireland.ie; May–Sept 9.30am–6.30pm; charge for visitor centre, ruins are free), with Romanesque doorways and transepts restored.

Access to **Banna Strand**, and a monument commemorating Roger Casement's landing from a German submarine in 1916, can be had around 3km (2 miles) north of Ardfert. The west-facing **Ballyheigue Strand** is popular for watersports and walking, with great views of the mountains of Dingle and the **Magharee Islands** across the bay.

The road continues to **Ballybunion**, a small, rather quaint seaside resort famous for its championship golf course, dramatic cliff walk and sandy beaches.

Further east and inland is **Listowel**, a quiet place that dates mainly from the late 19th century. It is known for Listowel Writers' Week, which takes place annually in late May (*see p.59*), and Listowel Races, a lively seven-day race meeting held in late September, originally a post-harvest celebration. **Listowel Castle** (The Square; tel: 086-385 7201; www.heritageireland.ie; free) dates from the 15th century and consists of two large ruined towers four storeys tall overlooking the River Feale and the town park.

The southwest

ACCOMMODATION

Southwest Ireland is notable for its many luxurious country-house hotels, which, for all their grandeur, seem to retain that quintessentially west-coast atmosphere of informality. Killarney, Dingle and Kenmare have a wide choice of accommodation options spanning all price ranges.

Killarney

Cahernane House Hotel
Muckross Road
Tel: 064-663 1895
www.cahernane.com
This elegant late Georgian house has a lakeside location with carefully tended grounds 1km (1¼ miles) outside town. The house is full of character, but most bedrooms are in a modern wing. **€€€**

Earls Court House
Woodlawn Road, off Muckross Road
Tel: 064-663 4009
www.killarney-earlscourt.ie
This 30-room guesthouse offers a high level of comfort and a warm, personal welcome in a quiet suburban location. **€€**

Friar's Glen
Mangerton Road, Muckross
Tel: 064-663 7500
www.friarsglen.ie
This attractive, traditional stone-fronted guesthouse is set in extensive grounds within Killarney National Park (which incorporates the Muckross Estate). It's ideal for a peaceful break. **€**

Hotel Europe
Fossa
Tel: 064-667 1300
www.theeurope.com
This large, luxurious modern hotel benefits from a stunning lakeshore location and excellent sporting facilities, including a swimming pool. The floor-to-ceiling windows enable guests to make the most of the mesmerising views. **€€€€€**

Killarney International Hostel
Killorglin Road
Tel: 064-663 1240
www.anoige.ie/hostels/killarney-international
It's worth joining the Youth Hostel Association (€20) to stay at this flagship hostel, a large 18th-century house in 30 hectares (75 acres) of gardens. It's located on a bus route 5km (3 miles) west of town. **€**

Loch Lein Country House Hotel
Fossa, Killarney
Tel: 064-663 1260
www.lochlein.com
Small, quiet hotel, newly built in a traditional style in a secluded spot 4km (2½ miles) from the town centre with distant lake views. Handy touring base for the Ring of Kerry. **€€€**

The Malton
Town Centre, Killarney
Tel: 064-663 8000
www.themalton.com
Located just across from the station, this hotel opened in 1854 to coincide with the arrival of the railway in Killarney. It has a grandiose pillared entrance portico, and inside is a lively bistro and bar. **€€€**

Ring of Kerry

Atlantic Villa
Knightstown, Valentia Island
Tel: 066-947 6839
www.anirish-experience.com
This family-run business occupies a solid-looking Victorian villa with individually decorated rooms and sea views. A self-catering apartment is also available. **€**

Brook Lane Hotel
Kenmare
Tel: 064-42077
www.brooklanehotel.com
This popular new hotel is built in traditional style just outside the village. It offers good value for money, with comfortable, well-appointed rooms, and leather arm-chairs and open fires in the lounge and restaurant. €€

Carrig Country House
Caragh Lake, near Glenbeigh
Tel: 066-976 9100
www.carrighouse.com
Exceptionally pretty Victorian manor in peaceful, well-tended lakeside gardens. The bedrooms are individually styled with antique furniture. The restaurant has a good reputation. The friendly owner-managers will help you plan your tours. €€€

The Final Furlong Farmhouse
Cahirsiveen
Tel: 066-947 3300
www.thefinalfurlong.com
This modern waterside B&B is situated a mile outside the village. The family who run it also keep horses, and guests can book a ride. Simple, impeccably clean and very friendly. €

Lakelands Farm Guesthouse
Lake Road, Waterville
Tel: 066-947 4303
www.lakelandshouse.com
Boats bob on the water at the end of the garden of this large modern fishing lodge on Lough Currane. Bedrooms are large, with great views of the hills and the sea. €

Park Hotel
Kenmare
Tel: 064-664 1200
www.parkkenmare.com
Splendid country-house hotel occupying a grand late 19th-century building with 4.5 hectares (11 acres) of grounds. It's famous for its understated charm, as well as its contemporary Irish cuisine. €€€€€

Parknasilla Resort
Sneem
Tel: 064-667 5600
www.parknasillahotel.ie
During its history, this rambling Victorian hotel has had many famous guests. It's located on a sheltered sea inlet, far from any other building, and has been discreetly modernised, with the addition of a pool and spa as well as self-catering options. €€€€€

The Dingle Peninsula
Dingle Skellig
An Daingean Harbour
Tel: 066-915 0200
www.dingleskellig.com
The only place in town with an indoor pool, the Skellig is popular with families and weekending couples. Built on the water's edge, it has a restaurant with a view of Dingle Bay, and a gorgeously sited open-air hot tub. The bar is a lively haven. €€€€

Emlagh House
An Daingean Harbour
Tel: 066-915 2345
www.emlaghhouse.com
A favourite with romantics, this 10-room Georgian-style guesthouse on the water's

Kenmare's Park Hotel enjoys a spectacular waterside setting and has an indoor-outdoor spa

edge combines luxury with a warm welcome. It features stylish decor, open fires, fresh flowers, original art and holistic treatments such as Swedish massage and reflexology in guests' own rooms. €€€

Grapevine Hostel
Dykegate Lane
Tel: 066-915 1434
www.grapevinedingle.com
This well-run private hostel in the town centre offers individual and dormitory accommodation in a large townhouse that's full of character, just a short step from Dingle's lively nightlife – and the launderette. Book well in advance. €

Heaton's Guesthouse
The Wood
Tel: 066-915 2288
www.heatonsdingle.com
Spacious two-storey house on an inlet 10 minutes' walk to the west of Dingle town. It looks – and feels – more like an affluent family home than a 14-room guesthouse.

The friendly owner-managers make everyone welcome, and the breakfast is certain to set you up for the day. €€

Tralee and North Kerry
Ballygarry House Hotel and Spa
Killarney Road, Tralee
Tel: 066-712 3322
www.ballygarryhouse.com
Family-run since the 1950s, Ballygarry is a 64-room hotel on the outskirts of town that retains its old-fashioned ambience. The lobby leads to a quiet library for residents, and locals enjoy the popular bar. €€€

Brook Manor Lodge
Fenit Road
Tel: 066-712 0406
www.brookmanorlodge.com
This B&B is a large pink house in open country 2km (1¼ miles) from Tralee, run by an enthusiastic young couple. It makes a good touring base, with large, comfortably furnished rooms, and an excellent breakfast served in the conservatory. €

RESTAURANTS

Dingle and Kenmare are the culinary hotspots in this region, while busy Killarney also has plenty of choice, to cater for its large number of visitors. Some of the best restaurants are in hotels, though there are some charming owner-chef establishments too.

Restaurant price categories
Prices are per person for two courses, not including drinks:

€ = below €20
€€ = €20–28
€€€ = €28–38
€€€€ = over €38

Killarney
Bricín
26 High Street
Tel: 064-663 4902
This unpretentious restaurant above a craft shop offers good honest food and friendly service. €

Chapter Forty
New Street
Tel: 064-667 1833
www.chapter40.ie

Busy and stylish contemporary restaurant, where chefs work with locally sourced produce under award-winning head chef Simon O'Regan. Extensive wine list, great buzz, dazzling presentation, delicious food. €€€

Gaby's Seafood
27 High Street, Killarney
Tel: 064-663 2519
www.gabysireland.com
Belgian owner-chef Gert Maes runs one of Ireland's finest seafood restaurants. The

Killarney's upmarket Chapter Forty focuses on locally sourced produce

superlative quality of the cooking is matched by the luxurious Continental-style baronial decor. €€€€

Killarney Golf and Fishing Club
Mahony's Point
Tel: 064-31034
www.killarney-golf.com
The clubhouse restaurant beside Lough Leane has one of the best views in Killarney. The menu is supplemented by daily specials, ranging from salads to hearty golfers' fare with chips. €–€€

Treyvaud's Restaurant
62 High Street
Tel: 064-33062
www.treyvaudsrestaurant.com
This bustling high-street restaurant is run by Swiss-Irish owner-chefs, who cook modern Irish cuisine for all occasions, from light lunches to à la carte dinners. Look out for local game on the menu in winter. €–€€

Ring Of Kerry
Bianconi's
Lower Bridge Street, Killorglin
Tel: 066-976 1146
www.bianconi.ie
Bianconi's is situated in an old coaching inn at the entrance to town, and has a dark

wooden Victorian interior. It is known for serving old-fashioned comfort food in a warm and friendly setting. €€

La Cascade
Sheen Falls Lodge, Kenmare
Tel: 064-664 1600
www.sheenfallslodge.ie
Expect impeccable service, luxurious surroundings and classic French cuisine. Main courses include fillet of turbot with cauliflower mousseline, and loin of lamb poached in olive oil. The desserts are sensational. €€€€

Fuchsia Restaurant
Knightstown, Valentia
Tel: 066-847 6051
A traditional wooden-fronted shop has been stylishly converted, with fuchsia-pink walls displaying local art. The hake bake is delicious, the lamb shank is faultless – though you must save space for the desserts too. €€

Lime Tree Restaurant
Shelbourne Street, Kenmare
Tel: 064-41225
www.limetreerestaurant.com
A place of character with consistently high-quality cooking and service. The wide-ranging menu contains a mix of mainstream, modern Irish and world cuisine. There's also an interesting wine list. €€

The Moorings
The Pier, Portmagee
Tel: 066-947 7108
www.themoorings.ie
Seafront pub-restaurant with a rustic pine interior warmed by an open fire. During the day it serves excellent bar food. €–€€

Mulcahy's Restaurant
36 Henry Street, Kenmare
Tel: 064-42383
www.kenmarerestaurants.com
Spacious, modern and eclectic in decor and food style. The innovative menu ranges from Thai, to Japanese fusion and Irish (plus vegetarian). The ingredients are organic. €€€

Listings

The Smugglers Inn
Cliff Road, Waterville
Tel: 066-947 4422
www.the-smugglers-inn.com
Landmark cliff-top restaurant where a talented father-and-son team run the kitchen. The locally sourced ingredients, including seafood, meat and game, are given the classic treatment but with a contemporary twist. €€€

Dingle
Ashe's Bar
Main Street, Dingle
Tel: 066-915 0989
www.asheseafoodbar.com
It's a cosy, quirky old-fashioned pub, a warren of nooks and crannies, but the menu is bang up to date, with prawn tempura, grilled oysters, rib-eye steak and squid salad. €€

The Chart House
The Mall, Dingle
Tel: 066-915 2255
www.charthousedingle.com
This charming stone-built cottage-restaurant is a renowned fine-dining establishment, and its innovative chefs make great use of local artisan food, fresh seafood and Kerry lamb. Desserts are a highlight. €€€

Chowder Café
Strand Street
Tel: 066-915 1061
Behind its traditional blue facade on the seafront, this lively spot serves a delicious chowder, in addition to a wide range of fresh fish, home-made burgers, good salads and a range of vegetarian options. There's a bistro-style dinner menu in summer. €

Out of the Blue
The Pier, Dingle
Tel: 066-915 0811
www.outoftheblue.ie
This basic tin hut beside the pier serves the freshest of seafood cooked to perfection in classic style. Book in advance to be sure of a table. €€€

Sammy's Store and Café
Inch Strand
Tel: 066-915 8118
www.inchbeach.ie
Amazing location right on the beach, with a child-friendly café and a bar. By day the menu features salads, burgers, soups and sandwiches, and at night there is a simple menu of fresh fish and steaks. €

Tralee and North Kerry
Allo's Bar and Bistro
Church Street, Listowel
Tel: 068-22880
Eat at the bar or share a long table in this lively gastro-pub. Artisan foods are a strong feature and the salads are outstanding. Dinner is a more formal affair in the adjoining restaurant. €€

Denny Lane Café
Denny Street, Tralee
Tel: 066-719 4319
www.dennylane.ie
This café brings a touch of metropolitan chic to Tralee, serving excellent coffee and infusions alongside home-made bakery items. The self-service selection of light dishes includes chicken roulade and lasagne. €

Kate Browne's Pub
Ardfert
Tel: 066-713 4055
This traditional thatched farmhouse is one of the best-known pub-restaurants in County Kerry. The menu features fresh seafood, steaks and a few lighter options. €€

Owner and chef at Dingle's Out of the Blue

NIGHTLIFE AND ENTERTAINMENT

Nightlife in the southwest revolves around pubs, and is at its liveliest in July and August, when live music is laid on most nights after 9.30pm. Set dancing is particularly popular in Kerry, as are *ceilidhs*: ask locally to find out what's on when.

Killarney

Gleneagle Hotel
Muckross Road
Tel: 064-663 1870
www.gleneagle.com
One of the biggest concert venues in Ireland, with a packed programme of big-name acts.

McSorley's Nite Club
College Street
Tel: 064-663 1282
www.mcsorleyskillarney.com
Large venue with live music and late bars open seven nights a week.

Ring of Kerry

Bridge Bar
Portmagee
Tel: 066-947-7108
Irish music and set dancing from 9.30pm on Fridays and Sundays, and Irish entertainment on Tuesdays in July and August.

Dingle

Almost every pub in Dingle has live music. Pick up a free magazine, *West Kerry Live*, at the Tourist Office for details of gigs not just in Dingle, but in the region as a whole.

An Droichead Beag
Main Street
Tel: 066-915-1983
This is the biggest pub in town, with live music most nights and set dancing on Wednesdays.

Tralee and North Kerry

Siamsa Tire
Town Park, Tralee
Tel 066-712-3055
www.siamsatire.com
The National Folk Theatre of Ireland puts on shows that celebrate traditional rural life through music, mime and dance. The centre also stages events for children.

Listings

SPORTS AND ACTIVITIES

The southwest is a prime destination for outdoor pursuits, with fine golf courses, excellent angling, walking and cycling routes, and opportunities for watersports.

Angling

Valentia Fishing
Tel: 066-947 6420
www.valentiafishing.com

Waterville Boats
Tel: 066-947 4800
www.discoverireland.com/southwests

Golf

Ballybunion Golf Club
Tel: 068-27146
www.ballybuniongolfclub.ie
Bill Clinton's statue adorns his favourite links.

Killarney Golf and Fishing Club
Tel: 064-663 1034
www.killarney-golf.com
Three courses, and outstanding scenery.

Tralee Golf Club
Tel: 066-713 6379
www.traleegolfclub.com
Seaside links designed by Arnold Palmer.

Waterville Golf Links
Tel: 066-947 4102
www.watervillegolflinks.ie
Tiger Woods's favourite European course.

There are many fine golf courses in the area

Walking and cycling

The Kerry Way is a 214km (133-mile) circular walking trail from (and to) Killarney. The Dingle Way is a 153km (95-mile) walking trail starting and ending in Tralee. Information on shorter hikes is available locally; also see www.discoverireland.com/southwest.

Hidden Ireland Adventures
Spórt Corrán Tuathail, Killarney
Tel: 064-662 2681
Con Moriarty specialises in guided ascents of Ireland's highest mountain. There are also less demanding routes on offer, to walk, scramble or climb.

The Mountain Man Outdoor Shop
Strand Street, Dingle
Tel 066-915 2400
www.themountainmanshop.com
The best place to hire a bicycle, replace walking equipment, plan an itinerary and make contact with other enthusiasts.

O'Sullivan's Cycles
Bishop's Lane, New Street, Killarney;
Tel: 064-663 1282
www.killarneyrentabike.com
Hire a bike with O'Sullivan's and explore the country roads and paths of Killarney.

Adventure centres and watersports

Jamie Knox Watersports
Maharees, Dingle
Tel: 066-713 9411
www.jamieknox.com
Arranges surfing lessons and equipment hire throughout the southwest.

Outdoors Ireland
Killarney
Tel: 086-860 4563
www.outdoorsireland.com
Offers help with all manner of outdoor activities, from hill walking (guides) to rock climbing, kayaking and adventure breaks.

Star Outdoors
Kenmare
Tel: 064-664 1222
www.staroutdoors.ie
This company organises kayaking, canoeing, sailing, boat hire and waterskiing.

Waterworld
Castlegregory, Dingle
Tel: 087 277 8236
www.waterworld.ie
Dive centre with accommodation. Also offers windsurfing and boat hire.

TOURS

In addition to the below, tours can be booked through the Killarney Tourist Office.

Bus tours and day trips

Bus Éireann has one bus a day from Killarney that travels around the Ring of Kerry and back to Killarney. It is only slightly more expensive to take an organised tour. Most bus tours run from Killarney and visit the Ring of Kerry and the Dingle Peninsula on day tours that last around 7 hours. The Gap of Dunloe is a popular 5–6-hour trip, with transport to the starting point near Beaufort, a pony and trap through the traffic-free mountain pass and a boat ride back to Killarney.

Bus Éireann
Killarney
Tel: 064-663 0011
www.buseireann.ie

Deros Tours
Main Street, Killarney
Tel: 064-663 1251
www.derostours.com
Minibus tours of Dingle, the Ring of Kerry
and the Gap of Dunloe.

Finnegan's Tours
The Square, Kenmare
Tel: 064-664 1491
www.kenmarecoachandcab.com
Minibus tours of the Ring of Kerry.

Boat trips and jaunting cars
Hire a jaunting car (a light, two-wheeled,
horse-drawn buggy) in Killarney at Muckross
Park or Kenmare Square in the town centre.

Seafari
Kenmare Pier
Tel: 064-668 3171
www.seafariireland.com
Two-hour eco-cruise of Kenmare Bay with
seal sightings guaranteed.

Tangney Tours
Tel: 087-257 1492
www.killarneyjauntingcars.com
Pre-book a jaunting car with hotel pick-up.
Tangney Tours (and Deros too – see *left
for details*) also operate lake cruises from
Ross Castle.

Walking tours
Richard Clancy
Tel: 064-663 3471
www.killarneyguidedwalks.com
Richard leads a two-hour walk of Killarney
leaving at 11am daily. Phone in advance to
book a place.

FESTIVALS AND EVENTS
Festivals in the southwest of Ireland tend to be low-key, friendly affairs, and are
often centred around the local landscape, traditional Irish culture and a great
passion for horses.

January
New Year Walking Festival
Glenbeigh, Co. Kerry
www.govisitireland.com
Walk off the excesses of the season and discover the best climbs and rambles near the
seaside village of Glenbeigh.

March
The Gathering Traditional Festival
Gleneagle Hotel, Killarney
www.thegathering.ie
A traditional music festival with concerts,
ceilidhs and workshops.

April
Féile nabealtaine.ie
Dingle, Co. Kerry
www.feilenabealtaine.ie

Five-day arts festival celebrating local culture.

July
Killarney Racing Festival
Ross Road, Killarney
www.goracing.ie/HRI/festivals
Five days of flat and National Hunt racing,
with a backdrop of mountain scenery.

Puck Fair
Killorglin, Co. Kerry
www.puckfair.ie
Traditional horse fair and entertainment.

August
Rose of Tralee International Festival
Tralee, Co. Kerry
www.roseoftralee.ie
Beauty competition and Irish cultural festival.

Limerick and the Shannon

Limerick is a modern city with a medieval core. Within easy reach of this historic city on the River Shannon is a region of ruined castles, ancient monuments, a dramatic coastline, spectacular caves and the eerie, moon-like landscape of The Burren, a treeless limestone plateau that is protected as a national park.

Limerick city

Population: 75,000

Local dialling code: 061

Local tourist office: Limerick City Tourist Office, Arthur's Quay; tel: 061-317 522; www.limerick.ie

Main police station: Henry Street; tel: 061-212 400

Main post office: Cecil Street; tel: 061-316 777

Main hospital: Limerick Regional Hospital, Dooradoyle; tel: 061-301 111

Airports: Shannon Airport; tel: 061-471 444; www.shannonairport.com

Station: Colbert Station; Parnell Street; rail: tel: 061-315 555; www.irishrail.ie; bus: tel: 061-313 333; www.buseireann.ie

Car-hire companies: Car Hire Ireland; no tel – book only online; www.carhireireland.com; Dooley Car Rentals; tel: 062-53103; www.dan-dooley.ie

Taxi companies: Limerick Taxis; www.limericktaxi.com; tel: 061-318 844

The western counties of Clare and Limerick constitute most of this prosperous region. Golfing, fishing, walking and surfing are among the most popular outdoor activities here. The Cliffs of Moher rise almost vertically out of the sea, and north of them lies The Burren, a region of limestone karst, rich in prehistoric remains and with over 1,000 species of plants.

By the time the waters of the River Shannon reach Limerick in the west, they have flowed over 386km (240 miles) through the central plain, widening out into Lough Allen, Lough Ree and Lough Derg. In the past, it was an important strategic barrier, dividing the ancient province of Connacht from Leinster and Munster, with very few crossing places. After hitting the important seaport and industrial centre of Limerick, the river still has another 97km (60 miles) to travel through the estuary to the open Atlantic. Limerick's position at the head of the Shannon estuary endowed the city with an often violent history. It is more than 1,000 years since Viking traders established a sheltered seaport here, but Limerick, the third-largest city of the Irish Republic, is full of reminders of its turbulent past, including the huge defensive bastions of King John's Castle.

Limerick city

The medieval centre of **Limerick**  is built on King's Island. Its Georgian quarter occupies the eastern bank, and expands westwards to include the modern shopping area around O'Connell Street. Until recently, Limerick resolutely turned its back on the wide, fast-flowing Shannon, arguably its most attractive asset,

Colourful Georgian houses in Limerick

The Locke Bar, on Limerick's Georges Quay

but dockside redevelopment has opened up magnificent river views. Gangland feuds among drug dealers has resulted in the city having high levels of crime in recent years, but the trouble is mainly confined to the outer suburbs. A regeneration programme is helping local communities to tackle the underlying social problems. Limerick's compact historic centre, meanwhile, is being promoted as a destination for short breaks, and it is as safe to visit as anywhere else in Ireland.

Medieval Limerick

An attractive riverside path, the Spokane Walk, skirts the Shannon and leads from the Tourist Information Centre at Arthurs Quay Park, and over a steel footbridge to King John's Castle, so that the entire medieval quarter can comfortably be visited on foot while enjoying riverside views. Quayside pubs with outdoor picnic tables add to the friendly ambience.

The **Tourist Information Centre** Ⓐ (tel: 061-317 522; www.discover ireland.ie/shannonregion; closed Sun except July–Aug) is a boldly designed modern building representing the outline of a ship, and the starting point of walking tours *(see p. 169)*. From here to King John's Castle is a short and interesting walk, which takes you largely along a riverside footpath and returns via the cathedral *(see right)*.

En route is the former waterfront Custom House, now the **Hunt Museum B** (tel: 061-312 833; www.huntmuseum.com; Mon–Sat 10am–5pm, Sun 2–5pm; charge), which houses an outstanding collection of 2,000 original works of art and antiquity. The collection, which was assembled by the medievalist John Hunt and his wife Gertrude, and left to the nation on his death in 1976, ranges from the 9th-century enamel Antrim Cross to Egyptian, Roman and Etruscan pieces, Chinese porcelain, a drawing by Picasso and masterworks by Leonardo, Renoir and the Irish artists Jack B. Yeats and Roderic O'Conor.

At the end of the walk is the impressive 800-year-old **St Mary's Church of Ireland Cathedral C** (tel: 061-310 293; www.cathedral.limerick-anglican.org; closed afternoons Nov–Feb; free), on King's Island. Built in the form of a cross, it is the oldest building in daily use in Limerick and incorporates both Romanesque and Gothic styles. The Romanesque West Door is magnificent, and the black oak misericorde (mercy) choir stalls are carved with animal features.

The top attraction in the medieval quarter, however, is the 13th-century **King John's Castle D** (tel: 061-411 201; www.shannonheritage.com; daily 9.30am–5.30pm, winter until 4.30pm; charge), also on King's Island. The castle is one of Ireland's most impressively sited Norman fortresses, with curtain walls and drum towers surviving. Climb one of the round towers for an excellent view of both river and town. An audiovisual display recounts Limerick's history from its foundation by the Vikings in AD992.

Georgian Limerick

Limerick is full of delightful architectural surprises. From Rutland Street,

Limerick

King John's Castle is the highlight of the medieval quarter

a brisk 20-minute walk through the main shopping area (allow more time if you're also window-shopping) leads to the spacious streets of the Georgian area, **Newtown Pery**. The tall, elegantly designed houses were built in the late 18th century and have brightly painted doors and semi-circular fanlights.

The Crescent **E** consists of smart, well-restored four-storey houses, most of which are now used as offices for accountants and solicitors and the like. From here, Barrington Street leads to Pery Square and the **People's Park,** where workers bask on the grass and eat their sandwiches at lunchtime.

The **Georgian House and Garden** **F** (2 Pery Square; tel: 061-314 130; www.georgianlimerick.com; Mon–Fri 9am–4pm; charge) is one of a terrace of six houses built around 1830. After renovation, it was furnished in period style, with its original architectural features reinstated in precise detail. It also houses a display relating to the 1999 filming of *Angela's Ashes*, based on Frank McCourt's moving memoir of growing up in the slums of pre-war Limerick.

South of Limerick city

The land to the south of Limerick city is rich agricultural land with low hills, adjoining the sheltered Shannon estuary in the west. Stone Age remains at Lough Gur comprise one of Europe's most complete Stone and Bronze Age sites. The lands around Adare were

City of youth

One reason why there are so many young people in Limerick is its university (www.ul.ie), a thriving institution founded in 1972 and currently with 11,000 students and 1,300 staff. Originally an Institution of Technology, the university is now strong in computing and engineering. Its campus at Plassey, 3km (1¾ miles) from the city centre (off the N24) is a showcase for contemporary architecture and design, and has a magnificent concert hall.

Thatched cottages and gardens in the chocolate-box village of Adare

settled in medieval times by three different monastic orders. A museum at Foynes celebrates the area's long connection with aviation.

Lough Gur

The Visitor Centre at **Lough Gur ❷** (tel: 061-385 186; www.loughgur.com; daily 10am–5pm, closed Sept–May; charge), built in the form of Neolithic huts, tells the story of pre-Celtic Ireland, dating back to 5000BC, when this site was inhabited. It has a horseshoe-shaped lake that is rich in bird life, and you can take a self-guided tour.

The **Grange Stone Circle** is 45m (150ft) across and contains about 100 boulders. More than 20 other stone circles, tombs, hut foundations, lakeside dwellings and ring forts have been excavated beside Lough Gur. The centre houses a collection of artefacts and has an audiovisual presentation introducing the site.

Adare

To the west is **Adare ❸**, one of Ireland's prettiest villages. Its stone-built, thatched cottages, originally built by the Earl of Dunraven to house the workers on his estate, are charming, and all have attractive front gardens. Nowadays, they mostly house craft shops and restaurants.

You can learn more at the **Adare Heritage Centre** (tel: 061-396 666; www.adareheritagecentre.ie; daily 9am–6pm; free except for special exhibitions), which has a helpful history display and a model of medieval Adare. Other highlights in the village include the 14-arch bridge, which dates from medieval times and leads to the **Augustinian Friary**, built in 1315. The cloisters were converted into a mausoleum for the Earl of Dunraven in 1826, and the church was restored in 1852.

Opposite the Dunraven Arms Hotel is the entrance to Adare Manor, orginally the seat of the earls of Dunraven but now an American-owned luxury hotel, **Adare Manor and Golf Resort**. It has twice hosted the Irish Open golf tournament and is regarded as one of Ireland's finest parkland courses. However, only golfers and hotel guests can pass the security barrier. The original 18th-century manor was enlarged in the Gothic Revival style in the mid-19th century. In its grounds are the ruins of the 14th-century **Desmond Castle** and of a 1464 Franciscan friary, accessible by a separate entrance.

Shannon estuary

On the south bank of the Shannon estuary, **Foynes ❹** played an important part in aviation history. In the late 1930s flying boats would land on the sheltered stretch of the Shannon between Foynes Island and the shore, having made the transatlantic crossing from Newfoundland. The award-winning **Foynes Flying Boat Museum** (tel: 069-65416; www.flyingboat museum.com; Mar–Oct 10am–6pm, Nov–Dec 10am–4pm; charge) commemorates those days with models and photographs, and includes the original terminal building, radio room and weather-forecasting equipment.

From Foynes, there is a pleasant drive along the wooded shores of the estuary. The turrets of **Glin Castle** are visible from the road, but the palatial home of the head of the Fitzgerald clan is no longer open to the public. **Tarbert ❺** is the embarkation point for the Shannon crossing (*see box*).

County Clare

Shannon Airport is located to the north of Limerick city, in an area

Foynes's transatlantic-crossing museum

> ### The Shannon ferry
>
> At Tarbert near the head of the Shannon estuary, a car ferry (tel: 065-905 3124; www.shannonferries.com; 7.30am–9.30pm on the half-hour) can take you across the wide estuary in 20 minutes to County Clare. This saves doubling back through Limerick city, a 137km (85-mile) journey, if you are heading for The Burren. The ferry is often accompanied by a pod of dolphins, whose presence will be announced over the loudspeakers. If the weather is fine, consider a return trip on the ferry as a foot passenger to enjoy the views and the sea air – wrap up warm, though, as it's always breezy.

formerly associated chiefly with ruined castles. There were once over 400 tower houses in the area, which was favoured for its good communication links and mild climate. Ennis (*see p.156*) is the county town and gateway to the west of Clare – arguably the most scenic part of the country. The area is known for its dramatic Atlantic coast that peaks in the Cliffs of Moher, and for the enigmatic limestone plateau of The Burren (from the Irish for 'stony place'), which forms the southern side of Galway Bay.

North of Limerick city

This is castle country, with ruined stumps of crumbling tower houses dotted around the place. Few are as imposing or as carefully restored as Bunratty, whose rectangular 15th-century keep is surrounded by four corner turrets, each topped with battlements and a set of flags.

Bunratty Castle and Folk Park ❻ (tel: 061-361 511; www.shannonheri tage.com; daily, castle 9am–4pm, park 9am–5.30pm, June–Aug until 6pm; charge) is firmly aimed at first-time visitors, and is good family entertainment. The castle contains furniture and paintings from the 15th and 16th centuries. The Folk Park behind it features reconstructed and fully furnished farmhouses, cottages and shops, set out as they would have been in the late 19th century. There is even a village street with a blacksmith, pub, drapery, print works and post office. Bunratty also organises enormously popular medieval banquets (*see p.168*).

Ennis ❼ is a busy market town, its attractive, small-scale commercial

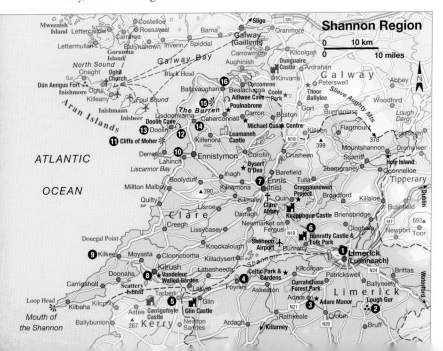

centre largely reconstructed in traditional style, and pedestrianised. The **Tourist Information Office** (tel: 065-682 8366; www.visitennis.ie) is on Arthurs Row, off O'Connell Street.

Ennis Friary is a Franciscan friary founded by the O'Brien kings of Thomond in the 13th century. The ruins, well preserved, consist of a nave, chancel, belfry and cloister (tel: 065-682 9100; Apr–Oct 10am–6pm; charge).

Playing the bodhrán at at an Irish Fleadh (music festival)

Ennis is known as a centre for traditional Irish music and dance. Performers and students flock to the Fleadh Nua, a competitive festival for musicians and dancers that is held annually at the end of May *(see p.169)*. At all times of the year, traditional musicians gather in the pubs of Ennis and hold impromptu music sessions, which can be enjoyed for the price of a drink. More formal, ticketed events are held at **Glór Irish Music Centre** (tel: 065-64 3103; www.glor.ie). The strikingly designed modern building hosts well-known touring acts on the Irish music scene *(see p.167)*.

In additional to its musical strengths, Ennis also has something of a multinational feel. Its proximity to Shannon Airport has meant that many people seeking asylum in Ireland were

Bunratty Castle is renowned for its medieval-style banquets

housed in the town while awaiting a verdict on their application, and opted to stay there when asylum was granted. Consequently, Ennis now has a sizeable West African population.

West Clare

Kilrush ❽, the nearest town to the ferry point, with a population of 2,650, is the biggest town on the coast of west Clare, and has a popular marina. The town was laid out in its current form, with attractive wide streets and a main square large enough to accommodate horse fairs, by a local landlord in the 18th century to complement his estate. Traditional livestock fairs (mainly horses, donkeys and sheep, with side stalls) are still held on the first Thursday in March, June and October.

Further round the coast, on the Atlantic coast of Clare (as opposed to the banks of the Shannon estuary) is

Kilkee ❾. The village has been rather overwhelmed by bland holiday-home developments (it is traditionally a favourite weekend spot for Limerick city people), but its centre retains an old-world charm.

The big attraction, however, is its west-facing beaches, where long rolling waves break on the sand after their Atlantic crossing. In fact, the beaches are impressive all the way up the coast to **Lahinch ❿**, which is also famous for its golf links. This stretch of coast has become the haunt of some of the world's leading surfers because of the immense waves (*see box, opposite*). The Clare waves suit surfers of all abilities when conditions are right, and surfing is the country's fastest-growing sport (*see p.30*).

Towering to 214m (702ft) high and stretching for 8km (5 miles), the **Cliffs of Moher ⓫** attract over 1 million visitors a year. You can park (charge) at

Kilkee's big attraction is its sandy beach

The Cliffs of Moher have more than a million visitors every year

the multimillion-euro **Visitor Centre** (tel: 065-708 6141; www.cliffsofmoher. ie; daily 9am–5pm, Mar–Apr and Oct until 6.30pm, May and Sept until 7pm, June–Aug until 9.30pm; free except for special exhibitions), which is built into the hillside and roofed with grass. The **Atlantic Edge Exhibition** includes a bird's-eye virtual-reality tour of the cliffs. In good weather, harpists and other buskers entertain outside, and there are some 600m (1,969ft) of pathways and viewing platforms to help you enjoy the spectacle without damaging the wildlife (this includes nesting seabirds from May to July). In clear weather you can see the Aran Islands offshore. Boat trips, which allow visitors to view the cliffs from a lower vantage point, are also popular (see p.169).

Further along the coast is **Doolin Cave** ⓬ (Pol an Ionáin; tel: 065-707 5761; www.doolincave.ie; daily 9am–5pm; charge), which shelters one of the world's largest free-standing stalactites, 'The Great Stalactite' (see box, p.162).

Doolin ⓭ itself (also called Road-ford on some maps) consists of a long straggle of B&Bs, hostels, hotels, restaurants and craft shops. There are also three pubs, which are renowned for traditional music. Some young musicians spend the whole summer camping here and learning from more experienced performers.

You can walk or drive to the pier, where fishermen land their catch in

Limerick and the Shannon

Riding the Aileens

The sea below the Cliffs of Moher is now recognised as one of Europe's top surfing destinations. A wave known as Aileens (after a nearby headland, Aill na Searach), reaches heights of over 9m (29½ft). Surfers are towed out by jetskis on lead-weighted boards to ride the vortex or 'barrel' at high speed back to shore. It is thrilling to watch, but strictly for the pros: one reason for the height of the wave is the shallow rocky reef below; it also has a strong rip, pulling the surfer straight towards the cliff face.

🚗 THE BURREN DRIVE

Drive through the rocky Burren, a treeless limestone plateau that fascinates botanists, geologists and archaeologists alike. Visit its Stone Age monuments, and take in the breathtaking views of Galway Bay and the Atlantic.

The Burren is a National Park covering 500 sq km (200 sq miles) of lunar-like limestone pavement, with unique flora and fauna and numerous megalithic remains, dating from the Stone and the Bronze ages, long before the arrival of the Celts.

Join the R478 where it crosses the N67 outside Lisdoonvarna, and continue for 9km (5½ miles) to Kilfenora. Here, **St Fachtnan's Cathedral** is an attractive 12th-century church with some finely carved effigies and three medieval high crosses. Next door, the **Burren Centre** *(see p.162)* shows a

short film introducing the unique landscape of The Burren.

The road now winds through the heart of The Burren, characterised by its limestone terraces, by huge erratic rocks that were deposited during the Ice Age and by relics of prehistoric man, including cairns, court graves, dolmens and over 400 stone forts. The whole area is a national park – for more information on this, see www.burrennationalpark.ie.

The land once had a thin covering of soil, but time, weather and the farming activities of prehistoric man denuded the surface, leaving the lunar-like region seen today. Meanwhile, under the ground, acid in the rainwater has seeped through the limestone to create pools and caves. Some 125 types of plant from Alpine, Arctic and Mediterranean zones flourish here, often growing up through the rock; they are at their best in April and May.

Continuing east, the left turn onto the R480 has an unmissable

The limestone Burren landscape

Tips

- Distance: 28km (17 miles)
- Time: A half-day
- Start: Lisdoonvarna
- End: Ballyvaughan
- A car is almost essential for this tour – it is also suitable for keen cyclists (be prepared for hills).
- Ballyvaughan is 30km (18½ miles) west of the N18 Galway–Limerick road (via the N67) and 49km (30 miles) south of the city of Galway, the starting point of the next chapter.

Lobster nets at Ballyvaughan, in County Clare

landmark, the beautifully proportioned ruins of **Leamaneh Castle**. (The edifice is not open to the public, and the surrounding lands are grazed by cattle.) The castle was built in two phases: the tower in 1480 and the manor in 1640.

The road between here and Ballyvaughan abounds in megalithic remains. A stone-walled car park has been built to accommodate visitors at the **Poulnabrone Dolmen**, a structure over 3m (10ft) high and The Burren's finest portal tomb, dating back to 2500BC.

The road then winds downhill through a series of corkscrew bends, with distant sea views, to **Aillwee Caves**. Fronted by a massive shop and flanked by separate attractions on birds of prey, this is one of the few Burren caves accessible to the public. The guided tour takes you for about 300m/yds through narrow passages into vast stalactitic chambers and past waterfalls.

Continue on to **Ballyvaughan**, a small fishing village on the southern shore of Galway Bay with

accommodation and good bar food at **Hyland's Hotel** (see p.166). Ballyvaughan is the starting point of the **Burren Way** (a marked walk) and a popular base for walkers.

The Burren Way has several sections, including the starting point in Ballyvaughan, that can be used for shorter walks. It runs from Ballyvaughan to Liscannor, a distance of 45km (26½ miles). The terrain varies from rocky ground, where only scrub grows, to magnificent wide 'green paths', and is largely off road.

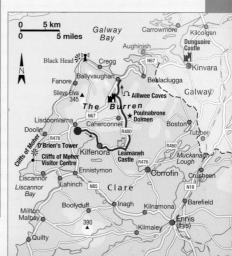

The Great Stalactite

The stalactite, which is over 600,000 years old, was discovered by two English cavers in 1952, and now measures more than 7m (23ft) long. You can see it on a one-hour tour (tel: 065-7075 761; www.doolincave.ie; daily 10am–5pm, on the hour; charge), with numbers limited to 20 people. A minibus driver will take you to the entrance of the cave, where you will be given a hard hat and torch before descending the 125 steps to a subterranean world. The cave is plunged into darkness, then, suddenly and stunningly, the subtly lit stalactite appears before you in the main chamber.

the evening. Boats leave from here for the Cliffs of Moher tour and for Inisheer, the smallest of the Aran Islands (*see p. 173*).

Slightly inland, **Lisdoonvarna** ⑭ developed as a spa centre thanks to the healing properties of its sulphurous spring water (the baths, alas, are no more). Today, its main claim to fame is its Matchmaking Festival (www.matchmakerireland.com) in September, when shy farmers meet women under the direction of Willie Daly, matchmaker, horse whisperer and publican (his bar is at 1 Main Street, in nearby Ennistymon).

To the south of Lisdoonvarna is **Kilfenora**, a tiny village that is famous for the Kilfenora Céilí Band, a group of local traditional musicians who celebrated their 100th anniversary in 2009, and tour throughout Ireland and to the UK and US.

Kilfenora is also the home of the **Burren Centre** (tel: 065-708 8030; www.theburrencentre.ie; June–Aug 9.30am–6pm, mid-Mar–May and Sept–Oct 10am–5pm; charge for the exhibition), which houses a tourist information point, exhibition area,

Matchmaking is big business in the former spa town of Lisdoonvarna

The area is also notable for its proliferation of plants from the Arctic, Alps and Mediterranean (*see box, p.164*). From the car, you may be unaware of any growth – to see the flora you need to look down, as much of it grows underground, beneath the porous limestone, and sprouts up from grykes (vertical crevices), between the clints (glacially polished horizontal surfaces), which occasionally wobble.

The **Caherconnell Visitor Centre** (tel: 065-708 9999; www.burrenforts. ie; Mar–Oct Mon–Sun 10am–5pm, July–Aug 10am–6pm; charge) explains the 'Cahers', the circular and walled farmsteads found throughout The Burren. There are more than 500 of them, including the spectacular Cahercummaun. The best preserved of these is found at Caherconnell.

A short distance to the north you will see what is unquestionably Ireland's best-known, most visited and most photographed megalithic burial tomb, the **Poulnabrone** ('the pool of the sorrows'), a portal dolmen with a huge capstone.

This ancient monument, which was constructed around 4,500 years ago, is now roped off for protection. It is strangely familiar, its image having been reproduced across the island on postcards, T-shirts, book covers and holiday brochures. It's a popular tourist spot, with numerous tour coaches stopping here daily.

A timeline on a signboard interprets the significance of the dolmen

craft shop and tearooms. There's an exhibition on The Burren and an informative video.

Next door to the centre is the 12th-century **St Fachtnan's Cathedral**, well worth a visit for its fine collection of medieval high crosses.

The Burren

Travelling east from Kilfenora, you come to the beautifully proportioned ruin of **Leamaneh Castle**, where you turn north, entering the extraordinary area that is **The Burren ⓯**, a place of geological and archaeological wonder – a karst landscape, hewn from stone. The name means 'rocky place', and everywhere there are giant boulders that were dropped by glaciers here. Some of these rock refugees have stood here for 15,000 years. With a patina all its own, it feels unlike anywhere else in Ireland – almost a different country.

and sets it in context with information on the surrounding flora. The dolmen was excavated in 1986, and the remains of 22 bodies – 16 adults and 6 children, male and female – were discovered. The bodies were estimated to be at least 1,500 years old.

From here, if you follow a road with hairpin bends down Ballyallaban Hill for 5km (3 miles), you will come to another natural wonder: **Aillwee Cave** (tel: 065-707 7036; www.aillweecave.ie; daily 9.30am–5.30pm, July–Aug 10am–6.30pm; charge), discovered in the early 1940s by a herdsman, Jacko McGann, who crawled into it to see what was there. A 35-minute guided tour through the cave incorporates caverns, bridged chasms, odd rock formations, pale threads of stalactites and waterfalls. The bones of a brown bear, a species extinct in Ireland for over 1,000 years, were found here.

Burren flora

More than 70 percent of Ireland's native flora, including 24 species of orchid and 25 types of fern, is found in The Burren. The best-known flower in this wild rock garden is the spring gentian *(gentiana verna)*, a dazzling small blue plant that can be seen in April and May. Search hard and you should be able to find it growing alongside brightly coloured magenta geraniums, early purple orchids, foxgloves, rock roses and swathes of creamy mountain avens, all sprouting from crevices in the pavements.

Heading north leads back to the coast and the picturesquely sited **Ballyvaughan** . Set on the shores of Galway Bay, it is the best base for exploring this unique landscape. It is also the starting point of the Burren Way walking route (*see p. 168*).

The Burren's Poulnabrone Dolmen, an iconic image of Ireland

ACCOMMODATION

Adare and Newmarket on Fergus are good alternatives to Limerick city, offering a relaxed rural setting and still being near Shannon Airport. While the best hotels in Limerick are new (or newly converted), elsewhere there are some venerable country house hotels. In west Clare things are simpler, but standards are high and competition is intense in the short season. Many places close between November and Easter.

Limerick city

Clarion Hotel
Steamboat Quay
Tel: 061-444 100
www.clarionhotellimerick.com
This boldly designed 17-storey hotel on the Shannon towers above the city. Facilities include a gym, sauna and pool. **€€**

Jurys Inn
Lower Mallow Street
Tel: 061-207 000
www.jurysinns.com
Popular chain hotel providing budget accommodation close to the shopping centre. **€**

No. 1 Pery Square
Pery Square
Tel: 061-402 402
www.oneperysquare.com
One of Limerick's finest Georgian houses is now a luxury hotel with sumptuously decorated bedrooms, and a lively brasserie. **€€€€**

Radisson Blu
Ennis Road
Tel: 061-456 200
www.limerick.radissonblu.ie/hotel-limerick
Modern business hotel in extensive grounds 5 minutes' drive from city centre and 15 minutes from Shannon Airport. **€€€**

South of Limerick city

Adare Village Inn
Main Street
Tel: 087-251 7102
www.adarevillageinn.com

A townhouse B&B in the village centre, with soundproofed, south-facing upstairs rooms. Owned and managed by the pub next door. **€**

Dunraven Arms Hotel
Adare
Tel: 061-605 900
www.dunravenhotel.com
Refurbished historic inn in a pretty village. Equestrian and golf holidays a speciality. **€€€**

Fitzgerald's Woodlands House Hotel
Knockanes, Adare
Tel: 061-605 100
www.woodlands-hotel.ie
Unpretentious modern hotel in a rural spot about a mile outside Adare. Benefits from a lively bistro and good leisure facilities. **€€**

County Clare

Ballinalacken Castle
Coast Road, Doolin
Tel: 065-707 4025
www.ballinalackencastle.com
Standing outside the village beside a ruined castle, this converted shooting lodge offers superb views of the Atlantic. **€€€**

The Burren Hostel
Lisdoonvarna
Tel: 091-566 999
www.sleepzone.ie
Formerly a three-star hotel, this well-run hostel is way above the average. All rooms are en suite, and it is surrounded by gardens. Great for families or small groups. The easiest way to book is via the website. **€**

Cappabhaile House
Ballyvaughan
Tel: 065-707 7260
www.cappabhaile.com
Purpose-built as a B&B, this large, unpretentious, stone-faced bungalow stands on the edge of The Burren, within walking distance of the lively village pubs. **€**

Dromoland Castle
Newmarket-on-Fergus
Tel: 061-368 144
www.dromoland.ie
If you can only afford to stay at one luxury hotel, choose this, for its awe-inspiring baronial grandeur. The castle overlooks its own lake and golf course. Friendly staff make everyone feel at home. **€€€€€**

Hyland's Burren Hotel
Ballyvaughan
Tel: 065-707 7037
www.hylandsburren.com
www.burrenwalkinglodge.com

Hyland's is a much-loved local institution. Most rooms have glorious views of the surrounding limestone hills. The Burren Walking Lodge, under the same management, is a simpler B&B. **€€** (Lodge **€**)

Gregan's Castle
Ballyvaughan
Tel: 065-707 7005
www.gregans.ie
A master-class in understated luxury, the guest rooms in this elegant Burren hideaway boast fine antiques and contemporary art, but are blissfully uncluttered, with no TV. The restaurant is renowned. **€€€€€**

Moy House
Milltown Malbay Road, Lahinch
Tel: 065-708 2800
www.moyhouse.com
The ultimate romantic retreat, this 18th-century country house has 6 hectares (15 acres) of grounds on a cliff top overlooking the wild Atlantic. **€€€€**

RESTAURANTS

Limerick's fine-dining restaurants compete with the restaurants of nearby country-house hotels (*see above* – jacket and tie may be required). West Clare is renowned for its seafood restaurants, though meat-eaters and vegetarians are also well catered for.

Restaurant price categories
Prices are per person for two courses, not including drinks:
€ = below €20
€€ = €20–28
€€€ = €28–38
€€€€ = over €38

Limerick city
The French Table
Steamboat Quay
Tel: 061-609 274
www.frenchtable.ie
The Strasbourg-born chef brings an authentic touch to the bistro-style menu at this relaxed waterfront restaurant. **€€€**

The Locke Bar and Bistro
3 George's Quay
Tel: 061-413 733
www.locke.bar.com

Nothing cutting-edge here, but it's good, traditional fare in a large riverside pub with tables outside. **€**

South of Limerick city
The Wild Geese
Main Street, Adare
Tel: 061-396 451
www.thewild-geese.com
Located in a tiny thatched cottage, this restaurant specialises in modern Irish cuisine. The food is beautifully presented, and the surroundings feel like a doll's house. **€€€**

Enjoying the sunshine at the riverside Locke Bar and Bistro

Morrissey's Seafood Bar and Grill
Doonbeg
Tel: 065-905 5304
www.morrisseysdoonbeg.com
Family-friendly restaurant offering local steaks and seafood from the grill. €€

Sheedy's Country House Hotel
Lisdoonvarna
Tel: 065-707 4026
www.sheedys.com
Super-fresh, locally sourced fine modern Irish cuisine from owner-chef John Sheedy. €€€

Vaughan Lodge
Lahinch, Co. Clare
Tel: 065-708 1111
www.vaughanlodge.ie
Stylish contemporary restaurant in a country-house hotel. Specialises in seafood. €€€

County Clare
J.P Clarke's Country Pub
Bunratty
Tel: 061-363 636
www.gallaghersofbunratty.com
This popular modern pub is a 10-minute drive from Limerick. Next door is Gallaghers Seafood Restaurant (€€€, evenings only), which is under the same management. €

NIGHTLIFE AND ENTERTAINMENT

Limerick has its classic pubs, Bunratty's medieval castle has been hosting banquets for generations, Ennis and Doolin are renowned for their traditional music scenes, and Kilfenora organises ceilidhs most weekends.

Limerick city
Dolan's Pub
3–4 Dock Road
Tel: 061-314 483
www.dolanspub.com
This lively waterfront pub offers traditional Irish music and singalongs most nights, as well as set dancing classes from May to September. Dolan's Warehouse, at the same location, presents live music with big-name acts.

The White House
52 O'Connell Street
Tel: 061-412 377
Traditional Georgian pub in the city centre, with poetry and music every Wednesday night at 9pm (free).

William G. South
The Crescent
Tel: 061-318 850
If you want to visit a pub that's remained almost unchanged since the old days described in Frank McCourt's memoir, *Angela's Ashes*, then try this one.

County Clare
Glór Irish Music Centre
Causeway Link, Ennis
Tel. 065-684 3103
www.glor.ie
A large modern venue used mainly for traditional Irish music concerts. It is one of the main venues for the Summer Music in Galway Festival in early August. Ennis also has half a dozen traditional music pubs, all

within a short walk of the Old Ground Hotel. Ask locally who is performing, when and where during your stay.

Gus O'Connor's
Fisher Street
Tel: 065-707 4168
www.oconnorspubdoolin.com

McDermott's
Lisdoonvarna Road
Tel: 065-707 4133
www.mcdermottspubdoolin.com

McGann's
Lisdoonvarna Road
Tel: 065-707 4133
www.mcgannspubdoolin.com

All three pubs are noted for traditional music.

Shannon Heritage
Bunratty Castle & Folk Park
Tel: 061-360 788
www.shannonheritage.com
Medieval banquets with cabaret are held nightly at Bunratty Castle, Knappogue Castle and Dungauire Castle from May to September. You will be welcomed by a medieval lord and served a bowl of honey-rich mead. Also features maidens with harps and fiddles, fleet-footed dancers and classical singers.

Vaughan's Barn
Kilfenora
Tel: 065-708 8004
Venue for ceilidhs and set dancing sessions.

SPORTS AND ACTIVITIES

Surfers now outnumber golfers, sea angling attracts many to the Shannon estuary, and the Burren Way remains one of the most popular walking routes in the country.

Angling
Carrigaholt Sea Angling Centre
Tel: 065-905 8209
www.fishandstay.com
Charter boat, equipment hire and tackle shop.

Golf
Adare Manor Golf Course
Tel: 061-605 274
www.adaremanor.com
Challenging parkland course.

Greg Norman's Doonbeg Golf Club

Doonbeg Golf Club
Tel: 065-905 5602
www.doonbeggolfclub.com
New Greg Norman-designed links course along 3km (2 miles) of Atlantic coast.

Lahinch Golf Club
Tel: 065-708 1003
www.lahinchgolf.com
Classic links course known as the St Andrews of Ireland.

Walking and cycling
The Burren Way is a 123km (76-mile) linear way-marked trail from Lahinch to Corofin, via the Cliffs of Moher. Sections are suitable for day walks. For good tips, see www.shannon regiontrails.ie for good tips. Your visit will be greatly enhanced by a specialist guide.

Burren Bike Hire
The Launderette, Ballyvaughan
Tel: 065-707 7061
Rents out all kinds of bikes and equipment.

Burren Guided Walks
Old Road, Fanore, Ballyvaughan
Tel: 065-707 6100
www.burrenguidedwalks.com
A variety of of walks, from short rambles to day-long hikes, are led by an experienced local guide.

Heart of Burren Walks
Kilnaboy
Tel: 065-682 7707
www.heartofburrenwalks.com
Themed walks of various lengths set out from Burren Display Centre, Kilfenora.

Watersports
Kilkee Diving and Watersports Centre
East End, Kilkee
Tel: 065-905 6706
www.diveireland.com
Diving, sailing and powerboating school in the sheltered waters of Kilkee Bay.

Lahinch Surf School
Ballyfaudeen, Lahinch
Tel: 087-960 9667
www.lahinchsurfschool.com
A team of hardcore surf dudes will teach you to ride the waves; all equipment provided.

TOURS

Bus tours depart from Limerick, for walkers the Shannon estuary has a resident pod of dolphins, while a boat trip is also a good way to view the Cliffs of Moher.

Bus tours
Barratt Tours
Limerick
Tel: 061-384 700
www.4tours.biz
For day trips to the Cliffs of Moher.

Walking tours
Angela's Ashes & Historical Walking Tour
Limerick Tourist Office
Tel: 061-327 108
www.freewebs.com/walkingtours
Walk led by a knowledgeable local guide.

Boat trips
Dolphin Watching
Kilrush
Tel: 065-905 1327
www.discoverdolphins.ie
Boat departs from Kilrush Marina.

O'Brien Cruises
Doolin Pier
Tel: 065-707 5555
www.obrienline.com
Offers trips to the Aran Islands, and one-hour cruises to the Cliffs of Moher.

FESTIVALS AND EVENTS

The area to the north and west of Limerick city is famous for traditional music, song and dance, and these are the mainstays of the festival scene.

Fleadh Nua
Gort Road, Ennis
Tel: 065-602 4276
www.fleadhnua.com
This eight-day celebration of traditional music with dance and song in late May features workshops, concerts and ceilidhs.

Willie Clancy Summer School
Miltown Malbay
Tel: 065-708 4148
www.oac.ie
The biggest traditional music summer school in Ireland is credited with the national revival of Irish set dancing.

The west – Galway and Mayo

Galway is often referred to as the most 'Irish' of cities. It is the gateway to Connemara's wild, romantic landscape and the remote Aran Islands at the very edge of Europe, where the Irish language is still spoken. Here in the far west, the huge sky seems to change by the minute, alternating between dazzling sun, fleeting clouds and bursts of rain.

Population: 51,000

Local dialling code: 091

Local tourist office: Galway City Tourist Office, Forster Place; tel: 091-537 700; www.discoverireland.ie/west

Main police station: Mill Street; tel: 091-538 000

Main post office: Eglinton Street; tel: 091-562 051

Main hospital: University College Hospital, Newcastle Road; tel: 091-542 222

Airports: Ireland West Airport, Knock; tel: 094-936 7222; www.knockairport.com; Galway Airport, Inverin; tel: 091-755 569; www.galwayairport.com

Trains: Galway Ceannt Station, Eyre Square; tel: 091-562 000; www.irishrail.ie

Buses: 091-562 000; www.bus eireann.ie; Citylink, Unit 1, Forster Court, Galway; tel: 091-564 163; www.citylink.ie

Car hire: www.carhireirealnd.com; Budget Car Rental; tel: 091-566 376; www.budget.ie/galwaycity. htm

Taxi companies: Big O Taxis; tel: 091-588 5858; www.bigotaxis.com

The western city of Galway has a compact city centre with numerous quaint shops, trendy boutiques and stylish cafés and pubs. The city has developed a unique personality, combining a strong Irish identity with exuberant cosmopolitan influences, epitomised by the broad cultural mix presented annually in the Galway Arts Festival *(see p.187)*.

Connemara is a land of lakes, bogs and mountains, but almost empty of people. Its farming and fishing communities traditionally clustered around the coast, while its interior was inhabited chiefly by sheep farmers.

Out in the Atlantic, the Aran Islands are home to an Irish-speaking community that keeps the customs of a much older Ireland, but has also adapted to the demands of modern tourism. The approach to County Mayo is dominated by Croaghpatrick, St Patrick's holy mountain, while Westport is a pleasant county town backing on to the island-studded Clew Bay.

Galway city and Bay

Vibrant **Galway city** ❶ has a colourful past. The medieval walled city grew up on the eastern bank of the River Corrib in the 13th century, developing as a thriving port for wine, spices and fish. It became known as the 'Citie of the Tribes' because of the 14 wealthy Anglo-Norman merchant families who ruled it as an independent city-state. Each family had its own mansion with stone-faced designs. Remnants of the buildings can be seen on a walk around the city.

Enjoying a drink on the lively and pedestrianised Shop Street

Eyre Square is decorated with fourteen flags

Galway city

Eyre Square ❹ is Galway's focal point and main public park. In 1963 US president John F. Kennedy made a speech here when given the freedom of the city. The square has recently been re-landscaped, giving it a much-needed facelift.

The **Discover Ireland Centre Galway** ❺ (Forster Street; tel: 091-537 700; www.discoverireland.ie/west; Mon–Sat 9am–5.45pm) is awash with booklets, maps, postcards and gifts.

Galway is so compact that visitors quickly feel at home. The main street between Eyre Square and the River Corrib is pedestrianised, and changes name four times – **William, Shop, High** and **Quay Streets** ❻. It is lined with shops, restaurants and pubs. Jugglers and buskers entertain at all hours. On spring and summer evenings many set up tables on the pavement, creating a Continental atmosphere.

The most notable church is the Anglican cathedral, the **Collegiate Church of St Nicholas** ❼ (tel: 091-564 648). Built around 1320, it is the largest parish church of the medieval period in Ireland. Outstanding features include the Crusader's Tomb with an inscription in Norman French, and a carved baptismal font of the late 16th century. The Saturday morning **farmers' market** beside the church is not to be missed.

Lynch's Castle **E** was the town house of the Lynch tribe and is now a bank. Its foyer has a series of wall panels on the castle's history. The imposing stone facade is decorated with carved panels and stonework, as well as gruesome gargoyles that include a lion devouring another animal.

The **Spanish Arch** **F** is the only remaining gate of the city walls, stands beside the Fishmarket, now a pedestrian plaza. It recalls the former trade with Spain, and leads to the **Long Walk** **G** where small ships are berthed, home to a large flotilla of swans. The **Galway City Museum**

H (Spanish Parade; tel: 091-532 460; www.galwaycity.ie; June–Oct Mon–Sat 10am–5pm, Sun 2–5pm, Oct–May closed Sun–Mon; free) occupies a fine new building. The ground floor covers the contemporary city, and two upper floors focus on medieval and post-Famine Galway.

From the museum a footpath runs along the riverside to the **Salmon Weir Bridge** **I**. It is the last bridge upstream before the waters of the Corrib River open out into Lough Corrib. In early spring (but sometimes later too) hundreds of salmon wait under the shadow of the bridge before making their way upstream to spawn in Lough Corrib.

Salthill **J** is just 3km (2 miles) along the coast, and offers an escape from the city streets, as well as tremendous views of the wide expanse of Galway Bay. This resort was built

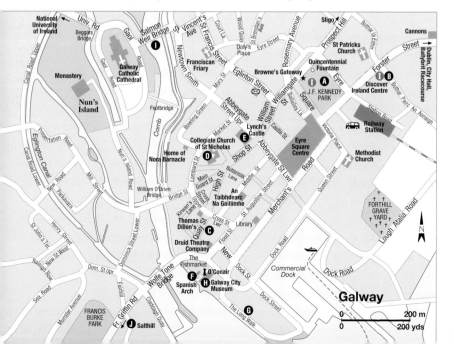

Galway

this lonely sentinel is floodlit, and hosts medieval banquets.

The Aran Islands

A trip to the **Aran Islands** (www.aran islands.ie) – Inishmore, Inishmaan and Inisheer – is well worth organising. As many as 2,000 day-trippers a day in peak season can visit the main island of Inishmore, which has a permanent population of 900, but most are on day trips. If possible, spend at least one night on the islands, to appreciate their isolation and peacefulness. Accommodation is plentiful, simple and inexpensive.

Everyday life is carried out in Irish (Gaelic), but the islanders speak English too. The islands contain many pre-Christian and early Christian remains. Bring waterproof clothes and wear shoes suitable for uneven terrain. Cars can safely be left at the mainland ferryport, **Rossaveal** ❸ (free).

in the early years of the 19th century, and has its quota of amusement arcades, discos and a fairground.

Galway Bay

Drive along the south shore of Galway Bay through **Kilcolgan** and **Clarinbridge**, where Galway's oysters are grown, to **Kinvara** ❷, a charming fishing village with a grassy quayside where traditional wooden 'hookers', used to carry turf across the bay in the old days, are berthed. Visitors enjoy its old-fashioned pubs and modern restaurants.

The floodlit **Dunguaire Castle** (tel: 061-360 788; Apr–Oct daily 10am–5pm; charge), a landmark to the village's north, is a four-storey tower house built in 1520. At night

---

Early music

While most people associate Galway with traditional music and street entertainment, there is another aspect to its musical life. The **Galway Early Music Festival** (www.galwayearlymusic.com), held annually in May, celebrates the culture of Europe from the 12th to the 18th century in music and dance. The programme of Baroque and Renaissance music features atmospheric candlelit concerts in the Church of St Nicholas (see p.171) as well as workshops, master-classes and street performances by internationally acclaimed ensembles.

Travel to the Aran Islands

Aran Island Ferries (tel: 091-58903; www.aranislandferries.com) operate daily services from Ros a' Mhil (Rossaveal) on the Connemara coast, with a bus link from Galway city. Book online, and get a deal including accommodation, or book at the Tourist Information Office in Galway. An air taxi service (hourly flights during peak season, €40 return) to the three islands is run by **Aer Arann Islands** (tel: 091-593 034; www.aerarannislands.ie) from Connemara Regional Airport, Inverin, a 45-minute drive west of Galway city (bus link from Galway city). The flight takes less than 10 minutes; the ferry journey to Inishmore is about 35 minutes.

Inishmore

Inishmore ❹, 'the Big Island' as the Aran folk call it, is 14km (9 miles) from tip to tip and only 3km (2 miles) across. Ferries dock at **Kilronan**. This is an island to explore on foot or rented bicycle (to reach Dún Aengus), given time, though minibuses and taxis are on standby for day-trippers. You can also hire pony traps for guided tours.

Dún Aengus (Mar–Oct daily 10am–6pm, Nov–Feb 10am–4pm; charge), a giant prehistoric fortress on the sheer edge of a cliff, consists of four semi-circular defensive walls. Apart from its historic interest, the view from its ramparts is one of the most striking imaginable. On a clear day the sweep of coastline from Kerry and Clare to the south, as well as the length of Galway to the western extremity of Connemara is visible. Colourful wild flowers, grazing cows, sheep and an abundance of bounding rabbits are to be found on the islands, and there are several other archaeological sites.

Hire a bicycle to explore Inishmore's classic Irish landscape

Cong ❼, a tiny, very pretty village on the opposite shore, was the location for John Ford's classic film, *The Quiet Man* (1952). The **Quiet Man Cottage** (tel: 094-954 6089; www. quietman-cong.com; daily 9am–5pm; charge) is a replica of the one in the film, a likeable romantic take on rural Ireland, aimed firmly at the American-Irish market. Cong is rich in antiquities, including the well-preserved remains of **Cong Abbey** (free), a 13th-century Augustinian foundation. From here, there is a lakeside walk to **Ashford Castle**, an imposing turreted mansion built in 1870 as a holiday home for the Guinness family. It is now a luxury hotel.

West Connemara coast

The attractive market town of **Clifden ❽**, known as 'the capital of Connemara' (in fact it is the only town), is pitched on a conical hill beneath wooded slopes and is a good base for exploring the region. Take a walk or a drive along the **Sky Road**, a scenic route above the town, to get a taste of the stunning sea and mountain scenery.

Connemara National Park ❾ (Letterfrack; tel: 095-41054; www. connemaranationalpark.ie; daily dawn–dusk, visitor centre May–Oct daily 9am–5.30pm; charge, park free) covers 2,000 hectares (5,000 acres) and is rich in wildlife. The Visitor Centre gives a good introduction to the local flora and fauna and has an indoor picnic area: handy in the Connemara weather.

Connemara

Connemara – a range of dramatic mountains and sparkling lakes – begins west of Lough Corrib. It is bordered by a coastline of rugged cliffs and small coves. Two ranges of moody mountains, the Twelve Pins and the Maumturks, dominate the views.

Around Lough Corrib

Lough Corrib ❺ extends 43km (27 miles) north from Galway; it is whipped by waves when the wind hurtles down the hillside. It's shallow and well supplied with islands and fish – salmon, trout, pike and perch. Take a cruise from the angling centre, **Oughterard ❻**, and sample the lake's tranquillity from the water.

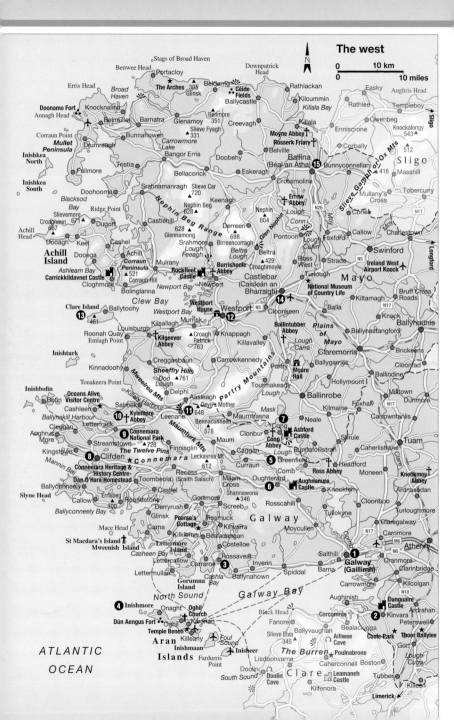

centre.com; charge) has live breeds, demonstrations of spinning and weaving, and a craft shop. Killary harbour has sheltered waters protected by mountains; sample its delights on a cruise *(see p.187)*. The floats and rafts are for farming mussels.

County Mayo

Mayo is a large, sparsely populated county consisting mainly of bog and mountains, with an exposed coastline battered by the Atlantic. It has long been synonymous with remoteness, poverty and emigration, but its unspoilt scenery is a magnet for outdoor-lovers. Historic Westport has expanded towards its quays, and is a popular destination year-round.

There are two routes from Leenane to **Westport**: via the spectacular **Doo Lough Pass** to **Louisburgh** or directly along the N59. Looming ahead you will see the unmistakable cone of **Croagh Patrick**, Ireland's holy mountain. The Reek, as it is known, is climbed in honour of St Patrick by more than 30,000 pilgrims – many of them barefoot – on the last Sunday in July. The Visitor Information Centre (Murrisk; tel: 098-64114; www.museumsofmayo.com; Mar–Oct 10am–5pm, closed end Oct–Mar) at the base of the mountain contains fascinating information about the archaeological discoveries on the summit. From the top, there are views of the bay and the hills of counties Mayo, Clare and Galway.

Picturesquely situated on the Carrowbeg River, **Westport** ⓬, a busy

Nearby is one of Ireland's most photographed buildings – the dramatically sited **Kylemore Abbey** ⓾ (tel: 095-41146; www.kylemoreabbey.com; exhibitions, café and craft shop: daily Mar–Nov 9am–5pm; free; Victorian walled garden mid-May–mid-Oct 10.30am–4.30pm; charge). This imposing late 19th-century limestone and granite neo-Gothic mansion rears up against a wooded backdrop on the far side of a lake. It was erected by a Liverpool merchant as a gift to his wife, who subsequently died tragically; she is commemorated by a chapel (charge). It is now a girls' boarding school, run by Benedictine nuns.

Leenane ⓫ at the head of **Killary Harbour**, Ireland's only fjord, marks the border between Galway and Mayo. The **Sheep & Wool Centre** (tel: 095-42323; www.sheepandwool

★ FESTIVAL FEVER

While the west of Ireland may be considered to have few formal provisions for the arts, it more than makes up for it with a jam-packed festival season, featuring writers, traditional music, the arts, horses, wooden boats and oysters. In Ireland the arts are synonymous with fun: usually family fun, with a wide variety of free entertainment from street parades to buskers and outdoor concerts. And if it rains, it's judged only to add to the enjoyment!

Galway, with its compact and largely pedestrianised city centre, is the ideal location for festivals. Everyone can walk from one venue to the next, and the car-free streets and piazzas are perfect for buskers, street theatre, human statues, circus acts and whatever is the latest performance trend. In such a small place, people quickly make friends, the lively programme providing a common interest and conversation topic.

Kilkenny Arts Festival is older and more serious, the Wexford Festival Opera is more specialised, and Cork's Midsummer Fest has better venues, but no other arts festival has the impact of Galway's two-week explosion of artistic activity in mid-July. Its highlight is the Macnas Festival Parade, when the local theatre company takes over the streets with giant papier mâché puppets. The Festival Big Top has major music acts, while the Town Hall Theatre showcases

Ladies Day at the Galway Racing Festival

premières of works by Irish playwrights and hosts major international companies. Leading writers, visual artists, comedians and dance companies add to a package that ensures the city never sleeps (www.galwayartsfestival.com).

The last day of the Arts Festival is followed by the opening of the Galway Racing Festival, another sleepless week, where the convivial atmosphere of the racecourse is carried back into the city every evening, as punters party the night away. Reputedly some people never get near the racecourse, but they have a ball anyway (www.galwayraces.com).

August is the time for traditional seaside regattas, the most picturesque being the Cruinniú na mBád (Gathering of the Boats) at Kinvara on Galway Bay. Traditional wooden sailing boats race across Galway Bay by day, while at night traditional Irish musicians entertain for free in the distinctive local style (www.kinvara.com/cruinniu).

In late September the focus shifts to Clifden, where the Connemara Pony Festival (www.cpbs), featuring showjumping and best-of-breed competitions, is the centrepiece of the Clifden Arts Festival, which runs for 10 days. Organised by the local community, the tiny town presents major Irish poets reading, recitals of classical music, comedy and free traditional Irish music and dancing displays (www.clifdenartsweek.ie).

And to top it all, on the second weekend in September, the opening of the oyster season is celebrated in Clarenbridge in a three-day festival of seafood, music and free entertainment (www.clarenbridge.com).

A local festival is a good place to catch traditional Irish music and dancing

A happy face: Irish festivals aim to be fun for all the family

market town with colourful shop fronts, retains some fine Georgian buildings. A walk around its tree-lined riverside mall, and the Octagon (its market place), is a pleasant experience. The town's quays, a 10-minute walk from its centre, are on **Clew Bay**, and the old warehouses have been nicely developed as tourist accommodation. This is the place for spectacular sunsets, to be watched, perhaps, from the terrace of one of the two waterside pubs.

Westport House & Pirate Adventure Park (tel: 098-27766; www.westporthouse.ie; May Sat–Sun, June–Sept daily noon–6pm; charge) is set in magnificent parkland on the outskirts of Westport and has attractions for children of all ages.

Heading west along the Clew Bay coast, **Clare Island** ⑬ can be reached by ferry from Roonagh Quay, Louisburgh (tel: 098-26525; www.clareisland.org). It is a rocky place with a population of 163 and worth visiting to learn the seafaring exploits of Grace O'Malley, or Granuaile (1530–1603), a pirate queen who preyed on cargo vessels. Late in her life she journeyed to London to do a deal with Queen Elizabeth I, negotiating in their only common language, Latin. The island holds much interest for the botanist and has a small hotel and B&Bs.

Castlebar and the north Mayo coast

To take a nostalgic look at what life in Ireland used to be like, visit the award-winning **National Museum of Country Life** (tel: 094-903 1755; www.museum.ie; Tue–Sat 10am–5pm, Sun 2–5pm; free) at Turlough Park, 8km (5 miles) from **Castlebar** ⑭, County Mayo's capital. The museum houses the **National Folklife Collection** documenting the domestic lives of people in rural Ireland from

Stock up on souvenirs in Westport

The striking visitor centre at the prehistoric site of Céide Fields

1850 to 1950. The displays are hugely appealing to both young and old. The award-winning modern building is in the grounds of a former stately home, and there is a good shop and café.

Heading up to the north coast of County Mayo, past Lough Conn, **Killala** and **Ballina** ⑮ have their own particular charms for the visitor. Killala rises above a small harbour, its skyline dominated by a pencil-thin 10th-century round tower and the spire of the Church of Ireland. Ballina, with its streets sloping down to the River Moy (www.rivermoy.com), is the largest town in Mayo and is internationally renowned for salmon fishing.

Continuing along the north Mayo coast road, you will be startled by the sight of a glass pyramid topping a large building. This is the visitor centre of the remarkable **Céide Fields** (pronounced *kay-jeh*) – (Ballycastle; tel: 096-43325; www.museumsofmayo.

com; June–Sept 10am–6pm, mid-Mar–May and Oct–Nov 10am–5pm; charge). An extensive Stone Age monument, the impressive site includes field systems, dwelling area and megalithic tombs dating back 5,000 years. The bog's rare wild flowers and the spectacular cliffs opposite the centre attract botanists, geologists and bird watchers.

Achill Island

Ireland's biggest offshore island is in fact connected to the mainland by a causeway. Achill, an Irish-speaking area, is now the location of numerous holiday villages, built during the boom years, which impinge somewhat on the scenery. However, Achill has some of the best beaches in Ireland, and it is still a pleasure to drive or walk around its cliffs on a fine day, enjoying the hedges of wild fuchsia and some stunning sea views. Follow signs for the Atlantic Drive.

ACCOMMODATION

Galway city has a wide choice of places to stay, from fashionable to functional, many of them within the historic centre. On the Aran Islands hospitality is simple, but you can expect an en suite bathroom. Connemara and Mayo have some country-house hotels, and many rooms offer sea, lake or mountain views.

Galway city and Bay

Adare Guest House
9 Father Griffin Place
Tel: 091-582 638
www.adarebedandbreakfast.com
Well-located, unpretentious accommodation with private parking, three minutes' walk from the city centre. Family-run for two generations, the plain rooms are well away from the centre's noise. It offers a good breakfast. **€**

The 'G'
Wellpark
Tel: 091-865 200
www.theg.ie
Contemporary, luxurious design with an extravagant sense of fun, designed by Galway-born milliner Phlilip Treacy, indulging his wildest fantasies. An edge-of-town location avoids Galway's traffic gridlock. **€€€€**

Park House Hotel
Forester Street, Eyre Square
Tel: 091-564 924
www.parkhousehotel.ie
Large, well-equipped family-run hotel in the heart of the city, a warehouse conversion offering high levels of comfort. There is a busy bar and lobby. Bedrooms have been triple-glazed against Galway's night-time noise. **€€**

The Aran Islands

Kilmurvey House
Inis Mór
Tel: 099-61218
www.kilmurveyhouse.com
B&Bs abound on the Aran Islands; reserve a room when booking your ferry or flight. Kilmurvey House is an 18th-century stone-

built house, at the foot of Dun Aengus, midway between the island's two villages, and serves dinner nightly. **€**

Ostan Inis Oirr
Lurgan Village, Inisheer
Tel: 099-75020
Whether you fly or take the ferry, this modest modern hotel, a short walk from both pier and landing strip, makes a comfortable base on the smallest of the Aran Islands. Traditional music is played nightly in the bar. **€**

Connemara

Abbeyglen Castle
Sky Road
Tel: 095-22832
www.abbeyglen.ie
Beautifully sited turreted mock castle, midway between the main town centre and scenic 'Sky Road' walk. Friendly staff, free afternoon tea and a loyal Irish clientele. **€€€**

Ballynahinch Castle Hotel
Recess
Tel: 095-31006
www.ballynahinch-castle.com
Historic house full of character, in the wilds of Connemara at the foot of one of the 'Twelve Bens', overlooking the Owenmore River. Extensive grounds, private salmon fishing and luxurious but tasteful decor. **€€€€**

Delphi Mountain Resort
Leenane
Tel: 095-42208
www.delphimountainresort.com
New spa and hotel aimed at those who enjoy a touch of boldly designed luxury while

enjoying the wilderness experience. Run by eco-aware owners, an organic kitchen is on-site. DVD players are provided but there is no reception for TV or mobiles. €€

Sleepzone
Leenane
Tel: 095-42929
www.sleepzone.ie
This former hunting lodge has stunning views over Ireland's only fjord and is a well-run hostel with over 100 beds in 21 en suite rooms. Outdoor pursuits are on the doorstep. It's a 6km (4 mile) walk or drive to the village, or there is a minibus available from Galway. €

County Mayo
Ashford Castle
Cong
Tel: 094-954 6003
www.ashford.ie
A castellated fairytale castle on Lough Corrib with very high standards of comfort and decor. Private golf course, tennis, fishing, boating, horse riding and shooting are part of the 'total resort' experience.
€€€€–€€€€€

Boffin Lodge
The Quay, Westport
Tel: 098-26092
www.boffinlodge.com

The idyllic location of Ashford Castle

Small and stylish traditional-style guesthouse in a tranquil location near Westport's quays, half a mile from the town centre. There are four-poster beds and steam rooms available. Close to a good choice of pubs and restaurants. €

Westport Plaza and Castlecourt Hotel
Castlebar Street, Westport
Tel: 098-55088
www.westporthotelsresort.ie
Neighbouring hotels in the town centre share the luxury pool and spa. Castlecourt is a comfortable traditional hotel, while the Plaza is a more snazzy (and expensive) boutique-style hotel with pleasantly luxurious bedrooms. €€–€€€

RESTAURANTS

There is a lively dining scene in Galway, but elsewhere places tend to be simple and traditional, serving fresh food in unpretentious surroundings. Some of the best restaurants are in hotels, which also serve reasonably priced bar food.

Restaurant price categories
Prices are per person for two courses, not including drinks:

$ = below €20
$$ = €20–28
$$$ = €28–38
$$$$ = over €38

Galway city and Bay
Ard Bia/Nimmo's
Spanish Arch
Tel: 091-561 114
www.ardbia.com
This compact waterside stone warehouse,

with bare wooden floors and quirky art on the walls, is an atmospheric café by day, ideal for a casual meal featuring local artisan food. More expensive meals are served in Nimmo's upstairs in the evening.
€–€€

The Malt House
Old Malt Arcade, 15 High Street
Tel: 091-567 866
www.themalthouse.ie
A quiet restaurant set in a charming old-world courtyard, but with cool and contemporary decor and a sophisticated menu of local seafood: try Galway Bay oysters with bacon and cabbage, or salmon in chilli broth. €€€

Mcdonagh's Seafood House
22 Quay Street
Tel: 091-565 001
www.mcdonaghs.net
A self-service chippy on one side, and a serious seafood restaurant on the other, McDonagh's is a Galway institution. The self-service bar also offers seafood chowder and a selection of seafood salads. €–€€€

Moran's Oyster Cottage
Kilcolgan
Tel: 091-796 503
www.moransoystercottage.com
The tiny thatched country pub is beside a wide weir and the Moran family's oyster beds. The front bar has been preserved, but there is also a large restaurant behind. From September to April try the local oysters; in summer fresh prawns, crab and lobster. €€

The Pier Head
The Quay, Kinvara
Tel: 091-638 188
www.pierheadkinvara
A corner bar in this pretty fishing village, with views of Dunguaire Castle and the sunset across the bay, is now an excellent restaurant. Sample mussels, skate and lobster, as well as locally sourced steak on the owner-chef's short, impeccably prepared menu. €€–€€€

The Aran Islands
Pier House Restaurant
Kilronan, Inishmore
Tel: 099-61471
www.pierhouserestaurant.com
Close to the ferry, with harbour views and outdoor tables, this unpretentious restaurant serves plenty of fresh seafood and bistro-style dishes like Connemara lamb shank, plus vegetarian specials. Home-made breads and desserts, and a decent wine list. €–€€

Connemara
Avoca Craft Shop
Letterfrack
Tel: 095-41058
Picnic tables overlooking a sheltered sea inlet will tempt you to stop, and Avoca's cafés are known for creating light, wholesome dishes, using local and artisan products. €

Mitchell's Seafood Restaurant
Clifden
Tel: 095-21867
Stone walls and an open fire make an atmospheric restaurant of this former shop. Local mussels are steamed in garlic, while fresh crab is served on home-made bread. €–€€

County Mayo
Healy's Hotel, Pontoon
Tel: 094-925 6443
www.healyspontoon.com
This modest country inn, favoured by fishermen, has turned its lounge bar into a restaurant, such is the demand for its simply prepared seafood, succulent steaks and tasty salads. But what most people remember is the stunning lake view across the road. €

The Ice House
The Quay, Ballina
Tel: 096-23500
www.theicehouse.ie
A refurbished riverside Victorian ice house now houses a striking, light-filled contemporary restaurant, part of a highly successful hotel and spa. Food is cutting-edge, mainly organic and local, served with panache. €€€

The Tavern Bar
Murrisk
Tel: 098-64060
Fishermen used to arrive with buckets of langoustines, starting the bar food tradition here. Today the menu also includes locally produced cheeses and meat. A more sophisticated restaurant (€€€) opens at night. €

NIGHTLIFE AND ENTERTAINMENT

For most of the west of Ireland (with the exception of Galway city) nightlife and entertainment revolve around the pub. Only Galway, Westport and Ballina have cinemas. Pub entertainment usually starts around 9.30pm, though there can be spontaneous music sessions at any time.

Clubs

GPO
Eglinton Street, Galway
Tel: 091-563 073
Dance club with bar full licence, open from about 11pm.

Pubs

The Bard's Den
Letterfrack, Connemara
Tel: 091-41042
Roadside bar, noted for its traditional music sessions.

Joe Watty's
Kilronan, Aran Islands
Tel: 099-20892
Traditional music is performed every night in summer.

Matt Molloy's
Bridge Street, Westport, Co. Mayo
Tel: 098-26655
Matt Molloy is the Chieftains' whistle and flute player, so it's no surprise that traditional music is a major feature.

Monroe's Tavern
Dominick Street, Galway
Tel: 091-583 397
Traditional music nightly, and set dancing sessions.

The Quays
Quay Street, Galway
Tel: 091-568 347
One of the best Galway music pubs, with three floors of bars.

Tig Coili
Mainguard Street, Galway
Tel: 091-584 294
Traditional music sessions daily.

Winkles Hotel
The Square, Kinvara
Tel: 091-637 137
Renowned music bar on Galway Bay, home base of accordionist Sharon Shannon.

Theatre

Druid Theatre Company
Druid Lane Theatre, Chapel Lane, Galway
Tel: 091-568 660
www.druidtheatre.com
One of Ireland's most successful repertory theatre companies, presenting a mix of new work and revivals.

Town Hall Theatre
Courthouse Square, Galway
Tel: 091-569 777
www.tht.ie
Theatre space shared by two of Druid and Galway's professional companies, Punchbag and Macnas, along with touring productions, comedy and variety.

Traditional Irish music in a Galway pub

SPORTS AND ACTIVITIES

The west is an area made for outdoor pursuits, traditionally golfing and angling, and also cycling and walking. New companies are providing facilities for kayaking, sailing, climbing and other activities. There is also a strong tradition of horse riding in Galway.

Adventure centres

Atlantic Adventure Centre
Lecanvey, Westport
Tel: 098-64806
www.atlanticadventurecentre.com
Canoeing, abseiling, rock climbing, boogie boarding and mountain climbing

Killary Adventure Company
Leenane
Tel: 095-43411
www.killaryadventure.com
From bungee jumping to kayaking and most outdoor things in between. Budget accommodation and family packages – 'from 8 to 80'.

Cycling

Clifden Cycle Hub
Tourist Office, Clifden
Tel: 095-21163
www.discoverireland.ie/cycling
Details of local bicycle hire, and maps of the looped cycle routes of Connemara.

Irish Cycling Safaris
Tel: 01-260 0749
www.irishcyclingsafaris.com
Choose a self-led tour of Connemara with pre-booked accommodation, bike hire, luggage transfer and route details, or join a group tour with organised stops, and a support van.

Horse riding

Dartfield Horse Museum and Park
Kilkeel, Loughrea
Tel: 091-843 968
www.dartfield.com
The museum is the base for Willie Leahy's riding trails and horse holidays. Book an hour's ride, or customise a residential holiday for children and adults, with cross-country challenges and/or trail riding on one of his 400 Irish-bred horses.

Riding on Cleggan beach, Connemara

Errislannan Manor Connemara Pony Stud
Clifden
Tel: 095-21134
www.errislannanmanor.com
Try one of the intelligent locally bred ponies on their home territory. Riding by the hour daily, longer treks, and holidays for unaccompanied children by arrangement.

Walking

There are four major way-marked trails in the west, and numerous scenic looped walks. See www.irishtrails.ie.

Connemara Safari Walking Holidays
Clifden
Tel: 095-21071
www.walkingconnemara.com
Forget your troubles on a five-day escorted walking holiday visiting three offshore islands.

Croaghpatrick Walking Tours
Westport
Tel: 098-26090
www.walkingguideireland.com
Enormously popular escorted walking tours in Mayo.

TOURS

A guided walking or bus tour of Galway city will leave you thoroughly familiar with its charms. It's especially worth making the effort to take at least one boat trip, to see the west from a new vantage point, and enjoy the abundant wildlife.

Walking tours

Galway City Tourist Information Office
Forster Place
Tel: 091-537 700
www.discoverireland.ie/west
For up-to-date details of the many walking tours of Galway city. Daily from 11am.

Bus tours

Galway Tour Company
Tel: 091-77066
www.galwaytourcompany.com
One of several companies offering open bus tours of Galway city and Salthill in summer and day trips to Connemara year-round. Tickets from Galway Tourist Information Office.

Boat trips

Generally run from April/May to September. Boats have bars, covered areas and seating.

Corrib Cruises
Oughterard, Co. Galway
Tel: 091-557 798
www.corribcruises.com
Daily cruises on Lough Corrib crossing to Cong and visiting historic Inchagoill Island.

Corrib Princess
Wood Quay, Galway
Tel: 091-522 033
www.corribprincess.ie
Covered launch sails from Galway city up the River Corrib to Lough Corrib in 90 minutes.

Killary Cruises
Leenane
Tel: 091-566 736
www.killarycruises.com
Ninety-minute cruises on the glassy calm waters of Killary Fjord.

Listings

FESTIVALS AND EVENTS

July and August are the big months for festivals, being the peak of the west's short summer, while September marks the opening of the season for local oysters.

July

Galway Arts Festival
www.galwayartsfestival.com
Two weeks in late July see Galway brimming with theatre, music, art and readings, a highlight being the Macnas street theatre parade.

Galway Races
www.galwayraces.com
The Arts Festival is followed by a week-long race meeting, famous for its atmosphere.

August

The Connemara Pony Show
www.cpbs.ie
Clifden is abuzz in the third week in August

for this major event. The local breed of horse changes hands for big money and shows its paces before the evening revelry.

Cruinniú na Bád Kinvara
www.kinvara.com/cruinniu
'The Gathering of the Boats' is a mid-August weekend of racing on Galway Bay with Galway hookers and other traditional wooden boats. Great spectating and great craic.

September

Clarenbridge Oyster Festival
www.clarenbridge.com
Celebrating the opening of the oyster season with free entertainment and demos.

Inland Ireland

Often overlooked, the inland counties are well worth exploring. Bogs, lakes and rivers dominate the region, making fishing and boating big attractions. The region is peppered with mansions and monasteries – including Clonmacnoise, Ireland's most important monastic site. New farmers' markets and espresso bars sit comfortably with centuries-old pubs and grocery shops.

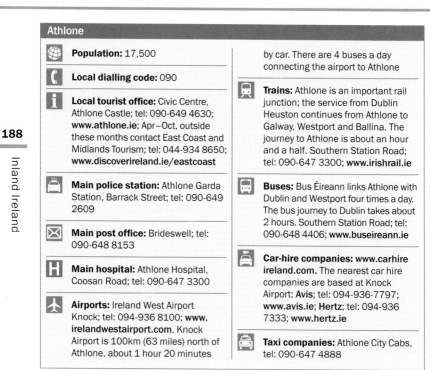

Athlone

Population: 17,500

Local dialling code: 090

Local tourist office: Civic Centre, Athlone Castle; tel: 090-649 4630; www.athlone.ie; Apr–Oct, outside these months contact East Coast and Midlands Tourism; tel: 044-934 8650; www.discoverireland.ie/eastcoast

Main police station: Athlone Garda Station, Barrack Street; tel: 090-649 2609

Main post office: Brideswell; tel: 090-648 8153

Main hospital: Athlone Hospital, Coosan Road; tel: 090-647 3300

Airports: Ireland West Airport Knock; tel: 094-936 8100; www.irelandwestairport.com. Knock Airport is 100km (63 miles) north of Athlone, about 1 hour 20 minutes by car. There are 4 buses a day connecting the airport to Athlone

Trains: Athlone is an important rail junction; the service from Dublin Heuston continues from Athlone to Galway, Westport and Ballina. The journey to Athlone is about an hour and a half. Southern Station Road; tel: 090-647 3300; www.irishrail.ie

Buses: Bus Éireann links Athlone with Dublin and Westport four times a day. The bus journey to Dublin takes about 2 hours. Southern Station Road; tel: 090-648 4406; www.buseireann.ie

Car-hire companies: www.carhireireland.com. The nearest car hire companies are based at Knock Airport: **Avis**; tel: 094-936-7797; www.avis.ie; **Hertz**; tel: 094-936 7333; www.hertz.ie

Taxi companies: Athlone City Cabs, tel: 090-647 4888

In a region marked by the relative absence of physical drama and bisected by the River Shannon, where bogland and lake account for much of the terrain, the counties of Longford, Laois, Offaly, Westmeath, Roscommon, Cavan and Monaghan have long been overshadowed by the coastal regions of the South and West. Long the preserve of anglers, now walkers, cyclists and other Irish weekenders are discovering the slower pace of life in its sleepy towns and villages. Many of these have been revitalised by young families moving to the region during the property boom to escape Dublin's high prices.

The southwest Midlands

Athlone is a busy administrative centre, and also the epicentre of the region's thriving lake and river cruising businesses, with good restaurants and lively bars. To the west is a sparsely populated region of low-lying bog, a fascinating ecological system. At Clonmacnoise there are major monastic remains, while Birr is an elegant Georgian town built around a magnificent castle.

Around Athlone

The origins of **Athlone** ❶ (www.athlone.ie), Ireland's geographic centre which straddles the River Shannon,

A traditional shop in County Westmeath

lie in its important strategic location as a river crossing, the first north of Limerick. Today it is the region's commercial and administrative centre. **Athlone Castle** (tel: 090-647 2107; www.athlone.ie; May–Sept daily 10am–5pm, closed Oct–Apr; charge) is a squat 13th-century building, which was badly damaged in 1690 when the Irish made a stand here against the advance of Cromwell's forces. The castle keep now houses a Folk Museum, and the **Tourist Office** (tel: 090-649 4630; www.athlone.ie; Apr–Oct).

The area behind the castle is being promoted as Athlone's 'Left Bank'. There are some nice townhouses dating from the 18th and 19th centuries, and several good restaurants and bars. The nicest thing to do in Athlone, between June and August, is to take a boat trip up the Shannon to Lough Ree *(see p.201)*.

Ballinasloe ❷ has long been an important crossing place of the **River Suck**. Every year during the first week of October, Europe's oldest horse fair takes place here; this is serious horse country, still hunted by the famous

The distinctive Athlone Castle

Galway Blazers. **Shannonbridge ❸**, where chocolate-coloured land banks stretch as far as the eye can, is the centre of Ireland's peat industry (*see box, opposite*).

Clonmacnoise ❹ (tel: 090-967 4195; www.heritageireland.ie; mid-Mar–Oct daily 10am–6pm, mid-May–mid-Sept until 7pm, Nov–mid-Mar daily 10am–5.15pm; charge) is one of Ireland's most important monastic sites, superbly located on a bend in the River Shannon. The monastery was founded in AD545 by St Kieran and was the burial place of the kings of Connaught and Tara. The earliest of the surviving ruins dates from the 9th century. The monastery was plundered from then onwards by the Irish, the Vikings and the Anglo-Normans until it was destroyed in the Elizabethan wars of the mid-16th century. Among the older surviving buildings of the complex are the shell of a small cathedral, two round towers, the remains of eight smaller churches and several high crosses. One of the churches, Temple Connor, was restored by the Church of Ireland in 1911 and is used for services.

Birr

Birr ❺ is an attractive Georgian town dominated by **Birr Castle and Demesne** (tel: 057-912 0336; www.birrcastle.com; Nov–Mar daily noon–4pm, Apr–Oct daily 9am–6pm; charge). Birr is a good example of Georgian town planning, with many original entrance fanlights and iron railings still intact. The gardens of Birr Castle cover 40 hectares (100 acres) and have more than 1,000 species of trees and shrubs with an especially

A high cross in the Clonmacnoise complex

In the Georgian town of Birr

bent. In the 1840s the 3rd Earl of Rosse built the Great Telescope which enabled him to see further into space than any of his contemporaries. The telescope, which has a 17m (56ft) tube and a 1.8m (6ft) mirror, has been restored to working order.

Walk along **Oxmanton Mall**, a tree-lined thoroughfare which leads from the castle gates past a row of elegant Georgian houses, to **Emmet Square**, the location of one-time coaching inn **Dooly's Hotel**, dating from 1747 (www.doolyshotel.com).

Lough Derg

Southwest of Birr is **Lough Derg** ❻, where the Shannon widens into a 50-sq mile (130-sq km) lake that is about 16km (10 miles) across at its widest point. The circular **Lough Derg Drive** (about 90km/55 miles) passes through a succession of pretty villages – peaceful, out-of-the-way places to stay that are gaining in popularity. Most visitors either have a boat or enjoy fishing on the lake. **Terryglass** is one of the prettiest villages near Lough Derg, although you

Inland Ireland

strong Chinese and Himalayan collection. The 17th-century castle is private, but its stable block now houses **Ireland's Historic Science Centre** (open as above). The owners of Birr Castle, the Parsons family, now the Earls of Rosse, have a strong scientific

Irish bogs

From the car window, bog looks like an unattractive treeless piece of brown waterlogged land. But get out and venture onto its spongy surface, especially in early summer, and you will realise why bogs are prized as wildlife habitats. Jewel-like wild flowers grow amid the pools, including butterwort and bell heather. Larks sing overhead, and snipes sit silently on their nests. Hares breed here too, and dragonflies and damsel flies. Peat has been a source of fuel in Ireland for over 1,000 years, and harvesting of turf for domestic use is still permitted in certain areas of Ireland, thanks to a derogation from EU law. There are over 1,500 raised bogs in Ireland; only 130 sites have been designated for protection.

US President Barack Obama enjoys a pint at Hayes Bar in his ancestral home of Moneygall

have to leave the main road to find the lake. **Dromineer** is right on the water, and has a ruined castle on its pier. Many of the people you meet in the pubs will be enjoying a holiday on a hired river cruiser.

To the east of Birr is an accessible range of low-lying hills, perfect for either leisurely strolling or serious hiking. The **Slieve Bloom Way** is a 32km (20-mile) circular trail through mostly uninhabited landscape and hidden vistas. The villages of Cadamstown or Kinnity make ideal starting points.

The southeast Midlands

This area of the midlands has much rich pasture. Mullingar is an important centre for cattle dealing. There are several impressive stately homes, all with interesting gardens and restored interiors. Note that the southeast Midlands area is only about an hour's drive from Dublin.

Great Irish houses

East of the Slieve Bloom Mountains, **Emo Court** ❼ (tel: 057-862 6573; www.emocourt.net; gardens: daily 9am–dusk, house mid-June–mid-Sept daily 10am–6pm; gardens, free, house, charge) is a fine Georgian

---

Obama's Irish roots

When Irish ancestry was first mooted for America's first black president it seemed like an Irish joke – Barack O'Bama? But researchers at Trinity College Dublin proved that President Obama's late mother, Ann Dunham, was a descendant of Falmouth Kearney, who left Moneygall in County Offaly in 1850, and settled in Ohio. The house where he lived is just a step from Ollie Hayes' Bar on Main Street. When Obama visited Ireland in May 2011, he and Michelle helicoptered in and drank a pint at this pub, putting Moneygall (population 289) firmly on the map (18km/12 miles south of Birr).

mansion on a big scale. It was built in 1792 for the Earl of Portarlington in the Classical style by James Gandon, best known for Dublin's Four Courts and Custom House *(see pp.78, 81)*. Approached via an avenue of splendid Wellingtonia trees, the house is certainly worth a visit. Pride of place goes to the domed rotunda, a mix of marble pilasters with gilded Corinthian capitals supporting the enormous blue painted dome. The gardens are planted with azaleas, rhododendrons and Japanese maples and feature a peaceful lakeside walk. Nearby is **Coolbanagher Church,** also designed by Gandon, which incorporates an intricate 15th-century font from an earlier church.

Charleville Forest Castle ❽ (tel: 057-932 3040; www.charlevillecastle.

ie; May Sat–Sun 2–5pm, June–Sept Wed–Sun 2–5pm, Oct–Apr by appointment; charge), to the north, a fine example of Gothic Revival style, was commissioned by Baron Tullamore in 1812. With its flag tower and castellated turrets rising high over an estate of pleasant woodland walks and gardens, the house is built of grey limestone with an internal gallery running the entire length of the garden front. Five avenues lined by Irish yew trees radiate from the house. The grounds contain many impressive trees including a 700-year-old oak.

Around Mullingar

The low-lying **Lough Ennel** on the road between Kilbeggan and Mullingar is a popular place for swimming, boating and fishing. The restored **Belvedere House and Gardens ❾** (tel: 044-934 9060; www.belvederehouse.ie; daily, Mar–Oct 10am–dusk, Nov–Feb 10.30am–4.30pm; charge) is remarkable for its terraced gardens descending in three stages to the shores of the lake. It has an attractive Georgian and Victorian interior, and the extensive gardens, dotted with large architectural follies.

Mullingar ❿, the chief town of County Westmeath, is said to produce Ireland's finest beef. **Tullynally Castle ⓫** (tel: 044-966 1159; www.tullynallycastle.com; May–Aug Thur–Sun and bank holidays 1–6pm; charge), to the north of Mullingar, is well worth a visit. The massive, grey-stone, turreted house overlooking **Lough Derravaragh** has been the seat of the Pakenham family,

Inland Ireland

Belvedere House Park and Gardens are set by a lake near Mullingar

★ THE IRISH BIG HOUSE

It was not until the 18th century, when the political situation stablised following the Battle of the Boyne in 1690, that Irish landlords commissioned buildings that were both graceful and grand, in keeping with their social status as the owners of many acres of land, and the chief employers of the landless natives. The 'big house' was the name given to the home of the local landlord by the Catholic tenants.

The 18th century, known as the Georgian period because of the successive reigns of four King Georges (1714–1830), was a period of distinctive country-house architecture, usually modelled on classical buildings.

To stabilise rebellious Ireland in the years following the Elizabethan wars, much land was given to Protestant English settlers, to increase the number of citizens who would be loyal to the Crown in times of trouble. This is why 'big houses' were built by Protestant landowners. Catholics were employed as servants and labourers, denied access to higher education at the time and barred from owning more than a modest amount of land.

Foreign architects were sought, as masters of the Palladian style. Italian and French 'stuccadores' vied with each other to produce the most ornate plaster ceilings, as can be seen at Emo Court and Belvedere House. The adjacent farm buildings and stables were cleverly disguised with pediments and other

Emo Court, located near the village of Emo in County Laois, is a large neoclassical mansion

decorations, deemed suitable to a gentleman's residence. The estates were generally self-sufficient, with walled gardens and heated glasshouses, and were supported by huge farms, where 1,600 hectares (4,000 acres) was not unusual.

The trend for spacious farmhouses with generous proportions persisted into the 19th century. But when land reform left the houses with greatly reduced estates, funds for the upkeep of the houses disappeared. While some are still family homes, many are also guesthouses, for example, Ashley Park House in County Tipperary, and the very grand Hilton Park in County Monaghan.

Today it is possible to stay at Hilton Park, situated in Co. Monaghan

Some houses were burnt out during the troubled years of the civil war that followed independence in the early 1920s. But far more houses were lost during the economic stagnation following independence, when owners of uninhabited houses were encouraged to remove the roofs, which led to an exemption from property tax. 'Big houses' held an ambiguous place in the Irish mind and were seldom valued for their beautiful craftsmanship, but were rather seen as unpleasant reminders of the years of British rule, and not part of the national heritage.

Today, while their architectural beauty is once again a matter of national pride, many Irish country houses open to the public emphasise the kitchen quarters and the servants' lifestyle, as is the case at both Strokestown House and Belvedere House. This is because this is where local people's ancestors would have worked; these memories are often kept alive by local historical societies.

The detail of servants' lives is recreated at Strokesdown House

now the earls of Longford, since 1655. The current family includes the children of the late British peer Lord Longford. There is an entertaining upstairs-downstairs guided tour, which includes the Great Hall, the library (one of Ireland's largest private collections, with over 8,000 volumes), the drawing room and the kitchen and laundry, fully equipped as in Victorian times.

The north Midlands

The famine museum at Strokestown Park vividly evokes this terrible disaster in the mid-19th century. Strokestown is only a short detour from the main road between Dublin and Sligo. Cavan and Monaghan, to the north of Dublin, are quiet agricultural backwaters, much beloved of anglers, and increasingly popular with weekenders heading for the area's new luxury hotel spas.

Famine Museum

If you can only visit one stately home in the Midlands, then opt for **Strokestown Park House and Famine Museum ⑫** (tel: 071-963 3013; www.strokestownpark.ie; daily house tours at noon, 2.30pm and 4pm; charge; museum and gardens daily 10.30am–5.30pm; charge). The fine Palladian mansion, at the centre of a large estate, was designed by Sir Richard Cassels in the 1730s, and stayed in the Mahon family until 1979. The kitchen is especially interesting. A gallery runs above it from which the lady of the house could oversee the staff without entering the kitchen itself. Tunnels to hide the movements of tradesmen and servants link the main block of the house to the kitchens and stables. The walled garden has also been restored.

Housed in the stable yard, the **Famine Museum** presents a vivid

A vintage tractor in the walled garden at Strokestown Park House

Fishing in Killykeen Forest Park

County Cavan

Landlocked County Cavan, neighbouring County Fermanagh to the north, emptied by emigration, bridges the two Irelands by providing the source of two great rivers: the **Shannon,** which flows south to the Atlantic, and the **Erne**, which flows north into Fermanagh's lakes. Both rivers are ideal for cruising.

Cavan ⓮ town is the site of a 14th-century Franciscan friary, of which only a belfry tower remains. **Killykeen Forest Park** (tel: 049-433 2541), 8km (5 miles) from Cavan town, covers 240 hectares (600 acres) of mixed woodland, offering a picturesque landscape of lakes, islands and woodland. It is especially popular with anglers and walkers, thanks to its forest walks and trails.

display tracing the history of the family and the estate linking this to the national events in 1845–50 which led to Ireland's Great Famine and the resulting mass emigration or death of more than 2 million people – almost one quarter of the population. It balances the history of the big house with the experiences of the peasants who worked the land. Moving documents record the pleas made to the Mahon family by tenants starving as a result of a devastating potato blight, and the responses they received.

South of Strokestown, **Roscommon ⓭** is a pleasant market town built on a low hill in the midst of rich cattle and sheep country. Roscommon Castle (freely accessible), originally a 13th-century Norman stronghold to the north of the town, is an impressive ruin on a green field site.

County Monaghan

Monaghan is a quiet, trim county of snug farmhouses and tranquil market towns, and lakes and rivers that draw fishermen. Its administrative centre, **Monaghan ⓯**, has a Market House dating from 1792, an imposing 19th-century Gothic Revival cathedral (St Macartan's) and a good **County Museum** (tel: 047-82928; Mon–Fri 11am–5pm, Sat noon–5pm; free) highlighting prehistoric relics and local heritage.

Rossmore Forest Park ⓰, 3km (2 miles) away, has several forest walks, a nature trail, a yew walk and good viewing points. The ruins of the 16th-century **Rossmore Castle** provide a viewing point to the surrounding countryside.

ACCOMMODATION

As much of this region is only an hour's drive from Dublin, it is a favourite weekend break destination, and has a big range of places to stay, from simple B&Bs for anglers to huge glitzy hotels offering luxurious spa breaks, and some lovely period country houses, small and large.

The southwest Midlands

Ashley Park House
Ardcroney, Nenagh
Tel: 067-38223
www.ashleypark.com
A charming family home in prettily decorated lakeside Georgian house, offering woodland walks and a rowing boat on the lake, evening meals and a wine licence. €€

The Maltings
Castle Street, Birr
Tel: 057-912 1345
www.themaltingsbirr.com
Very popular budget accommodation in a converted stone malthouse, with a picturesque riverside setting by Birr Castle. Friendly and welcoming, especially to children. €

Sheraton Athlone Hotel
Gleeson Street, Athlone
Tel: 090-645 1000
www.sheratonathlonehotel.com
Athlone's newest hotel shines high over the town, a 12-storey tower of glass providing spectacular views. An excellent pool and spa facilities, and a contemporary restaurant opening onto a pleasant roof garden. €€€

Wineport Lodge
Glasson, Athlone
Tel: 090-643 9010
www.wineport.ie
Enjoy very comfortable rooms facing the setting sun in a peaceful lakeside setting. Also offers a luxury spa with a range of treatments and cedar hot tub, strikingly designed restaurant, boat jetty and an adjacent golf club. €€€

The southeast Midlands

Eskermore House
Daingean, Tullamore
Tel: 086-824 9574
www.eskermore.com
A sympathetically restored early Georgian farmhouse in the heart of the picturesque Bog of Allen, offering rural peace one hour from Dublin. The proprietor can arrange activity holidays and provide evening meals. €

The north Midlands

Hilton Park
Near Clones, Co. Monaghan
Tel: 047-56007
www.hiltonpark.ie
In the Madden family since Samuel, a friend of Dr Johnson, bought it in 1734. One of the best country houses open to guests: a magnificent place and warm family welcome. €€€

Riverside House
Cootehill, Co. Cavan
Tel: 049-555 2150
www.cootehilltourism.com
Farmhouse B&B (and self-catering option) on a working dairy farm, favoured by anglers and those seeking peace and tranquility. Dinner by arrangement or restaurants in nearby town. €

Slieve Russell Hotel and Country Club
Ballyconnell, Co. Cavan
Tel: 049-952 6444
www.slieverussell.ie
A phenomenon. One of the first of a wave of new hotels, with a luxury interior contrasting with the Disney-like exterior. There is a pool, Jacuzzi and fine food to tempt. €€€

RESTAURANTS

The best selection of restaurants and bar food is to be found in Athlone and at the boating centres around Lough Derg. Many places serve the excellent local beef, but fresh seafood is popular too. The keynote is fresh local produce.

Restaurant price categories

Prices are per person for two courses, not including drinks:

$ = below €20
$$ = €20–28
$$$ = €28–38
$$$$ = over €38

The southwest Midlands

Larkin's Pub
Portroe, Nenagh
Tel: 067-23232
www.larkinspub.com
Thatched country pub on the shores of Lough Derg, with outside tables. Staples such as seafood chowder and Irish stew in the day; more ambitious dishes in the evening. **€–€€**

The Old Fort
Shannonbridge
Tel: 090-967 4973
www.oldfortrestaurant.com
Enjoy the novelty of eating in a restored fort, built in 1819 as a defence against Napoleon. Daytime coffee shop and evening restaurant, in very atmospheric surroundings. **€€**

The Thatch Bar
Crinkle, near Birr
Tel: 057-912 0682
Just a mile south of Birr, this traditional thatched pub has good bar food and a formal restaurant in the evening. Fare includes steaks and lamb, as well as local ostrich. **€€**

Wineport Lodge
Glasson, Athlone
Tel: 090-643 9010
www.wineport.ie

The penthouse at Sheraton Athlone Hotel

Outstanding contemporary dining in a seductive lakeside setting. A magnet for gourmets with seasonal menus for the adventurous eater, such as game, eels and turf-smoked charcuterie. Excellent wine list. **€€€€**

The southeast Midlands

Castle Durrow
Durrow, Co. Laois
Tel: 057-873 6555
www.castledurrow.com
An imposing 18th-century house, now a hotel. There is a spacious bar for informal meals (€) and the dining room at the rear is a romantic spot, with impeccable service. **€€€€**

Morrissey's Pub and Grocery Store
Abbeyleix
Tel: 057-873 1281
This little heritage town's pride is this wood-panelled emporium. One of Ireland's best preserved pubs, dating from 1775, its simple menu includes a slap-up all-day breakfast. **€**

The north Midlands

Andy's Bar and Restaurant
Market Street, Monaghan
Tel: 047-82277
www.andysmonaghan.com
Cheerful family-run pub restaurant that has won many awards over the years. Ingredients are sourced locally, such as the garlic Monaghan mushrooms (the main local crop). **€€**

Macnean House and Bistro
Blacklion, Co. Cavan
Tel: 071-985 3022
www.macneanrestaurant.com
Owner/celebrity chef Neven Maguire offers up a nine-course Prestige Menu. Considered one of the best restaurants in Ireland. **€€€€**

NIGHTLIFE AND ENTERTAINMENT

This is a rural area without much formal entertainment and without a strong musical tradition. The pub is the best bet for hearing about any up-and-coming events.

Pubs

Anchor Inn
Grand Canal, Vicarstown, Co. Laois
Canalside pub with good traditional music sessons every Monday from 10pm, more frequent in summer.

Angler's Rest
Main Street, Ballyconnell, Co. Cavan

Traditional bar, popular with visitors to the area; live music on some evenings.

Dooley's Hotel
Birr
Tel: 057-912 0032
www.doolyshotel.com
Liveliest spot for miles around, with regular weekend discos.

SPORTS AND ACTIVITIES

The big attraction in this area is cruising on the Shannon and on Lough Derg. There is excellent walking and quiet roads for cycling, while the region is an angler's paradise. Watersports on the region's many lakes are popular too.

Angling

The fisheries of the Shannon, Lough Derg and the River Suck are prolific in pike.

Central Fisheries Board
Tel: 01-836 0606
www.cfb.ie
Contact the board for up-to-date information on licences and conservation measures.

Irish Flycraft Tackle Shop
Abbeyleix
Tel: 086-845 1257
www.irishflycraft.com

Laois Angling Centre
Coolrain
Tel: 057-873 5091
www.laoisanglingcentre.ie
Equipment hire and tuition.

Cruising

Cabin cruisers can be hired by the week or for short breaks. Season runs May to September.

Emerald Star
Portumna, Co. Galway

Tel: 071-962 76333
www.emeraldstar.ie

Athlone Cruisers Ltd
Jolly Mariner Marina, Athlone
Tel: 090-647 2892

Silver Line Cruisers
Banagher, Co. Offaly
Tel: 057-915 1112
www.silverlinecruisers.com

Cycling

Hire a bicycle and explore some of the region's cycling and mountain bike routes. The Mullingar Cycle Hub has three loops starting from the town, and there are designated cycle paths in Lough Boora Woodland.

M. Kavanagh (Cycle Hire)
Railway Street, Portlaoise
Tel: 057-862 1357
www.discoverireland.ie/cycling

Walking

The biggest attraction is the Slieve Bloom Way, a 70km (43-mile) route through Laois and Offaly, with panoramic views and largely off-road paths. Also popular is the Grand Canal Way, which goes from Dublin's outskirts across the central plains, via Clonmacnoise's monastic settlement, past sleepy canalside villages for 130km (80 miles) to Shannon Harbour, Co. Offaly; **www.irishtrails.ie.**

Stock up on bait in Carrick on Shannon

Watersports

Lakes and rivers to suit all watersports enthusiasts, from speedboat trips to kayaking.

Bay Sports
Hodson Bay, Athlone
Tel: 090-647 3383
www.baysports.ie
Activity centre with kayaking, rowing, sailing raft buildings and powerboat trips.

Lilliput Adventure Centre
Dysart, Lough Ennell, Mullingar
Tel: 044-922 6789
www.lilliputadventure.com
Canoeing, hill walking and rock climbing for groups or individuals.

TOURS

River and lake cruising is the main form of guided tour in the region. To get a taste of its pleasures, take a 3-hour or 90-minute guided cruise. From Athlone you can opt to go upriver to scenic Lough Ree, or downriver to the monastic site at Clonmacnoise.

The Viking
Athlone
Tel: 090-647 3383
www.vikingtoursireland.ie

Silver Line Cruisers
Banagher, Co. Offaly
Tel: 057-0915 1112
www.silverlinecruisers.com

FESTIVALS AND EVENTS

Lacking the spectacular scenery of coastal Ireland, and the venues of the bigger cities, Inland Ireland has to try harder to attract visitors, leading to some unusual and highly enjoyable festivals.

June
Flatlake Literary & Arts Festival
www.theflatlakefestival.com
Offbeat arts festival at the lovely Hilton Park stately home.

July
Mullingar Agricultural Show
www.mullingarshow.com
A must for lovers of country pursuits.

August
National Stradbally Steam Rally
www.irishsteam.ie
Working demonstrations and carnival atmosphere.

Birr Vintage Week
www.birrvintageweek.com
Vintage cars, fancy dress, arts trails and entertainment.

The northwest

Sligo, Leitrim and Donegal in the northwest of Ireland combine Stone Age burial sites and island-studded lakes with echoes of William Butler Yeats. A rocky coastline with long sandy beaches, Irish-speaking villages, Christian pilgrimages with pagan origins, and the heathery slopes of Glenveagh National Park make this a particularly intriguing region to explore.

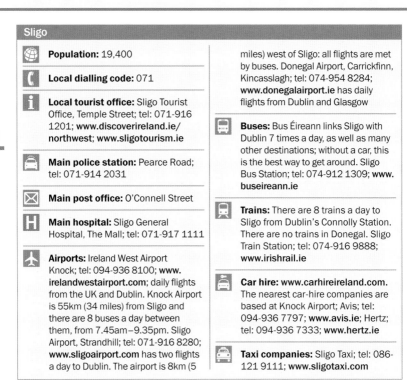

Sligo

Population: 19,400

Local dialling code: 071

Local tourist office: Sligo Tourist Office, Temple Street; tel: 071-916 1201; www.discoverireland.ie/northwest; www.sligotourism.ie

Main police station: Pearce Road; tel: 071-914 2031

Main post office: O'Connell Street

Main hospital: Sligo General Hospital, The Mall; tel: 071-917 1111

Airports: Ireland West Airport Knock; tel: 094-936 8100; www.irelandwestairport.com; daily flights from the UK and Dublin. Knock Airport is 55km (34 miles) from Sligo and there are 8 buses a day between them, from 7.45am–9.35pm. Sligo Airport, Strandhill; tel: 071-916 8280; www.sligoairport.com has two flights a day to Dublin. The airport is 8km (5 miles) west of Sligo: all flights are met by buses. Donegal Airport, Carrickfinn, Kincasslagh; tel: 074-954 8284; www.donegalairport.ie has daily flights from Dublin and Glasgow

Buses: Bus Éireann links Sligo with Dublin 7 times a day, as well as many other destinations; without a car, this is the best way to get around. Sligo Bus Station; tel: 074-912 1309; www.buseireann.ie

Trains: There are 8 trains a day to Sligo from Dublin's Connolly Station. There are no trains in Donegal. Sligo Train Station; tel: 074-916 9888; www.irishrail.ie

Car hire: www.carhireireland.com. The nearest car-hire companies are based at Knock Airport; Avis; tel: 094-936 7797; www.avis.ie; Hertz; tel: 094-936 7333; www.hertz.ie

Taxi companies: Sligo Taxi; tel: 086-121 9111; www.sligotaxi.com

Sligo, a land of bright lakes and dramatically carved valleys left behind when the last Ice Age retreated 10,000 years ago, is rich in archaeology and history. Almost every hilltop has a passage grave, every lake a defensive artificial island, a crannog, every river confluence a castle, a friary, a priory. County Leitrim's quiet, lake-strewn countryside and unspoilt environment are gaining popularity. The most northerly county on the island, Donegal is known for its scenery of mountains, glens, strands and lakes. Apart from the fishing, boating and bird watching, tourists come for hill walking, horse riding, cycling and traditional music.

Sligo

Sligo town, closely associated with the poet, playwright, senator and Abbey Theatre co-founder William Butler Yeats, is the county's tourist magnet. To the west lie miles of open beaches, and to the north mountains rise like jutting tablelands dominating the skyline. The area is well endowed with prehistoric sights. Sligo also has a strong Irish music tradition, dating back over generations.

Surfers' coast

Like bookends, the county begins and ends with seaside resorts. **Enniscrone**

Easky beach is popular with surfers

Meadows in Co. Sligo

on the shores of Killala Bay is at the western end, and at the other is Bundoran, a few miles across the county border in Donegal. From Enniscrone, follow the surfers' coast through **Easky**. Look out for beach establishments offering seaweed baths, a traditional treat in this area.

Carrowmore

At **Carrowmore ❶**, 8km (5 miles) southwest of Sligo town, the 6,000-year-old Bronze Age graves of Ireland's largest megalithic cemetery (Visitor Centre; tel: 071-916 1534; www.heritageireland.ie; May–mid-Oct daily 10am–6pm; charge) are easily approached, scattered across the tussocky fields. Above them, on the western horizon, on top of 328m (1,078ft) **Knocknarea**, is the vast cairn, 70m long by 11m high (200ft by 35ft), consisting of 40,000 boulders. It is named Mebh's (pronounced Maeve's) Cairn, supposedly for the 1st-century AD Mebh of Connaught whose lust for glitz, baubles and fine clothes would put many a modern royal princess in the shade. The best approach is from the south.

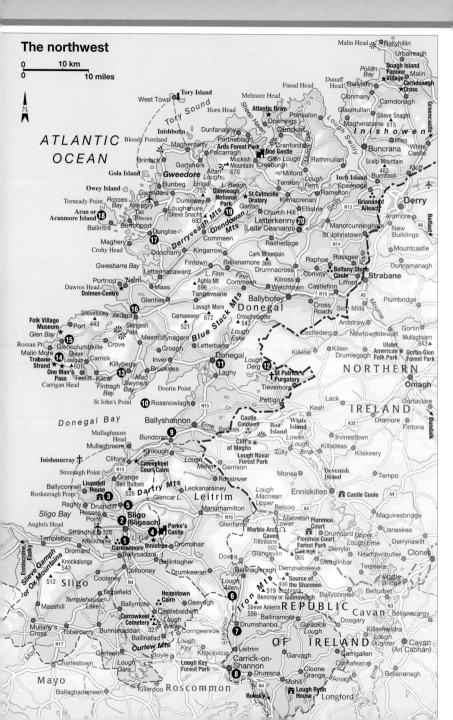

Sligo town is known for its connections with W.B. Yeats

Sligo town

Founded by the Normans in the 13th century, **Sligo ❷**, a sheltered seaport on the fast-flowing Garavogue River, grew into a prosperous town. Today, with its diverting narrow streets and traditional shop fronts, Sligo town is the business hub of the northwest and makes an ideal base for exploring the region. The waterfront has been developed and cafés, bars and restaurants offer alfresco dining, allowing you to watch swans gliding along the Garavogue.

W. B. Yeats (1865–1948) spent his childhood holidays here, and wrote passionately about the place: his legacy is to be found all around. The **Yeats Memorial Building** (Hyde Bridge; tel: 071-914 2693; www.yeats-sligo.com; Mon–Fri 10am–5.30pm; charge) is the venue for the Yeats International Summer School every August. A permanent Yeats photographic exhibition is on display and the River Café offers refreshment. A bronze statue of the poet stands across the bridge. The **Sligo County Museum** (tel: 071-911 1679; Tue–Sat 9.30am–5pm; free) contains Yeats's letters, a complete collection of his poems, photographs of his funeral, and his Nobel Prize citation.

The arts and theatre thrive in Sligo. The **Model Arts and Niland Gallery** (The Mall; tel: 071-914 1405; www.themodel.ie; Tue–Sat 10.30am–5.30pm; free) is an extensively renovated school and one of Ireland's leading cultural spaces, a multidisciplinary arts centre featuring a fascinating collection of Irish art, with works by Jack Yeats and Paul Henry.

Yeats Country Drive

Lissadell House ❸, one of the many places in the area associated with the poet Yeats, is no longer open to the public *(see box, p.206)*. The Yeats Country Drive, a signposted route, begins to the southeast of Sligo town and follows the north side of beautiful **Lough Gill ❹** swinging south into County Leitrim, at the elegant 17th-century lakeside **Parke's Castle** (Fivemile Bourne; tel: 071-916 4149; www.heritageireland.ie; May–Oct daily 10am–6pm; charge) and continues to **Dromahair** and the 15th-century Creevylea Abbey ruins. The final stage of the journey, a visit to Yeats's **Lake Isle of Innisfree**, or a tour of Lough Gill, can be taken with local boat companies. Innisfree is a tiny island, just a mile square, and poor weather can make it difficult to replicate Yeats's vision.

The northwest

Ben Bulben in Mullaghmore

re-interred here in the dour little Protestant Church of Ireland's graveyard.

Northwest Lakelands

Long beloved of anglers, the quiet charms of County Leitrim have now been discovered by other people – a place so watery, with so many rivers and lakes, large and small, as well as the west's heavy rainfall, that it is sometimes referred to as 'Leaky Leitrim.'

Leitrim

North of Mullaghmore, Leitrim dips its toes into 4km (2½ miles) of the Atlantic, before the shoreline reaches the Drowse, one of the best of salmon rivers and the boundary with Donegal. **Lough Allen** ❻ bisects the tiny county of lakes and rushes, meandering rivers, bumpy roads, crumbling farmhouses, drumlins (low rounded hills) and neglected fields. The writer John McGahern (1934–2006) moved to Leitrim in later life, and worked a small farm there. He described its quiet rural charms lovingly in his novels (including *Amongst Women*) and stories. Many other writers, artists and

The Yeats brothers spent their holidays at windswept **Rosses Point**, 6km (4 miles) northwest on the R291. The view across to Knocknarea is inspiring.

North of Sligo, 9km (5½ miles) on the N15, is tiny **Drumcliff** ❺, at the foot of the majestic cliffs of Ben Bulben. Although he died in France, Yeats by his own request was

Lissadell House

The light of evening, Lissadell, / Great windows open to the south, / Two girls in silk kimonos, both / Beautiful, one a gazelle. The girls were poet Eva Gore-Booth and her sister Constance, later Countess Markievicz. Constance, while under a death sentence for her heroic part in the 1916 Easter Rising, was the first woman to be elected to the British House of Commons. She never took the seat, preferring Ireland's equivalent, the Daíl.

Her childhood home, Lissadell House, a large classical building in cut grey limestone on the north shore of Drumcliff Bay, is still standing, and has been fully renovated. Now a private home, it is closed to the public due to a public rights of way dispute, and is unlikely to reopen. However, it can be seen from a distance, and large open-air concerts (inaugurated by Leonard Cohen in 2010) are held there in the summer.

people seeking a slower pace of life (often organic smallholders) have been attracted to the county, in part by its low property prices.

Leitrim has much in its favour. There is a necklace of lakes in the northwest linking the rivers Shannon and Erne via the Ballinamore–Ballyconnell Canal – marketed as the Shannon-Erne Waterway. From spring to winter, the banks of the lakes and rivers are dotted with the big green umbrellas of visiting fishermen. Hired cruisers ply the canal, while amid the watermeadows, bird watchers spy on heron, warblers, corncrakes and cuckoos.

Drumshanbo ❼, at the southern tip of Lough Allen, is the liveliest place in Leitrim, and is a good place to hear Irish music.

Carrick-on-Shannon is an attractive and lively place to visit

Roscommon

The county town, **Carrick-on-Shannon** ❽, is a buzz of activity, much of it centred on the riverside and bustling marina with its opulent cruising boats, quality restaurants and luxury hotels. A walk around town with its attractive shop fronts is rewarding. Carrick boasts some striking architecture including the remarkable Costello Memorial Church, a tiny Catholic chapel on Bridge Street which is the smallest in Ireland. The tourist office (tel: 071-962 0170; www.leitrimtourism.com) is based in the Old Barrel Store, at the Marina.

Donegal

Donegal's long indented coast is pounded by Atlantic storms, while inland it is a sparsely populated county of hard-working small farmers. Its rocky coves, the hilly expanses of Glenveagh National Park and the phenomenally long sandy beaches attract visitors, from mainland Europe and the UK, but also from the neighbouring Northern Ireland, for whom it is an attractively different destination right on the doorstep.

Beaches

County Donegal contains seven Blue Flag beaches recognised for their safety as well as the quality and cleanliness of water and recycling facilities. The beaches start at **Bundoran** ❾, known for its marine wildlife and magnificent **Tullan Strand**. It is a popular centre for surfing. Regular sea angling and sightseeing trips with whale, seal, porpoise and dolphin-watch cruises are available in the summer (*see p.216*).

The northwest

★ FORTIFIED IRELAND

Ireland's successive waves of invaders – Celts, followed by Vikings followed by the Normans and then the English – created a society constantly on the defence, living in fortified homes that began with the crannog, fenced-in lake-islands, and ring forts made of stone or earth. Monasteries built round towers to keep their treasures safe from the Vikings, while the Normans brought a wave of elaborate castle-building and the English introduced fortified homes and walled towns.

Irish homesteads were fortified from the earliest days, due to a constant state of tribal warfare and persistent cattle rustling. People and livestock were locked in overnight in hilltop forts, surrounded by tall ramparts of rock or earth, or on crannogs, lake-islands surrounded by willow fences. There are between 30,000 and 40,000 ring forts around Ireland, dating from the Iron Age to Early Christian times. There is a fine example of the stone-rampart

fort in Donegal, Grianan of Aileach. The Irish for fort is *dún*, reflected in place names containing dún or don.

The reputed wealth of Irish monasteries attracted Viking invaders, so the round tower evolved from a bell tower and vermin-proof storehouse to a place to keep the gold and silver altar vessels safe. The only entrance is high up, and the ladder was taken in after the last person in. Some 70 towers remain, including one at Drumcliff, dating from

The impressive edifice of Donegal Castle

AD574, and an unusual one on Tory Island off Donegal.

The Irish clan chiefs built simple stone castles, usually a square stone tower with narrow windows, built on high ground at a strategic point, close to fresh water, and with panoramic views, enabling the defenders to spot any unusual activity, such as potential invaders, for miles around. After the Norman invasion in the 12th century, castles became more substantial, and more elaborate, with curtain walls, and corner towers enclosing a circular courtyard. Ballymote Castle in Sligo, built by Richard de Burgo, the 'Red Earl' of Ulster, in 1300 was said to be the strongest fortress in Connaught.

Castles were often remodelled, as fashions changed. Parke's Castle on Lough Gill is a fortified home dating from the early 17th century, which was remodelled from a 16th-century tower house, a widespread phenomenon. Tower houses had the disadvantage of dark lower floors, and flights of steep narrow stone steps to access the better-lit rooms above. The stairs were built narrow, so that one man with a sword could repel anyone trying to enter from below.

From the Elizabethan wars right up to the late 17th century, many settlers from England and Scotland lived in fortified walled towns, including Derry, Waterford, Limerick and Athenry, or retreated to them in times of tension between the rebellious 'native Irish' and the settlers, loyal to the English crown.

King John's Castle in Limerick is a classic example of a Norman castle

209

Fortified Ireland

Fortifications such as Easkey Castle provide a backdrop to life in the northwest

Rossnowlagh , Bundoran's smaller quieter cousin round the coast to the north, is also a base for surfers. The extensive Blue Flag beach is very popular with families, and there are lifeguards during the summer months.

Donegal Bay

Donegal ⓫, the lively county town, has a busy market square that is congested with tourist traffic all summer. Donegal Castle (tel: 074-972 2405; Mar–Oct daily 10am–6pm, Nov–Feb Thur–Mon 9.30am–3.30pm; charge) is an impressive 15th-century fortified home, with a castle keep and adjoining Jacobean mansion, built by the O'Donnell clan. It is furnished throughout, and is pleasantly landscaped. Apart from tourism, the weaving and making up of tweeds is the main industry, and Magee's, the town's largest shop, is the industry's principal outlet. Weavers and other craft workers can be seen at work at **Donegal Craft Village** (tel: 074-972 2225; www.donegalcraftvillage.com; Mon–Sat 10am–5pm, Oct–Apr Tue–Sat 10am–5pm), which has a good collection of shops and a tearoom.

Donegal is the nearest town to **Lough Derg** ⓬, with its tiny Station Island, the focal point for a major act of pilgrimage, St Patrick's Purgatory. Supposedly, St Patrick spent 40 days here, praying, fasting and expelling evil spirits. The traditional ritual involves a three-day stay, walking barefoot, while praying, with two meals a day of black tea and dry toast or oatcakes. There is now a 'light' option, consisting of a prayerful day trip. It is a peaceful spot to visit and view from the shore; The island, now covered with buildings, looks from a distance like a Canaletto painting.

The road west of Donegal town runs past Bruckless, where there are

The safe and clean Bundoran beach *(see p.207)* is popular with both families and surfers

Donegal town is a busy tourist hub

oysters and mussels for sale, to Ireland's biggest fishing port, **Killybegs** . The **Maritime & Heritage Centre** (tel: 074-974 1944; www.visitkillybegs.com; Mon–Fri 10am–6pm, July–Aug also Sat–Sun 1–5pm; charge) explains Killybeg's fishing traditions and the tradition of hand-knotting carpets. Donegal carpets, handmade in pure wool, are a luxury product that can be seen in Dublin Castle and the Oval Room in Washington.

Kilcar, on the craggy, beautiful coastline to the west, is a traditional tweed-making centre, now a popular holiday resort with good traditional music. Continue west through **Carrick**, to reach 601m (2,000ft) **Slieve League** ⑭, whose sheer cliffs – among the highest sea cliffs in Europe – plunge a scary 235m (765ft) into the sea. You can drive most of the way to the summit. Walk the final stretch to the railed-in viewing point. The views across Donegal Bay back to the north Mayo coast, and out to the open Atlantic, are, when not shrouded in mists, spectacular – and vertiginous.

The **Slieve League Cultural Centre** (tel: 074-973 9077; www.sliabhleague.com; daily 10.30am–5pm) houses a tea shop with artisan food and home-baking and a craft gallery, as well as archaeological, geological and tourist information.

Glencolumbkille

Glencolumbkille ⑮, at the head of Glen Bay, is enfolded in green hillsides. Over 40 prehistoric dolmens, souterrains and cairns have been catalogued in this area, some 5,000 years old. Four cottages in the **Folk Village Museum** (tel: 074-973 0017; www.glenfolkvillage.com; Easter–Sept Mon–Sat 10am–6pm, Sun noon–6pm; charge) present the very basic traditional living conditions over the centuries.

At **Ardara** ⑯, the Heritage Centre (tel: 074-953 7905; Easter–Sept Mon–Sat 10am–6pm, Sun 2–6pm; charge) has a tourist information point, awash in season with Northern Ireland's holidaymakers buying Guinness, tweeds, Aran sweaters and fishing tackle, while tapping their toes to fiddlers. This area is renowned for traditional music.

The Rosses

Continue north to **Dungloe** ⑰, capital of the Rosses, a raggedly charming peninsula of islands, trout lakes and inlets. From **Burtonport**, a 25-minute ferry service (tel: 074-952 0532; www.arranmoreferry.com) runs to **Aranmore Island** ⑱, with its 900 souls, dry-stone walls, holiday cottages and an abundance of wildlife.

The northwest

Glenveagh National Park

Glenveagh National Park ⓳ (tel: 074-913 7090; www.glenveaghnationalpark.ie; daily 10am–6.30pm) forms 400 hectares (10,000 acres) of the most beautiful part of County Donegal. With its castle (guided tour only; hours as above; charge) and its formal French and Italian gardens against a backdrop of wild mountains, the park has a further surprise in the Regency-style **Glebe House Gallery** (tel: 074-913 7071; Easter and June–Sept Sat–Thur 11am–6.30pm; charge), which displays the late artist Derek Hill's collection: small paintings by Degas, Renoir, Picasso and the primitive painters of Tory Island. Don't miss picturesque **Gartan Lough**, 5km (3 miles) south via a narrow bog road. **Colmcille Heritage Centre**, Churchill, (tel: 074-913 7306; Easter–Sept Mon–Sat 10.30am–6.30pm, Sun 2–6pm; free) tells the story of the saint through an audiovisual display.

Tory Island

Tory Island, 14km (9 miles) off the coast, appeals to bird watchers (corncrakes, nesting seabirds), walkers and lovers of unusual, remote places. The 140 resident islanders are Irish-speakers, a courtly, hospitable bunch, who ensure that overnight visitors are entertained with music, dance and stories. The islanders were encourage to paint by Derek Hill and usually have paintings to sell. The treeless landscape has a lighthouse at its flat end, and steep cliffs at the other. Antiquities include a round tower and a tau cross.

Ferries leave from Bunbeg (1 hour 45 mins) year-round, and Magheroarty (40 mins) Apr–Oct (tel: 074-953 1340; www.toryislandferry.com).

Letterkenny ⓴, the prosperous county town on the River Swilly 16km (10 miles) to the southwest, is useful as a touring base.

Glenveagh Castle is a 19th-century castellated mansion

ACCOMMODATION

Donegal has a great choice of places to stay, nearly all set amid great scenery. Choose between a classic beachside hotel, a quiet rural B&B, or lively traditional hotel in the town centre. In Sligo, there's an affordable castle on offer, while the lakelands offer a choice of rural retreats.

Sligo

Markree Castle
Coolooney
Tel: 071-916 7800
www.markreecastle.ie
Massive castellated mansion on a 400-hectare (1,000-acre) estate of gardens and parkland that has been in the Cooper family for 350 years. One of the more affordable castle hotels, with enormous bedrooms, 11km (7 miles) south of town. €€€

Riverside Suites Hotel
Millbrook, Sligo Town
Tel: 071-914 8080
www.riversidesuiteshotelsligo.com
This recent addition to Sligo town offers a choice of one- or two-bedroom suites with a riverside setting and use of the local fitness suite. Book online for large discounts. €€

Sligo Southern Hotel
Strandhill Road
Tel: 071-916 2101
www.sligosouthernhotel.com
A 'superior' 3-star hotel, next to the railway station, with its own leisure centre. Although the interior is a little faded, the hotel is excellent value; upgrade to a superior room for great views and a private Jacuzzi bath. €–€€

Northwest Lakelands

Bush Hotel
Carrick-on-Shannon, Co. Leitrim
Tel: 071-967 1000
www.bushhotel.com
This historic coaching inn in the centre of this bustling riverside town has been given a major makeover, and is now a 'boutique'

hotel. While the bars and lounges retain a traditional demeanour, bedrooms have contemporary decor. €€

Glebe House
Ballinamore Road, Mohill, Co. Leitrim
Tel: 071-963 1086
www.glebehouse.com
In 20 hectares (50 acres) of farmland and mature trees, this beautifully restored former Georgian rectory is a perfect rural retreat, with a warm family welcome. Breakfast is served until noon. Self-catering houses available. €

Temple House
Ballymote, Co. Sligo
Tel: 071-918 3329
www.templehouse.ie
Real old-world atmosphere and luxury accommodation at this imposing lakeside Georgian mansion overlooking a 13th-century Templar castle. Boating and woodland walks on-site. An excellent touring base. €€€

Donegal

Ard na Breatha Guesthouse
Drumrooske Middle, Donegal Town
Tel: 074-972 2288
www.ardnabreatha.com
An award-winning restaurant and guesthouse, 2km (1¼ miles) outside Donegal town. The bedrooms are light, bright and spacious, and there is a lounge with a small 'honesty bar'. Breakfast choices include the 'full Irish', smoked salmon and pancakes. €

Harvey's Point Country Hotel
Lough Eske
Tel: 074-972 2208

Listings

www.harveyspoint.com

A modern luxurious lakeside complex with sports facilities, 6km (4 miles) from town on the shores of Lough Eske, beneath the Blue Stack Mountains. The restaurant is seriously good, offering French cuisine. €€€

Ionad Siúl Walking Lodge
Glencolumbille
Tel: 074-973 0302
www.ionadsuil.ie

Aimed firmly at walkers, this 11-room guest-house offers bed without breakfast – you make your own in the well-equipped kitchen. All rooms are en suite, clean and spacious, and it is set in the spectacular and remote countryside of Glencolumbcille. €

Malin Hotel
Malin, Inishowen
Tel: 074-937 0606
www.malinhotel.ie

Situated at the tip of the Inishowen Peninsula, this is a comfortable hotel that is also the hub of the small town, with a good restaurant and lively bar. A great base for walking; they also organise equestrian breaks. €€

Rathmullan House
Lough Swilly, Letterkenny
Tel: 074-915 8188
www.rathmullanhouse.com

A large, luxurious country-house hotel with grounds leading to a mile-long sandy beach. Beautiful gardens, period-style rooms, indoor pool, all-weather tennis courts, spa treatments and excellent restaurant. €€€€

Sand House Hotel
Rossnowlagh
Tel: 071-985 1777
www.sandhouse-hotel.ie

Midway between Bundoran and Donegal town, this large, well-run hotel is right on the beach and will please all the family. Within easy reach of three top golf courses. €€€

RESTAURANTS

The northwest has excellent locally reared beef, lamb and poultry, and a peerless supply of fresh seafood. The pub grub is generally good, especially by the sea, but many of the best restaurants are in country hotels.

Restaurant price categories

Prices are per person for two courses, not including drinks:

$ = below €20
$$ = €20–28
$$$ = €28–38
$$$$ = over €38

Sligo
Hargadon's Bar
4–5 O'Connell Street
Tel: 071-915 3709
www.hargadons.com

One of Ireland's great traditional pubs, the interior of Hargadon's is little changed since it opened over 150 years ago. But it has added a restaurant, serving hearty fare at lunch and dinner – from oysters with chorizo to bangers and mash or fish paella – at great prices. €

Montmartre
1 Market Yard, Sligo
Tel: 071-916 9901
www.montmatrerestaurant.ie

Small, chic restaurant near the Tourist Office, with a French owner and staff, this is Sligo's leading fine-dining destination (dinner only). The classic menu is well judged – baked hake with beurre blanc, lamb rump with herb crust. Children welcome. €€€

Nimmo's Bar
Pier Head Hotel, Mullaghmore
Tel: 071-916 6171
www.pierheadhotel.ie

Seafood is the star here, as you would expect from a bar (with outside tables) over-looking the pier. Their pan-fried crab claws

Fresh crab on the menu

are famous, or try the Lissadell mussels. Non-seafood options include golden-fried brie, and fillet steak. **€–€€**

Source
1-2 John Street;
tel: 071-914 7605
www.sourcesligo.ie
A magnet for serious foodies, Source showcases local artisan produce in its bustling central premises, including an all-day café-restaurant and a wine bar (from 3pm) which serves farmhouse cheese platters and Irish stew in addition to Spanish tapas. **€–€€**

Northwest Lakelands
Oarsman Bar
Bridge Street, Carrick-on-Shannon, Co. Leitrim
Tel: 071-962 1733
www.theoarsman.com
Family-run gastro-pub with a warm, friendly atmosphere. Light snacks are served in the bar, and the first-floor restaurant is the busiest in this riverside boating town, using locally sourced ingredients, organic where possible. Great desserts. **€–€€**

Victoria Hall
Quay Road, Carrick-on-Shannon, Co. Leitrim
Tel: 071-962 0320
www.victoriahall.ie
Victorian parochial hall near the waterfront, nicely converted to a spacious bistro, with white walls and pale wood. Serves Thai and Irish dishes, including a bento box containing both starters and mains. **€–€€**

Donegal
The Beach House Bar & Restaurant
Swilly Road, Buncrana
Tel: 074-936 1050
www.thebeachhouse.ie
In a gorgeous spot right on the pier with great views across Lough Swilly, head chef Niall Gorham cooks exciting dishes and sources as much local and organic produce as possible; the fish is as fresh as it comes. **€€**

Danny Minnie's Restaurant
Annagry, The Rosses
Tel: 074-954 8201
www.dannyminnies.com
Well-established family-run restaurant, not far from the airport, offering classic cooking in a romantic candlelit atmosphere with antiques and fresh flowers. Offers a set dinner and a wide-ranging à la carte menu. Also has accommodation. **€€€**

Herons Cove
Rossnowlagh Road, Ballyshannon
Tel: 071-982 2070
www.heronscove.ie
Close to the beach and the picturesque harbour at Creevy Pier, this family-run restaurant offers the best of Irish cuisine and hospitality. The tastefully designed dining room serves excellent steaks and fresh seafood. **€€**

The Mill Restaurant
Figart, Dunfanaghy, Co. Donegal
Tel: 074-913 6985
www.themillrestaurant.com
Exceptional restaurant and guesthouse in a converted flax mill beside a lake. Owner-chef Derek Alcron is renowned for accomplished creative cooking. Study his amazing menu with an aperitif beside the open fire. **€€€€**

Weeping Elm Restaurant
Rathmullan House, Co. Donegal
Tel: 074-915 8188
This restaurant is in an outstanding country-house hotel, a large 19th-century house on the shores of Lough Swilly. Chef Ian Orr supports the 'slow food' movement, and uses produce from the walled garden. **€€**

Listings

NIGHTLIFE AND ENTERTAINMENT

Once north of Sligo, you make your own nightlife and entertainment. There are some good traditional music pubs: ask locally about ceilidhs, set dancing and other events.

Pubs

Anderson's Thatched Pub
Elphin Road, Carrick-on-Shannon
Tel: 087-228 3288
5km (3 miles) south of town; nightly sessions in summer.

An Poitín Still
Main Street, Carrick-on-Shannon
Traditional music on Friday.

The Corner Bar
Main Street, Ardara,
Co. Donegal
Tel: 074-954 1736
One of several pubs in the village with music most nights.

O'Donnell's Bar
The Diamond, Donegal Town
Tel: 074-972 1049
Traditional music most nights.

Ostán Loch Altan
Gortahork, Co. Donegal
Tel: 074-913 5267
Good spot for set dancing.

Theatre
Blue Raincoat Theatre Company
The Factory, Sligo
www.blueraincoat.com
Adventurous professional company.

Hawkswell Theatre
Temple Street, Sligo
Tel: 071-916 1518
www.hawkswell.com
Hosts a diverse programme of entertainment.

The Model
The Mall, Sligo
Tel: 071-914 405
www.themodel.ie
Small performance space and cinema.

SPORTS, ACTIVITIES AND TOURS

Angling, golf and hiking, the traditional outdoor pursuits in the area, have now been joined by watersports, especially surfing. The long sandy beaches, where you can often walk for miles without seeing other people, are a major attraction.

Angling
The Northwest has some major salmon and sea-trout fisheries, and offers a wealth of opportunities for coarse angling. Fisheries Ireland has details: www.fisheriesireland.ie.

Cycling
Bike Shop
Donegal Town
Tel: 074-972 2515

Cranks Bicycle Hire
Sligo Town
Tel: 087-956 4086

Kingfisher Cycling Trail
Tel: 071-985 6898
www.cycletoursireland.com
A mapped and signposted cycle route through various counties.

Golf
There are magnificent links courses along the Atlantic seaboard, and well-established parkland courses elsewhere.

Donegal Golf Club
www.donegalgolfclub
One of the most highly rated.

Surf beach, Strandhill

Walking

Mount Errigal is a fairly easy ascent from the car park at Dunlwey on the R521. The Bloody Foreland coastal walk is best done at sunset, to understand how it got its name. Glenveagh National Park provides fine walking in the Derryeagh Mountains; Slieve League near Carrick in Donegal and the Blue Stack Mountains are also popular; **www.irishtrails.ie.**

Walking and Talking in Donegal
www.walktalkdonegal.com
Sean Mullan leads walking weekends for in the Rathmullan area. The price (about

€200) includes food, accommodation and guided hikes.

Walking Ireland
www.walkingireland.ie
Walking weekends in Donegal; local guides.

Watersports and surfing

Easkey, Enniscrone, Strandhill and Budoran are the surfing hotspots.

Donegal Adventure Centre
Bundoran
Tel: 071-984 2418
www.doneraladventurecentre.net
Surfing, kayaking, body boarding.

National Watersport Centre
Ballyshannon
Tel: 071-982 2922
www.discoverireland.ie/northwest
Surfing, sailing, windsurfing and canoeing.

West Coast Surf School
Strandhill
Tel: 086-306 7053
www.westcoastsurfschool.com

FESTIVALS AND EVENTS

Festivals in the area tend to be low-key events, often involving traditional music, walking or fishing in addition to the arts.

June
An Tóstal
www.antostalfestival.ie
Family-oriented music festival in Drumshanbo on the June bank holiday weekend.

July
Earagail Arts Festival
www.eaf.ie
Bilingual two-week-long arts festival across north Donegal.

August
Ballyshannon Folk Music Festival
www.ballyshannonfolkfestival.ie
Early August weekend of Irish folk music.

Yeats Summer School
www.yeats-sligo.com
Sligo's annual two-week celebration of the poet late July to August.

September
Hills of Donegal Celtic Festival
www.discoverbundoran.com
Celebrating links between Scotland, the north of England and Donegal with music, dance and history.

October
Sligo Festival of Baroque Music
www.modelart.ie
Excellent festival of Baroque music.

Belfast

Belfast has successfully reinvented itself as a short-break destination. Visitors love its imposing Victorian buildings, its booming retail centre and its fascinating industrial past, which is fast becoming its greatest tourist asset. Bars and restaurants are thriving, partly due to the warmth of the people, while the up-and-coming Cathedral quarter showcases all that is best in the arts.

Population: Belfast: 500,000

Local dialling code: 028

Local tourist office: Belfast Welcome Centre, 47 Donegall Place; tel: 028-9024 6609; www.gotobelfast.com

Main police station: Police Service of Northern Ireland Headquarters, Brooklyn House, 65 Knock Road, Belfast; tel: 028-906 5000

Main post office: Central Post Office Headquarters, Castle Place, Belfast; tel: 0845-722 3344

Main hospital: Royal Victoria Hospital, 274 Grosvenor Road, Belfast; tel: 028-9024 0503

Media: *Belfast Telegraph*, *Belfast News Letter*; free from tourist offices: *What About*, *Belfast in Your Pocket*

The Victorian and Edwardian architecture of Belfast ❶ resembles Leeds or Liverpool in England, rather than the Georgian elegance of Dublin, just 160km (100 miles) south. But Northern Ireland's capital has other strengths. A low-rise, open city, framed between lofty green Cave Hill and the great blue bowl of Belfast Lough, it is dotted with lovely parks and open spaces and is surprisingly easy to get around.

Above all, it's the people of Belfast who remain its great attraction. Belfast people are among the friendliest you will meet, with an easy and down-to-earth sense of humour. And, ironically, it is precisely that synthesis of Ulster Scots and native Irish, so long a source

of division, that gives the people of Belfast their distinct personality.

Belfast is the home town of the legendary *Titanic*, whose luxurious embellishment symbolised the apex of Belfast's Edwardian heyday as one of the world's greatest ports, and whose watery fate pre-dated Belfast's own long industrial and manufacturing decline. Now the city, rejuvenated with the help of huge investment from the UK government, has been enjoying new popularity as a short-break destination.

The city centre

The city radiates out from City Hall and the magnificent Victorian streetscape of Donegall Square. North of the square is a largely pedestrianised shopping area, leading to the Cathedral Quarter, where a major new arts centre will cement its reputation as Belfast's new cultural district. The waterfront to the east is being developed on both banks, the new visitor centre, Titanic Belfast, and the Odyssey enhancing the city's attractions. To the south, Great Victoria Street has several notable buildings, before reaching Shaftesbury Square, gateway to the University district.

Donegall Square area

Dominating the city centre in Donegall Square is the 1906 **City Hall**  (tel: 028-9027 0456; www.belfastcity. gov.uk/cityhall; tours Mon–Fri 11am, 2pm, 3pm, Sat 2pm, 3pm; free).

The grand interior of City Hall

The city's historic trade is commemorated in the street names

Dubbed a 'Wrenaissance' building due to its shameless borrowing from St Paul's Cathedral in London, it is at the heart of Belfast. Famed for its marbled halls, its plush Council Chamber has resounded to some of the liveliest debate in the history of public affairs. The portraits of the lord mayors in the corridors reflect Belfast's divided history, a long line of formally dressed unionists eventually reaching the first Catholic (SDLP) lord mayor in 1997. Not until 2002, with Sinn Féin's informally attired Alex Maskey, do you find a Republican. The surrounding gardens are a favourite summer lunchtime spot.

Linen Hall Library (tel: 028-9032 1707; www.linenhall. com; Mon–Fri 9.30am–5.30pm, Sat 9.30am–4pm) on Donegall Square North is a revered public-subscription library, founded in 1788 as the Belfast Reading Society and later renamed to reflect the city's linen-producing heritage. Now it has an intriguing collection of books, comfortable armchairs and a pleasant café. Take a literary waking tour to find out more (*see p.233*). The **Belfast Welcome**

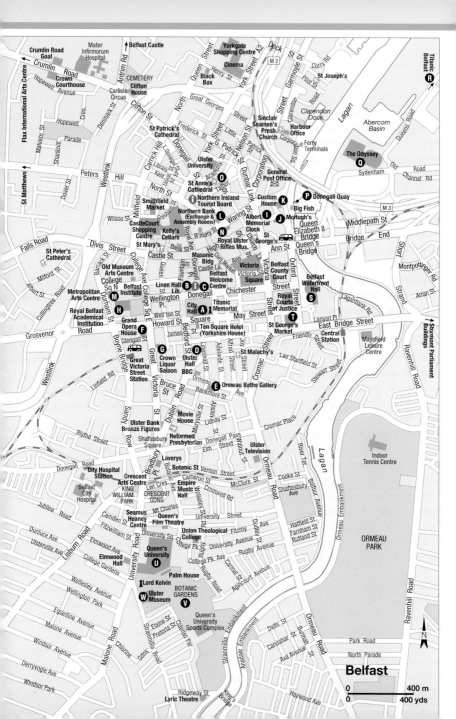

Belfast transport

Airports: Belfast International Airport (30km/19 miles north of city); tel: 028-9448 4848; **www.belfastairport.com**; Ulsterbus – a branch of Translink – operates an Airbus service every 15 minutes into the city centre from 6.50am to 6.15pm. The service is less frequent in the evenings. The one-way fare is £7 and round-trip £10. A single taxi fare from the International Airport into the city centre is £25 and journey time is 30 minutes. **George Best Belfast City Airport** (6km/4 miles east of city); tel: 028-9093 9093; **www.belfastcityairport.com**; bus services run to the city centre every 20 minutes from 6am to 10pm. The round-trip costs £3. Taxi fares are £10 from the City Airport into the city centre and journey time is 15 minutes. **City of Derry Airport** (8km/5 miles east of city); tel: 028-7181 0784; **www.cityofderryairport.com**; a direct bus service, the Airporter, links both Derry and the Belfast International and City airports. The journey costs £17.50 one-way, round-trip £27.50

 Train station: Central Train Station, East Bridge Street, Belfast; tel: 028-9066 6630; www.translink.co.uk

 Bus station: Europa Buscentre, main bus depot, Great Victoria Street, Belfast; tel: 028-9066 6630

 Port: Port of Belfast, Corporation Square, Belfast; tel: 028-9055 4422; **www.belfast-harbour.co.uk**

 Car hire: Avis, tel: 0844-544 6036; **www.avis.co.uk**; Hertz, tel: 028-9073 2451; **www.hertz.co.uk**; Budget, tel: 028-9023 0700; **www.budgetbelfast.co.uk**

 Taxis: Fonacab, tel: 028-9033 3333; **www.fonacab.com**; Value Cabs, tel: 028-9080 9080; **www.valuecabs.co.uk**

Centre **C** (47 Donegall Place; tel: 028-9024 6609) is the place to pick up maps and brochures.

On the south side of City Hall several buildings from Belfast's linen-producing era remain, including an old warehouse, now a chic hotel, **Ten Square** (10 Donegall Square South; tel: 028-9024 1001), whose Linenhall Street facade has some interesting carvings, typical of the work of the celebrated architect Charles Lanyon (1813–89) *(see box, p.222)*. On the west side is Bedford Street, home to the distinguished **Ulster Hall D** (No. 30; tel: 028-9033 4400; www.belfastcity.gov.uk/ulsterhall). Built in 1862 as a music hall, it now hosts rock and classical concerts, and cultural events, and is home to the Ulster Orchestra.

Around the corner at 18a Ormeau Avenue, one of Belfast's leading art galleries has been established at a beautifully converted Victorian bathhouse. The **Ormeau Baths Gallery E** (tel: 028-9032 1402; www.ormeaubaths.co.uk; Tue–Sat 10am–5.30pm) has regular exhibitions of leading contemporary Irish and international artists.

Great Victoria Street area
Despite damage from bombs and planners, **Great Victoria Street**, which runs down to Shaftesbury Square, has several of Belfast's

A visit to the Crown Liquor Saloon is a must when in Belfast

architectural jewels. It is also the location of the much-bombed four-star Hastings **Europa**, a base for hundreds of journalists during the Troubles and a tourist attraction in itself. The twin-domed **Grand Opera House** 🄵 (tel: 028-9024 1919; www.goh.co.uk) has a plush brass and velvet interior, gilded elephant heads supporting the boxes, and excellent acoustics. Thanks to its now extended wing space, the venue, where Sarah Bernhardt, Orson Welles and Laurel and Hardy all appeared, can now house the grandest West End productions.

Walk to the south and take time to enjoy Guinness and oysters at one of the world's most beautiful Victorian pubs, the **Crown Liquor Saloon** 🄶, (tel: 028-9024 3187; www.crownbar.com). Its tiling and stained-glass windows were the work of some of Italy's finest craftsmen, in Belfast to work on Catholic churches and the White Star liners, in the 1880s.

Lanyon's legacy

Charles Lanyon (1813–89), an English architect, carpet-bagger and engineer, is the man responsible for the exotic look of many Belfast buildings. He conferred on the city's new bank buildings the majestic solidity of the palazzi of northern Italian merchant princes. Meanwhile, Queen's University's spoof Elizabethan quad unashamedly borrows from Oxford's Magdalen. His Doric facade of the Union Theological College promises dour Presbyterianism, while his Palladian Custom House intimidates. Lanyon was also responsible for 14 churches. Although a philanderer who openly bought election votes, Lanyon ended up knighted, becoming the city's mayor and a Conservative MP.

College Square East reveals one of the city's finest buildings, Sir John Soane's dignified redbrick **Royal Belfast Academical Institution** , a renowned boys' grammar school dating from 1814 with over 1,000 pupils; it is familiarly known as 'Inst.'

Central district

The area north of Donegall Square to St Anne's Cathedral is largely pedestrianised. In Queen's Square the **Albert Memorial Clock** was, until its recent restoration, threatening to rival the Leaning Tower of Pisa, while the renovated **McHugh's Bar** claims to be housed in Belfast's oldest building. Lanyon's glorious **Custom House**, where Anthony Trollope once worked, looks over Custom House Square, Belfast's premier

Look closely at the Big Fish sculpture to see the history of the city

outdoor venue, used for all kinds of events, from carnivals to live concerts.

The historic 1769 Exchange and Assembly Rooms were converted to the **Northern Bank** by Sir Charles Lanyon. With the completion of Belfast's brand new flagship home for the arts, the **Metropolitan Arts Centre** (St Anne's Square; tel: 028-9023 5053), six storeys tall, with two theatres, three art galleries and dance studios and a price tag of £13m (due to open in early 2012) the development of the Cathedral quarter into a cultural district to rival Dublin's Temple Bar is gaining credibility.

Worth visiting on Waring Street is the **Royal Ulster Rifles Museum** (tel: 028-9023 2086; www.army museums.org.uk; Mon–Fri 10am–12.30pm, 2–4pm, Fri until 2.30pm; charge). Further along the neo-Romanesque **St Anne's (Belfast) Cathedral** (tel: 028-9032 8332; www.belfastcathedral.org) dates from the beginning of the 19th century. Its striking stainless-steel 'Spire of Hope' was added in 2007. Check out the mosaic roof over the baptistery, composed of 150,000 pieces of glass. On the cathedral's east side in Talbot Street is the **Home Front Exhibition**, which gives an in-depth account of wartime Northern Ireland.

Waterfront area

Donegall Quay is the place to catch the Lagan Boat Company's fine tours *(see p.233)* and see local sculptor John Kindness's now famous **Big Fish**, a 10m (32ft) salmon whose ceramic 'skin' tells the history of Belfast.

QUEEN'S QUARTER WALK

Based around the distinguished Queen's University, this walk explores the university district, an eclectic mix of elegant wine bars, scruffy student cafés, excellent bookshops and impressive architecture.

Begin the walk at the tranquil **Botanic Gardens**, an oasis of greenery within the city, laid out in the mid-19th century on land that slopes down to the River Lagan. Make sure to visit the architect Sir Charles Lanyon's restored curvilinear **Palm House**, with its exotic flora, and the **Tropical Ravine**, a miniature sunken rainforest. Also within the garden, at the southwest corner, is the **Ulster Museum**, which explores the geological, biological, sociological and industrial history of Northern Ireland.

Sir Charles Lanyon's graciously designed Queen's University

It has recently emerged from a £27 million renovation project, which has added a spacious atrium, and brought it into the 21st century. Its natural science areas are highly recommended, as is its photographic archive of the Troubles. Children will enjoy Peter the Polar Bear, and the Egyptian mummy, Takabuti.

Leave the gardens by the Stranmillis Road exit. A short excursion to the south brings you to the pleasant village atmosphere of **Stranmillis** and a line of shops and cafés, including a wide range of ethnic eateries, stretching down to the riverside towpath along the Lagan. One of the pleasures of the university area is the many well-kept Victorian redbrick houses in tree-lined streets off the main through-roads.

Returning north along University Road the imposing courtyard and redbrick facade of **Queen's University** are on the right. Lanyon based the quadrangle on the Tudor-style quad of Magdalen College, Oxford. There are over 100 listed buildings around the campus and surrounding area; to learn more you can visit the **Welcome**

Tips

- Distance: 1.6km (1 mile)
- Time: A half-day
- Start: Botanic Gardens
- End: Crescent Arts Centre
- Several buses run south from Donegall Square to the Botanic Gardens, the starting point of the walk. To walk takes about 15 minutes.

Bookfinders Café is a delightful place where you can peruse the shelves, glass in hand

Centre in the main quad building, which has information and maps; it also organises guided tours. One of the highlights is the new library at Queen's in **College Park**, a £50 million building that opened in 2009, and contains over 1.5 million books.

North of Queen's is the atmospheric **Bookfinders Café**, which features a fine selection of second-hand tomes that you can enjoy with a bowl of soup, a cup of coffee or a nice glass of wine. Appropriately, it is across the road from the **Seamus Heaney Centre**, named for the Ulster-born 1997 Nobel laureate, one of many distinguished alumni. It is a centre of literary research and creative writing, fostering the next generation of poets and novelists. It often hosts readings by local and visiting writers.

Leave University Road by **University Square**, lined with Victorian terraces, to arrive at **College Park**, which leads to student-filled Botanic Avenue. Look out for shabby-chic **Café Renoir** (at No. 95), a great stop for morning coffee, as well as the excellent crime bookshop **No Alibis** (at No. 83).

Shaftesbury Square, at the top of Botanic Avenue, was once an integral part of Belfast's 'Golden Mile', established during the Troubles to boost the city's tourism. Celebrity chef Paul Rankin's acclaimed restaurant **Cayenne** can be found here (see p.230). To the south of Shaftesbury Square is a fine Victorian building dating from 1873, which now houses the **Crescent Arts Centre**, a lively arts and community centre with an auditorium, gallery and café.

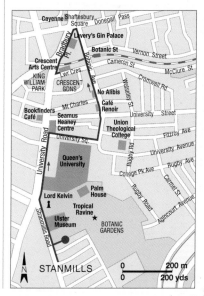

Across the River Lagan, in the newly named Titanic Quarter, **The Odyssey**  (Queen's Quay; tel: 028-9045 1055; www.odysseyarena.com) is a venue for sporting events and pop concerts, and hosts the interactive discovery centre **W5** (tel: 028-9046 7700; www.w5online.co.uk; Mon–Thur 10am–5pm, Fri–Sat 10am–6pm, Sun noon–6pm; charge), with nearly 200 interactive exhibits, a tenpin bowling alley and cinema. The city's newest and most talked-about attraction, the **Titanic Belfast**  visitor centre opens in early 2012 and tells the liner's story as well as the wider theme of industrial heritage. Clad in diamond glazing, the bow-shaped facade of the six-storey building reflects the lines of the ship. Its shard-like appearance is created from 3,000 different-shaped panels, each folded from silver anodised aluminium sheets into asymmetrical geometries which catch the light like a cut diamond. For opening hours visit www.gotobelfast.com.

South along the Lagan is the copper-domed **Belfast Waterfront Hall**  (2 Lanyon Place; tel: 028-9033 4455; www.waterfront.co.uk), a forerunner of Belfast's renaissance when built in 1997 and a venue for top international performers.

At the corner of Oxford Street and May Street, **St George's Market** , Ireland's oldest covered market, has been elegantly refurbished and now has many stalls selling superb locally produced food, including cheeses, organic meats, fish and seafood, and plants. The Friday **Variety Market** (6am–2pm) has many of those food stalls plus books, antiques and more.

University area

Based around Sir Charles Lanyon's distinguished Queen's University,

Live entertainment at St George's Market

Enjoying the sun in the Botanic Gardens

Queen's University

Queen's University , its blue-tinged red brick at its best near dusk, is one of Lanyon's delights, designed in the Tudor style of Oxford's Magdalen College. There are over 100 listed buildings around the campus. The 'Walkabout Queen's' leaflet from the **Queen's Welcome Centre** (tel: 028-9097 5252; www.qub.ac.uk/centre; Mon–Fri 9.30am–4.30pm, Sat–Sun 10am–1pm) provides a signposted tour. Don't miss the Great Hall, which Lanyon based on the medieval great halls of the Oxbridge universities *(see box, p.222)*. The **Naughton Gallery** (tel: 028-9097 3580; www.naughtongallery.org) in the Lanyon Building houses the university's art collection and often hosts interesting touring exhibitions.

Belfast Botanic Gardens

South of the University, the **Belfast Botanic Gardens** (tel: 028-9031 4762; www.discovernorthernireland.

Queen's quarter is a curious mixture of student haunts, elegant academia and Belfast's designer-label heartland, the Lisburn Road. This long tree-lined avenue is studded with fine restaurants, chic bars, delis and boutiques. It's also home to many of Belfast's finest private art galleries.

Cafés of Belfast

In recent years café culture has been part of the transformation of Belfast. Here are the top five to seek out:

- **Black Box Café** (18–22 Hill Street; tel: 028-9024 4400) offers comfy sofas, delicious scones, cookies and cakes, and free newspapers.
- **Made in Belfast** (Wellington Street; tel: 028-9024 6712) serves snacks and informal lunches with warming soups and goat's cheese.
- **Avoca Café** (Arthur Street; tel: 028-9027 9950) specialises in oversized scones topped with jam and clotted cream.
- **Harlem Café** (Bedford Street; tel: 028-9024 4860) is where lattes and laptops combine; it is a focal point for the media and PR crowd.
- **Caffé Avanzo** (College Street; tel: 078-7034 7316) is best when you take a seat outside, weather permitting, and enjoy the chimes of the Millennium Clock at the Fountain Shopping Centre opposite.

Stormont

Belfast's most iconic edifice is the grand **Parliament Buildings**, known as Stormont for its location in East Belfast (off the Upper Newtownards Road, about 5km/3 miles from the city centre; tel: 028-9076 0556). The plain classical facade has a central portico and dates from 1928–32. It was built because the 1920 Government of Ireland Act created the need for a separate parliament in Belfast. In 1972 it ceased to function as a parliament house and the British government transferred its functions to Westminster. Since the Belfast Agreement of 1998 (also known as the Good Friday Agreement) it is once again the home of the government of Northern Ireland, known as the Northern Ireland Assembly. Visitors don't have access to the building but can walk the 120 hectares (300 acres) of grounds (daily 7.30am–dusk), including the impressive mile-long driveway.

com; 7.30am–dusk; free) contain another Lanyon gem, his curvilinear **Palm House** (Apr–Sept Mon–Fri 10am–noon, 1–5pm, Sat–Sun 1–5pm, Oct–Mar until 3.45pm; free), recently restored. In the **Tropical Ravine**, water drips from banana leaves into a miniature sunken rainforest.

On the park's Stranmillis Road boundary, the **Ulster Museum** Ⓦ (Botanic Gardens; tel: 028-9044 0000; www.nmni.com; Tue–Sun 10am–5pm; free), which reopened in 2009 following remodelling, has a 23m (75ft) high atrium that leads into fascinating history, art and science galleries. The museum also has a new enclosed rooftop gallery to house its glass, jewellery and Belleek collections.

A display at Ulster Museum

ACCOMMODATION

There is plenty of choice in Belfast, whether you opt for a contemporary hotel in the city centre, a historic warehouse conversion or traditional guesthouse accommodation in the leafy University district.

Accommodation price categories

Prices are for one night's accommodation in a standard double room (unless otherwise specified):

£ = below £80
££ = £80–150
£££ = £150–200
££££ = over £200

City centre

Benedicts Hotel
7–21 Bradbury Place
Tel: 028-9059 1999
www.benedictshotel.co.uk
Good-value boutique-style hotel with an excellent restaurant, which uses local produce. **£**

Fitzwilliam Hotel
1–3 Great Victoria Street
Tel: 028-9044 2080
www.fitzwilliamhotelbelfast.com
Unassuming from the outside, the interior is contemporary and sleek. The kitchen is overseen by Michelin-starred chef Kevin Thornton. **£££**

Jurys Inn Belfast
Fisherwick Place, Great Victoria Street
Tel: 028-9053 3500
www.jurysinns.com
Jurys bring their popular per-room formula to Belfast, with this spacious, modern 190-room hotel on the Golden Mile. **££**

Malmaison Belfast
34–38 Victoria Street
Tel: 028-9022 0200
www.malmaison-belfast.com
This imaginative conversion of two beautiful Victorian warehouses is situated near the city centre and the Cathedral quarter. Rooms are bordello-themed, and the hotel has a popular brasserie and Art Deco-style bar. **£££**

The Merchant Hotel
35–39 Waring Street
Tel: 028-9023 4888
www.themerchanthotel.com
Formerly a richly ornamented Italianate bank headquarters, this opulent hotel aims to be ranked for luxury and service alongside Claridge's in London. **££££**

Ten Square Hotel
10 Donegall Square South
Tel: 028-9024 1001
www.tensquare.co.uk
A listed Victorian linen warehouse has been transformed into an ultra-luxury hotel with oriental decor and an emphasis on style. Right in the centre of town at Donegall Square. **£££–££££**

University area

Avenue Guesthouse
25 Eglantine Avenue
Tel: 028-9066 5904
www.avenueguesthouse.com
Located between Lisburn and Malone roads, this is a lovingly restored Victorian townhouse 10 minutes' walk from the city centre. **£**

Camera Guesthouse
44 Wellington Park
Tel: 028-9066 0026
www.cameraguesthouse.com
A beautiful 19th-century terraced house on a leafy street near the Botanic Gardens. The rooms are basic, but the delightful breakfasts – with cafetière coffee, potato cakes and fresh orange juice – cannot be faulted. **£**

Duke's at Queens
65–67 University Street
Tel: 028-9023 6666
www.dukesatqueens.com
Behind a redbrick Victorian facade, the design here is cool and contemporary. Well located near an array of bars and restaurants, and a 10-minute walk to the city centre. **££**

Listings

An Old Rectory
148 Malone Road
Tel: 028-9066 7882
www.anoldrectory.co.uk
Charming former rectory, this guesthouse serves a particularly fine breakfast. **£**

Tara Lodge
36 Cromwell Road
Tel: 028-9059 0900
www.taralodge.com

Well located just off Botanic Avenue, Tara Lodge combines the facilities of a hotel with the friendliness of a guesthouse. Spacious, comfortable rooms and helpful staff. **££**

Wellington Park Hotel
21 Malone Road
Tel: 028-9038 1111
www.wellingtonparkhotel.com
Smart contemporary-style Best Western. Live music in the popular Wellie Bar. **££**

RESTAURANTS

Eating out is one of Belfast's greatest lures, with a wealth of talented chefs at work. Restaurants cater for every taste and offer good value for money to boot. There is also a thriving café scene in the centre and around the university.

Restaurant price categories

Prices are for a standard two-course meal with a beer or glass of wine:

£ = below £15
££ = £15–25
£££ = £25–40
££££ = over £40

City centre

La Boca
6 Fountain Street
Tel: 028-9032 3087
www.labocabelfast.com
La Boca is a buzzing little place with live music, big steaks and great service. The all-day bistro menu of Argentinian and Spanish specials is supplemented by an afternoon *picadas* (small plates) menu, offering manchego cheese, olives and cured meats. **££**

Cayenne
Shaftesbury Square
Tel: 028-9033 1532
www.cayenne-restaurant.co.uk
Run by celebrity chef Paul Rankin, this funky restaurant is famed for its pan-Asian cooking, served alongside Irish favourites such as sirloin with horseradish gratin. **££**

The Edge
May's Meadows, Belfast
Tel: 028-9032 2000
Overlooking the Waterfront; soak up the view from the balconies and enjoy local seafood. Good service and value. **£–££**

The Ginger Bistro
7–8 Hope Street
Tel: 028-9024 4421
www.gingerbistro.com
Excellent value at Simon McCance's bistro just off Great Victoria Street. Try the fried spiced squid or a perfect rib-eye steak. Classic desserts such as raspberry crème brûlée and sticky toffee pudding are a highlight. **£**

Mourne Seafood Bar
34–36 Bank Street
Tel: 028-9024 8544
www.mourneseafood.com
One of the city's favourites, this seafood bar serves up the daily catch from the owners' beds in Carlingford Lough, and the ports of Annalong and Kilkeel. **£–££**

Tedfords
5 Donegall Quay
Tel: 028-9043 4000
www.tedfordsrestaurant.com
Once a ship's chandlers, this place retains a nautical theme and the menu favours seafood. Creative food and a good-value wine list. **£££**

Zen
55–59 Adelaide Street
Tel: 028-9023 2244
www.zenbelfast.co.uk
Zen (behind City Hall) leads the way for both traditional and cutting-edge Japanese cuisine. Eat upstairs in spectacularly chic surroundings with booth-style seating or downstairs where you can choose from the sushi bar. **££**

University area
Beatrice Kennedy
44 University Road
Tel: 028-9020 2290
http://beatricekennedy.co.uk
Located in a Victorian terrace that has retained its original character. Soft jazz, fresh flowers and candles create an intimate setting for a fusion menu; the home-made food speaks for itself. **££**

Metro at Crescent Townhouse Hotel
13 Lower Crescent
Tel: 028-9032 3349
www.crescenttownhouse.com
This elegant brasserie off Botanic Avenue offers modern Irish and British cooking with a twist: try the slow-roast pork belly, game stew or duck confit. Also has a vegetarian menu and an excellent wine list. **£££**

Shu
253 Lisburn Road, Belfast
Tel: 028-9038 1655
www.shu-restaurant.com
Ultra-modern with courteous service, this spot offers well-chosen ingredients, classic brasserie-style menus, consistently good cooking and value for money. There is also a vegetarian menu. Children are welcome.
£–££

NIGHTLIFE

Belfast has some great pubs where landlords take pride in maintaining the original decor. The best known is the Crown Liquor Saloon *(see p.222)*, a Victorian gin palace that flourished in this industrial city, but those below are also well worth a visit.

Pubs
The Duke of York
7 Commercial Court
A former journalists' pub (though most famous for former barman Gerry Adams), hence the printing artefacts. Old-fashioned intimate vibe and with a good mix of live music and disco.

The John Hewitt Bar
51 Donegall Street
Once a newspaper office, originally set up by the socialist poet John Hewitt. Traditional pub interior and bar food, plus music three nights a week. Closed Sundays.

The Kitchen Bar
36–40 Victoria Square
Now located in a spacious old Victorian warehouse, with live traditional Irish music and jazz.

McHugh's Bar
29–31 Queen's Square
Built in 1711, this is Belfast's oldest listed building. See a collection of memorabilia relating to Belfast and munch on bar food.

The Northern Whig
2 Bridge Street
Trendy and popular with businesspeople.

Drinkers outside the Duke of York

ENTERTAINMENT

Theatre, classical music and film are all well catered for in Belfast, as befits a major city with a thriving university. The rebuilt Lyric Theatre is not to be missed.

Grand Opera House
Great Victoria Street
Tel: 028-9024 1919
www.goh.co.uk
This glorious 1895 building is Belfast's biggest entertainment venue, staging drama, musicals, ballet and pantomime.

Lyric Theatre
Ridgeway Street
Tel: 028-9038 5685
www.lyrictheatre.co.uk
Northern Ireland's only full-time theatre, the Lyric reopened in spring 2011 after an £18m rebuild. Offers a diverse repertoire of classical, popular and contemporary drama.

Ulster Hall
30 Bedford Street
Tel: 028-9033 4455
www.ulsterhall.co.uk
Built in 1862 as a music hall, Ulster hall hosts a variety of sporting events, rock gigs, choral and classical music concerts and beer festivals.

Waterfront Hall
2 Laynon Place
Tel: 028-9033 4455
www.waterfront.co.uk
A multipurpose venue offering comedy, theatre, music and acrobatics, with two exhibition galleries.

SPORTS AND ACTIVITIES

Spectator sports are an important part of Belfast life, with ice hockey, football and rugby especially popular, but for those looking to get active, cycling is a great option, as is walking in the lovely countryside around the city.

Cycling
For an overview of routes and information visit: **www.cycleni.com.**

Belfast Bike Tours
Tel: 078-1211 4235
www.belfastbiketours.com
This company organises tours of up to two hours for £15.

Bikedock
79–85 Ravenhill Road
Tel: 028-9073 0600
www.bikedock.com
Hire a bicycle from here.

Football (soccer)
Windsor Park
South Belfast
www.irishfa.com
This is the home venue for Northern Ireland's international football matches, as well as the home of Linfield Football Club, who play in the IFA Premiership (the Irish league).

Ice hockey
Odyssey Arena
Tel: 028-9073 9074
www.belfastgiants.com
Home of the Belfast Giants, who play here most weekends.

Rugby
Ravenhill Stadium
Tel: 028-9049 3222
www.ulsterrugby.com
Ulster Rugby play their European Cup and inter-provincial matches at Ravenhill grounds in the southeast of the city.

TOURS

The city's rich historical past, including a fascinating industrial history, makes it well worth taking a guided walk or bus ride to learn more about Belfast.

Boat Trips
The Lagan Boat Company
Donegall Quay
Tel: 028-9033 0844
www.laganboatcompany.com
Guided boat tours, including *Titanic*-themed.

Bus tours
Belfast City Sightseeing Tours
Tel: 028-9032 1321
www.belfastcitysightseeing.com
See the city-centre sights from an open-top bus. Tours before 2pm include Stormont.

Taxi tours
Belfast City Black Taxi Tours
Tel: 028-0903 01832

www.allirelandtours.com
Increase your understading of Northern Ireland's politics on a 75-minute tour in a black taxi visiting Loyalist and Nationalist sights.

Walking tours
Belfast City Walking Tours
Tel: 028-9029 2631
www.belfast-city-walking-tours.co.uk
General and special-interest walks, with focuses like the *Titanic* and Victorian Belfast.

Belfast Welcome Centre
47 Donegall Place
Tel: 028-9024 6609
Get Northern Ireland info here, or join a literary or historical pub tour (May–Oct).

Listings

FESTIVALS AND EVENTS

Belfast is strong on showcasing the vibrant local arts scene.

March
Saint Patrick's Day Carnival
www.belfastcity.gov.uk
Enjoy a carnival winding through the city centre on 17 March and a free concert mixing pop and traditional music.

April–May
Cathedral Quarter Arts Festival
www.cqaf.com
Live music, dance, performance and children's events bring the city-centre streets to life all day and into the early hours.

July–August
Féile an Phobail
www.feilebelfast.com
Concerts, debates, tours, drama and international acts playing alongside Irish talent as West Belfast's community celebrate their unique culture.

October
Belfast Festival at Queen's
www.belfastfestival.com
A major arts festival, showcasing the best of international art and performance, and Northern Ireland's vibrant cultural scene, based around Queen's University.

At the Glitter and Sparkle Halloween Ball, part of the Belfast Festival

Northern Ireland

The visual evidence of Northern Ireland's civil strife is increasingly hard to find, allowing the country's traditional attractions – gorgeous lakes and glens, a stunning coastline and a wealth of golf courses – to take their place in the spotlight. In its prestigious role as City of Culture 2013 the city of Derry/Londonderry plans to share the diversity of the area and its extraordinary history with the rest of the world.

Derry/Londonderry

Population: Derry (100,000)

Local dialling code: 028

Local tourist office: Derry Visitor and Convention Bureau, 4 Foyle Street; tel: 028-7126 7284; www.derryvisitor.com

Main police station: Police Service of Northern Ireland, Strand Road, Derry; tel: 028-7136 7337

Main post office: Custom House Street, Derry

Main hospital: Altnagelvin Area Hospital, Glenshane Road, Derry; tel: 028-7134 5171

Surprisingly for such an historically troubled area, it's sometimes hard to be sure of the exact location of the border between the Republic and Northern Ireland. Partly this is because it snakes its way along 18th-century county boundaries through farming land that is sometimes bleak, more often breathtakingly beautiful, taking little account of natural boundaries such as rivers, or of the cultural differences that separate Republican-minded Roman Catholics and British-oriented Protestants. Houses straddle it so that, as the joke has it, a man may sleep with his head in the United Kingdom and his heart in the Republic of Ireland.

Political expediency accounts for the absurdities. The intention was to redraw the border rationally after partition in 1920 left six of the nine counties of the ancient province of Ulster (Antrim, Down, Armagh, Derry, Fermanagh and Tyrone) under British rule, and a Boundary Commission was set up to advise. But in the end the British and Irish governments, both hoping to avoid further trouble, suppressed the commission's report and left things as they were. Had they decided differently, much of the subsequent conflict might have been averted.

Derry/Londonderry

Across the border from Donegal is the county of Londonderry and its famously friendly chief city, whose very name has long been a bone of contention for its main two communities. Catholics refer to Derry, for both county and city, while Protestants stick to Londonderry, with officialdom increasingly resorting to the clumsy **Derry/Londonderry** in an effort to maintain neutrality, resulting in the local nickname 'Stroke City'. Though it was scarred by the Troubles, there has been increasing redevelopment since the peace process began during the 1990s.

Derry/Londonderry ❷ is buzzing with excitement and pride after winning its bid for 2013 City of Culture, a date which will also commemorate 400 years of the founding of the city. Derry's regeneration plans put arts and culture at the heart of its redevelopment, with a focus on harnessing the creative energy that now pulses through the modern city. In 2011 the

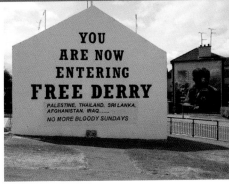

The infamous signage at the Bogside, Derry

spectacular £14.5m **Peace Bridge** ❶ for cyclists and pedestrians across the River Foyle was opened. It is seen as a symbolic unification of all communities living in the city.

Derry city

The city's growth was financed by London guilds, which in 1613 began creating the last walled city in Europe. Its purpose was mercantile success, and you can still see traces of its former economic confidence in the ornamental facades of the old shirt-making factories, which provided the city with its livelihood for generations. The **walls** ❷ (tours tel: 028-7134 7176; charge, otherwise free access), 20ft (6m) thick and complete with watchtowers and cannon, are marvellously intact.

Two 17th-century sieges failed to breach the walls, earning the sobriquet 'maiden city'. Some say the city still has a siege mentality, a theory reinforced by the IRA's daubed slogan 'You are now entering Free Derry'. This was the name given to the **Bogside** ❸, a densely populated Roman Catholic housing

Out and about in Derry city

estate, when its inhabitants barricaded it against the police in 1969. Their grievances were old ones. After Ireland's partition in 1920, the city's governing Unionists had fixed constituency boundaries to ensure a 'permanent' majority for themselves in what was a mainly nationalist area – an artificial majority that wasn't overturned until the mid-1970s.

A good way to experience the political history of the Bogside is to visit the **Bogside Artists** (46 Derry Street; tel: 028-7137 3842; www.bogside artists.com), whose studio is in the centre of the area. Guided tours of all 12 murals are available. The award-winning **Tower Museum** 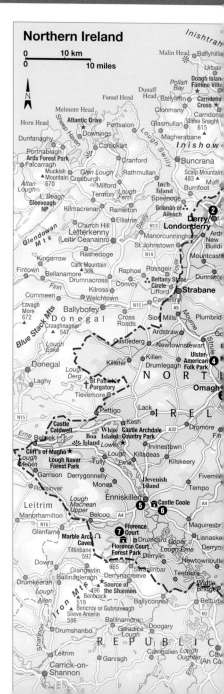 (Union Hall Place; tel: 028-7137 2411; www. derrycity.gov.uk/museums; Tue–Sat 10am–5pm, with exceptions July–Aug; charge) skilfully uses audiovisuals and photography to tell its story from both sides of the sectarian divide.

Streets from the city's original four gates (Shipquay, Ferryquay, Bishop's and Butcher's) converge on The Diamond, a perversely square-shaped market place at the top of Shipquay Street, the steepest main thoroughfare in Ireland. At the bottom of the street, the **Guildhall** (Guildhall Square; tel: 028-7137 7335; Mon–Fri 9am–5pm; free), one of those Tudor Gothic structures popular in Northern Ireland, clearly shows the influence of the London merchants. In 2011 a £3m repair programme which included restoration of the stonework, roof, windows and stained glass was carried out on the Guildhall – and the famous Guildhall clock also had a makeover – the first since 1891.

Derry's Guildhall (see p.136)

The best place to enquire about all tourist information is the **Derry Visitor and Convention Bureau F** (44 Foyle Street; tel: 028-7126 7284; www.derryvisitor.com). Free Derry Tours (Gasyard Centre, Lecky Road,

238

Brandywell; tel: 028-7126 2812) take you through the history of the Bogside and Fountainwell areas, pivotal locations during the Troubles. Tours begin at 10am and 2pm daily.

Inland to Tyrone and Fermanagh

County Tyrone is dominated by the Sperrin Mountains, laced with scenic walks and trails. During tough times in the 1800s, Tyrone's strong Presbyterian work ethic spurred many to seek their fortune in America. Northern Ireland claims that 11 US presidents have had roots in the province. Ulster's links with the US are celebrated at the unique Ulster-American Folk Park. Fermanagh in the southwest is the province's lakeland playground: a third of it is under water. Proof that political divisions are less of a barrier these days

Derry City

0   200 m
0   200 yds

Creggan Street
William Street
Little Diamond
Frederick St
Eglinton Pl
Fahan Street
Butcher St
Listannon Park
Listmoor St
BOGSIDE **C**
Westland Street
Bogside Artists
Rossville Street
Double Bastion
Roaring Meg
St Columb (Long Tower Church)
Lecky Rd
Barrack Street
St Columbas Wm
Long Tower St
Abbey St
Rossville Street
Chamberlain St
High St
Waterloo
Magazine St
Butcher's Gate
City Wall **B**
Society St
Fahan Street
Royal Bastion
St Augustine's
Verbal Arts Centre
Bishop St
Bishop's Gate
Court House
Bishop Street Without
The Fountain
Upper Bennett St
Lwr James St
Gr James St
Void Art Gallery
Sackville St
Waterloo Place
Tower Museum **D**
Shipquay St
Shipquay Gate
Harvey St
Castle St
Bloody Sunday Monument
Butcher's Gate
The Nerve Centre
First Derry Presbyterian
St Within
Palace St
London St
Deanery
St Columb's Cathedral
Wapping Lane
Custom House
Harbour Museum - Genealogy Centre **A**
Peace Bridge
Guildhall **E**
Bank Place
Derry Craft Village
Bloody Sunday Centre
Millennium Forum
Richmond Shopping Centre
Linenhall St
Ferryquay St
Pump St
Playhouse Theatre
Ferryquay Gate
Artillery St
New Gate
Ferry Quay
Haywin Street
John Street
Foyle Street
Foyle Road
Central Library
Water St
Orchard Gallery & Cinema
Rialto
Market St
Foyleside Shopping Centre
Bridge Street
Carlisle Road
Derry Visitor & Convention Bureau **F**
Abercorn Road
Embankment
Foyle Street
River Foyle
King St
Workhouse Museum
Waterside Link
WATERSIDE
Derry Station
Duke Street

N

Airports: Belfast International Airport (30km/19 miles north of city); tel: 028-9448 4848; **www.belfastairport.com**; most international arrivals land at Belfast. City of Derry Airport (8km/5 miles east of city); tel: 028-7181 0784; **www.cityofderryairport.com** has flights from the UK. From the City of Derry Airport a direct bus service, the Airporter, links both Derry and the Belfast International and City airports. The journey costs £17.50 one-way, round-trip £27.50. Derry City Airport to Derry city centre is £12

 Trains: Derry Railway Station, Duke Street, Waterside; tel: 028-9066 6630; **www.translink.co.uk.** Northern Ireland Railways departs for Derry from Central Station, East Bridge, Belfast; tel: 028-9066 6630. The other main cities or towns connected to Belfast by train are Lisburn, Portadown and Newry to the south, as well as northbound to Carrickfergus, Larne, Ballymena, Coleraine and Derry in the northwest. Tickets can be bought online or at the bus station. There's a free 10-minute shuttle service from the train station to the west bank of Derry. During weekdays trains leave Belfast for Derry at two-hourly intervals

 Buses: Ulster Bus, Foyle Street; tel; 028-7126 2626; **www.translink.co.uk.** The Europa Buscentre in Belfast is the hub for departures to Derry as well as provincial towns. Express journey time to Derry is 1 hour 40 minutes; an alternative service takes 2 hours. If you want to tour Northern Ireland by train or bus an ilink ticket allows unlimited travel. It costs £15 per day, or £55 per week. One-day journeys from Belfast to other cities and towns cost from £10 return

 Car hire: Avis, tel: 0844-5446 036; **www.avis.co.uk**; Hertz, tel: 028-9073 2451; **www.hertz.co.uk**; Budget, tel: 028-9023 0700; **www.budgetbelfast.co.uk**

 Taxi companies: The main taxi firms that serve both Belfast and Northern Ireland are Fonacab and Value Cabs. Fonacab, tel: 028-9033 3333; **www.fonacab.com**; Value Cabs, tel: 028-9080 9080; **www.valuecabs.co.uk.** In Derry, Foyle Delta Cabs, tel: 028-7126 3905 is the biggest operator; **www.foyledeltacabs.com**

Northern Ireland

can be seen in the restoration of the Ballinamore–Ballyconnell cross-border canal: you can now travel all the way to Limerick by inland waterway.

County Tyrone

As you drive into **Omagh ❸**, the county town of Tyrone, the religious fragmentation of Northern Ireland is immediately apparent. On the right is the Presbyterian Church (Trinity); on the left, the Methodist Church; next, St Columba's Church of Ireland; then the Gothic spires of the Roman

Garden of Light

In August 2008, on the 10th anniversary of the Omagh bombing, an unusual and very moving memorial – the Garden of Light – was opened. A heliostatic mirror in the memorial park tracks the sun and directs a beam of light onto 31 small mirrors, each etched with the name of a victim. These in turn bounce the light via another hidden mirror onto a heart-shaped crystal in an obelisk at the bomb site.

The Ulster-American Folk Park is an outdoor museum which tells the story of emigration

Catholic Church of the Sacred Heart, a poor man's Chartres Cathedral. There are many more. The joining of the Rivers Camowen and Drumragh to form the Strule make the location pleasant enough, but Omagh is more a town for living (and praying) in than for visiting. Locals still recall the Saturday afternoon in August 1998 when a car bomb exploded in the town centre, killing 31 people and injuring more than 200 (see box, p.239). Although, in the eyes of most people, the Troubles have ended, the murder by dissident Irish Republicans of a Roman Catholic police officer, Ronan Kerr, near Omagh in 2011, was a reminder of the fragility of the peace process.

The Mellon banking family of Pittsburgh, having traced their roots to 4 miles (6km) north of Omagh, off the A5, endowed the **Ulster-American Folk Park** ❹ on the site at Camphill (tel: 028-8224 3292; www.nmni.com; Mar–Sept Tue–Sun 10am–5pm, Oct–Feb Tue–Fri 10am–6pm; charge). To illuminate the transition made by the 18th-century emigrants, craftsmen's cottages, a schoolhouse, a blacksmith's forge and a Presbyterian meeting-house from the Old World have been rebuilt on a peat bog alongside log cabins, a Pennsylvania farmstead and a covered wagon from the New World. Peat is kept burning in the cottages, and there are demonstrations of candle-making, fish-salting and horse-shoeing as well as periodic 'living history' re-creations of battles between redcoats and native Americans. An indoor exhibit recreates the main street of an Ulster town 100 years ago. A replica of an emigrant ship links the continents. The award-winning park has a number of annual celebrations, including Fourth of July and an Appalachian and bluegrass festival.

County Fermanagh

The county town, **Enniskillen** ❺, a Protestant stronghold since Tudor times, is built on an island between two channels of the River Erne as it flows from **Upper** to **Lower Lough Erne**. In summer, pleasure boats (tel: 028-6632 2882; www.ernetours ltd.com; June–Aug daily 2.15 and 4.15pm, May, Sept, Oct Tue, Sat, Sun, with exceptions) ply the lakes, while visitors cruise them in their hired craft (Manor House Marine, Killadeas; tel: 028-6862 8100; www. manormarine.com).

Blakes of the Hollow pub in Enniskillen

The town's strategic importance is shown by **Enniskillen Castle** (tel: 028-6632 5000; www.enniskillen castle.co.uk; July–Aug daily 2–5pm, May, June and Sept Mon–Sat, Oct–Apr Mon–Fri; charge). The earliest parts date from the 15th century and the imposing water gate from the late 16th century. The castle houses two museums, one specialising in prehistory, the other in military relics.

Enniskillen is rich in small bakeries and butcher's shops, and there's a convivial atmosphere as farmers mix with townsfolk in the local hostelries (*see box, left*). Confusingly, the main street, best viewed from the head of the 108 stairs of **Cole's Monument** (Forthill Park; tel: 028-6632 3110; mid-Apr–Sept 1.30–3pm; charge) changes its name six times between the bridges at either end. One of the best-preserved towns in Northern Ireland, Enniskillen has several appealing areas, not least the **Buttermarket** (Mon–Sat 10am–5pm) in the centre, a restored 19th-century courtyard specialising in crafts and art galleries.

Two miles (3km) southeast of Enniskillen on the A4 is Ireland's finest classical mansion, **Castle Coole** ❻ (National Trust; tel: 028-6632 2690; www.nationaltrust.org.uk; June–Aug daily 11am–5pm, mid-Mar–May and Sept Sat–Sun only, with exceptions, grounds daily 10am–dusk;

Blakes of the Hollow

Generally agreed to be one of the great classic pubs of Ireland, Blakes of the Hollow (6 Church Street; tel: 028-6632 0918), with its unusual red-painted exterior, has been in the same family since 1887. Renowned for serving a fine pint of Guinness and a classic Irish coffee, it is the sort of place that seemed unlikely ever to change. But even Blakes has had to move with the times, and now has a restaurant, the Café Merlot, serving bistro-style food on the lower ground floor, and a fine-dining restaurant, Number 6, on the top floor. Thankfully the food is every bit as good as their pints, and well worth sampling.

charge). Completed in 1798, it is a perfect example of late 18th-century Hellenism and has furniture dating from before 1830. A state bedroom is presented as it was for George IV. The park lake's graylag geese were established here 300 years ago.

A few more miles southwest on the A32, towards Swalinbar across the border, **Florence Court**  (National Trust; tel: 028-6634 8249; www. nationaltrust.org.uk; house: May–Sept daily 11am–5pm, Mar–Apr and Oct Sat–Sun only, with exceptions, grounds daily 10am–dusk; charge) is a beautiful 18th-century mansion. Contents include fine rococo plasterwork and period furniture. The grounds feature an ice house, a water-powered sawmill, a walled garden, extensive park and woodland and a yew tree reputed to be the parent of all Irish yew trees. You can sample home-made delights served in the Stable restaurant.

In and around Armagh

To the east is County Armagh, known as the Apple Orchard of Ireland. During the 1980s and 1990s, its southern acres earned the less inviting sobriquet of Bandit Country, thanks to terrorist activity near its border with the Republic. The area has now put its turbulent past behind it and is attracting tourists, especially to the Ring of Gullion, a scenic driving and walking route in South Armagh.

Armagh city

Its county town of **Armagh** ❽ symbolises the problematic dualism of Northern Ireland. Its two striking cathedrals – one Protestant, one Catholic, both called **St Patrick's** – sit on opposite hills like, someone once said, the horns of a dilemma. The two communities live mostly in separate parts of the city, with little interaction,

Armagh's dualism encapsulated in street signs

Georgian architecture can be seen around Armagh

1801; www.armagh.co.uk; Sept–June Mon–Sat 10.30am–5.30pm, July–Aug until 8.30pm, Sun 2–8.30pm; charge). This explains St Patrick's connections with the city, including the 9th-century Book of Armagh. The book, written in 807 by the scribe Ferdomnach, is a precious historic record because of the information it provides about the elusive St Patrick.

Two miles (3km) west of the city, off the A28, is the high-tech **Navan Centre** (tel: 028-3752 1801; Apr–Sept daily 10am–7pm, Oct–Mar until 4pm; charge), celebrating Emain Macha, which was Ulster's Camelot around 600BC, making it Europe's oldest Celtic site. Access to the hilltop is free.

County Down

County Down stretches from Belfast Lough south to the Mourne Mountains, better known in song as the Mountains of Mourne, a favourite Irish emigrant lament. There are several pretty resort towns on the coast, including Newcastle and Ardglass. Downpatrick is rich in associations with Ireland's patron saint, while Strangford Lough with its numerous islands is also the site of some interesting early Christian remains.

The Mourne Mountains

The Mournes are 'young' mountains (like the Alps) and their chameleon qualities attract walkers. One moment the granite is grey, the next pink. You walk by an isolated

Northern Ireland

although increasingly they join together for ecumenical gatherings and social functions.

Armagh is known for its dignified Georgian architecture. At one end of an oval **Mall** – where cricket is played in summer – is a classical courthouse, at the other a jailhouse. Access is free into the gardens of the 1790 Observatory that accommodates Ireland's main **Planetarium** (College Hill; tel: 028-3752 3689; www.armaghplanet.com; Mon–Fri 1–5pm, Sat 11.30am–5pm, pre-booking essential for shows; charge). Astronomical shows have been enhanced by a major refurbishment to the Digital Theatre. There are also interactive exhibitions and an outdoor Astropark with scale models of the planets.

In the city centre is **St Patrick's Trian** (English Street; tel: 028-3752

★ ON THE TRAIL OF ST PATRICK

Ireland's patron saint is one of the best known of all time, and his feast day on 17 March is celebrated by thousands of people with no direct Irish connections. He is usually pictured as an elderly man in green vestments, with snakes writhing at his feet. Unlike St Christopher, St Patrick was a historical figure, albeit one whose real story is embellished by legend. Ancient pilgrimages are still observed today in his honour.

St Patrick was a Roman Briton living in southwest England or Wales, the son of wealthy parents. As a teenager he was kidnapped and taken to Ireland where he was sold into slavery. He was a shepherd on Slemish Mountain near Ballymena, County Antrim, which is where he found faith. God told him to run away and find his ship, so he escaped and travelled some 320km (200 miles) south to Wexford, where a boat was waiting.

On his return to Britain, he converted to Christianity and became a priest. One night he dreamt that he heard the Irish calling him to come and convert them, so in AD432 he returned to the land where he had been a slave. He founded the first church in Ireland at Saul, outside Downpatrick. Today a replica and a round tower stand in its place. His grave is believed to be beside Downpatrick Cathedral.

Downpatrick Cathedral, where St Patrick's remains are thought to be

Much of our knowledge of St Patrick comes from a pastoral letter he wrote in endearingly bad Latin, which survived in the Book of Armagh, now housed in Trinity College, Dublin. Meanwhile, legends grew up around his figure, which have far wider currency than the true story. He is said to have struggled with demons for 40 days and nights on the summit of Croaghpatrick in County Mayo; even today thousands of pilgrims climb the mountain every year on the last Sunday in July, many of them barefoot, like their parents and grandparents before them.

St Patrick is said to have had another mighty struggle with demons in a cave on Station Island on Lough Derg in County Donegal, and for over 1,000 years people have been making a three-day pilgrimage. Everyone on the island arrives fasting, and goes barefoot. An enormous number of prayers are said, while walking traditional paths called 'stations'. Nobody sleeps for the first night, and the one meal a day permitted consists of dry toast or oatcakes and black tea.

St Patrick is closely associated with Armagh, whose hill is topped by two cathedrals, one Catholic, one Protestant. In the Protestant Cathedral's stained-glass window St Patrick is pictured as a young man in sandals dressed in the Roman style, reflecting the historical reality. The Catholic Cathedral's windows show the familiar elderly bishop in green robes, an image dating from the early 17th century, which has become the predominant one.

The traditional depiction of St Patrick at Armagh's Catholic Cathedral

Learning about the saint's story at the St Patrick Centre in Downpatrick

On the trail of St Patrick

farmhouse, and within moments are in the middle of a wilderness. Much of the range can only be reached on foot, and it is a great destination for walkers. **Slieve Donard** ⑩, the highest peak at 850m (2,796ft), has exhilarating panoramic views.

At the foothills of the Mournes, **Newcastle** ⑪ is east Down's main resort, with a fine, sandy beach, an inordinate number of cake shops and the celebrated Royal County Down Golf Club, one of the world's top 10 links courses. Several forest parks – **Donard**, **Tollymore**, **Castlewellan** (charges) – are good for riding (on a pony or bicycle). This is an area that invites you to unwind and is bemused by people being in a hurry.

Downpatrick

Northeast of Newcastle, approaching the southern shores of Strangford Lough is **Downpatrick** ⑫, which has a Georgian air and a cathedral supposedly built on the site of St

Patrick's first stone church. The saint himself is said by some to be buried here. You can follow his story in a high-tech interactive exhibition with audiovisuals at the **St Patrick Centre** (Lower Market Street; tel: 028-4461 9000; www.saintpatrick-cenre.com; June–Aug daily 9.30am–6pm, Apr–May and Sept Mon–Sat 9.30am–5.30pm, Sun 1–5.30pm, Oct–Mar Mon–Sat 10am–5pm; charge), itself the hub of Downpatrick's famous week of celebrations around St Patrick's Day, 17 March. A hundred metres/yards or so away, the atmospheric **Downpatrick and County Down Steam Railway** (tel: 028-4461 5779; www.downrail.co.uk) runs weekend events between June and September and special holidays.

Strangford Lough

The conservation area of **Strangford Lough** ⑬ is noted for its myriad islands, most of which are sunken drumlins, the smooth glacial hillocks

Walking in the lush Tollymore forest park

This tower house on the shore of Strangford Lough dates from around 1550

gentrify some of its fast-food bars and souvenir shops to do justice to the new marina packed with yachts and cruisers. Rowing around the bay in hired punts and fishing trips from the pier are evergreen attractions. It is a busy town with a weekly open-air market, plenty of pubs and eating places, parkland and a leisure centre with heated pools. The best beach is nearby **Ballyholme Bay**, a sandy arc which can become very crowded.

The A2 from Bangor to Belfast runs through what locals enviously describe as the Gold Coast. This is stockbroker country, where lush lawns meet mature woodland, with hillside sites that lure the well-heeled. **Cultra**, 10km (6 miles) from Bangor, has leafy lanes and the resplendent Culloden Hotel. They go in for yachting, golf and horse riding around here.

that characterise County Down's landscape. **Mahee Island** , accessible by bridge, has a golf course and the remains of **Nendrum Abbey** (Visitor Centre; tel: 028-9181 1491; Easter–Sept daily 10am–6pm, Oct–Easter noon–4pm; free), an early monastery. **Castle Espie** (Wild-fowl and Wetlands Trust; tel: 028-9187 4146; www.wwt.org.uk; daily 10.30am–dusk; charge), on the shores of Strangford Lough, is home to Ireland's largest collection of ducks, geese and swans. **Comber** , at the head of Strangford Lough, was a linen town and still has a working mill. The town centre retains its old character, despite the developers, with cottage shops and a square.

Belfast Lough

Bangor was originally a small seaside resort, noted for its abbey. The rejuvenated seafront still has to

Northern Ireland

Silent Valley Mountain Park

The remote **Silent Valley Reservoir** (Head Road, Kilkeel (B27); tel: 028-9074 1166; www.niwater.com; daily 10am–dusk; charge), in the heart of the Mourne Mountains, has as its centrepiece a large dam, which supplies Belfast and County Down with water. It is such a peaceful and beautiful spot that Northern Ireland Water provides facilities for the numerous visitors (about 50,000 a year) who seek out its tranquillity. These include a restaurant and information point, and a shuttle service (May–Sept) from the car park to the dam.

Carrickfergus has a wonderfully authentic castle to explore

Nearby, at the restored Cultra Manor, is the award-winning **Ulster Folk and Transport Museum** ⑱ (tel: 028-9042 8428; www.nmni.com; Mar–Sept Tue–Sun 10am–5pm, Oct–Feb Tue–Fri 10am–4pm, Sat–Sun 11am–4pm; charge), which brings social history to life. Farmhouses, cottages, churches and mills have been painstakingly reconstructed. Freshly made soda bread, a local speciality, is sometimes baked over a traditional peat fire. On another part of the site the Transport Museum has its own fascination; exhibits range from horse-drawn chariots right up to a prototype of the ill-fated Belfast-built DeLorean sports car. There is a *Titanic* exhibition and the state-of-the-art X2 Flight Exhibition, where you can simulate flying. From here it's a straight run into Belfast.

County Antrim

Antrim, which stretches north of Belfast as far as the Giant's Causeway, is one of the scenic highlights of Northern Ireland. The Causeway

St Patrick's green and other tall tales

St Patrick didn't banish the snakes from Ireland because there were none. Ireland has no snakes, moles, or weasels either. After the last Ice Age, some 10,000 years ago, Ireland was cut off from Europe before these creatures made it across the landbridge. Other misinformations connected with the saint include what the shamrock, associated with the saint, actually is: not a botanical species, but the winter-resting stage of the white clover plant. And the national colour of Ireland is not St Patrick's green. In heraldry the national colour of Ireland is blue; Ireland's heraldic flag shows a gold harp on a blue background, known as St Patrick's blue.

Coastal Road, along the east-facing coast, gives access to Antrim's celebrated Glens, peaceful spots with traditional farms. The north coast, with its famous Giant's Causeway, is a favourite holiday spot for Belfast people, with bracing resorts and the romantic ruins of Dunluce Castle to explore.

Carrickfergus

Carrickfergus ⓭, north of Belfast, is another market and dormitory town. Its big synthetic-fibre plants are empty now – a contemporary monument to its industrial past. More interesting is the imposing 12th-century Norman **Castle** (The Marine Highway; tel: 028-9335 1273; Easter–Sept daily 10am–6pm, Oct– Easter until 4pm; charge). Set beside the harbour, it still attracts attention for its authenticity. It is a real castle

Driving on the Antrim coast road

in every sense, with a portcullis, ramparts, chilling dungeons, cannons and a regimental museum in the keep. Looking to the new age of leisure, the town's **marina** has 300 berths. The parish church of St Nicholas (with stained-glass windows to Santa Claus) is 12th-century.

Antrim coast road

The rewards of continuing along the coast are spectacular views of brown moorlands, white limestone, black basalt, red sandstone and blue sea along the **Causeway Coastal Road ⓴**. The road, designed in 1834 by Sir Charles Lanyon as a work of famine relief, opened up an area whose inhabitants had previously found it easier to travel by sea to Scotland than overland to the rest of Ireland. At various points, you can turn into one or other of Antrim's celebrated nine glens – **Glenarm, Glencloy, Glenariff, Glenballyeamon, Glenaan, Glencorp, Glendun, Glenshesk** and **Glentaisie** – and into another world of peaceful landscapes, still traditionally farmed.

Ballygalley ㉑, at the start of the famous scenic drive, has a 1625 fortified manor house (now a hotel) and, inland from the coast road, a well-preserved old mill and pottery. **White Bay** is a picnic area around which small fossils can be found. **Glenarm** has a beautiful park adjoining a fussy castle, home of the earls of Antrim. **Carnlough** has a fine harbour and, running over its main street, a white bridge built in 1854 to carry limestone from the quarries to waiting boats. The village of **Waterfoot** is the entrance to **Glenariff Glen**, a deep wooded gorge. Wild flowers carpet the upper glen in spring and early summer, and rustic footbridges carry walkers over the Glenariff River, past postcard-pretty waterfalls.

About 2km (1¼ miles) to the north, **Cushendall**, 'capital of the Glens', is a picturesque village. It has a good beach and is a popular sailing centre. Ten kilometres (6 miles) further on, **Cushendun ㉒**, is a village of white cottages, graceful old houses and friendly pubs, has been captured on countless canvases and is protected by the National Trust.

North Antrim coast

The north coast begins at **Ballycastle ㉓** setting for an end-of-August agricultural fair, held since 1606 *(see p.255)*. The **Ballycastle Museum** (59 Castle Street; tel: 028-2076 2942; July–Aug daily noon–6pm; free)

concentrates on the folk social history of the Glens. A seafront memorial marks the spot where, in 1898, Guglielmo Marconi first seriously tested wireless telegraphy. He made his historic transmission between here and **Rathlin Island ㉔**, 13km (8 miles) off the coast. The island, whose population has slumped from 2,000 to 80 since 1850, makes its living from farming and fishing and attracts geologists, botanists and bird watchers; there is a reserve (tel: 028-2076 3948) visited by an estimated 250,000 birds of 175 species. A ferry (tel: 028-2076 9299; daily year-round; reservations advised) makes the journey from Ballycastle in 45 minutes. There is one pub, a hotel, a guesthouse and a youth hostel.

Eight kilometres (5 miles) west, off the A2, is the **Carrick-a-rede Rope Bridge** (tel: 028-2076 9839; Mar–Oct daily 10am–6pm, Nov–Feb 10.30am–3.30pm; charge), which swings over

The extraordinary Giant's Causeway

Giant's Causeway Visitor Experience opened to the public. The building, which uses locally quarried basalt, is sunken into the ground and blends seamlessly into the landscape. One of the most pleasant ways to reach the Giant's Causeway is on the narrow-gauge **steam train** from Bushmills (daily July, Aug and Easter; Sat–Sun Mar–Oct; charge).

The distillery at **Bushmills** ㉖ (Distillery Road; tel: 028-2073 3218; www.bushmills.com; guided tours: Mar–Oct Mon–Sat 9.15am–5pm, Sun noon–5pm, Nov–Feb Mon–Fri 9.30am–3.30pm, Sat–Sun 12.30–3.30pm; charge) boasts the world's oldest whiskey-making licence (1608). Old Bushmills, Black Bush and Bushmills Malt, made from local barley and the water that flows by in St Columb's Rill, can be tasted and bought after a tour.

About 3km (2 miles) along the coast road are the romantic remains of **Dunluce Castle** (tel: 028-2073 1938; www.ni-environment.gov.uk; Apr–Sept daily 10am–6pm, Oct–Mar 10am–4pm; charge). Poised on a rocky headland beside sheer cliffs, the ruins of this 14th-century stronghold are huge and dramatic. In the graveyard of the adjacent ruined church are buried sailors from the Spanish Armada galleass *Girona*, which was wrecked on nearby rocks in 1588 with 1,300 men on board and was located on the seabed in 1967. Many of the *Girona*'s treasures are in Belfast's Ulster Museum.

251

Northern Ireland

a 24m (80ft) chasm, allowing salmon fishermen and brave tourists access to a rocky promontory. Travelling on past cliffs and white surfers' beaches, you will come upon the romantic ruins of **Dunseverick Castle.**

Giant's Causeway

The castle is at the eastern end of the **Giant's Causeway** ㉕, an astonishing assembly of more than 40,000 basalt columns, mostly perfect hexagonals formed by the cooling of molten lava. The tallest, in the **Giant's Organ**, are about 12m (39ft). The formal approach is via the visitor centre run by the National Trust (44 Causeway Road; tel: 028-2073 1855; www.nationaltrust.org.uk; car park charge). In 2012 the new £18.5m glass-fronted

ACCOMMODATION

Northern Ireland's greatest strength is its wealth of old-fashioned country hideaways, with a genuine warm welcome. Large modern hotels are the exception rather than the norm, but they also make a point of welcoming visitors warmly. Both offer great value.

Derry/Londonderry

Ardtara Country House
8 Gortead Road, Upperlands, Maghera
Tel: 028-7964 4490
www.ardtara.com
Deep in Seamus Heaney country, this elegant Victorian manor house has large, luxuriously furnished rooms with garden views and original fireplaces. Good touring base. **££**

Radisson Blu Roe Park Hotel
Roe Park, Limavady
Tel: 028-7772 2222
www.radissonroepark.com
Eighteenth-century mansion with a large modern extension built on a hill in rolling countryside. Bedrooms are in the modern wing, and are spacious and luxurious with views of the golf course or the garden. **££**

Inland to Tyrone and Fermanagh

Grange Lodge
7 Grange Road, Dungannon
Tel: 028-8778 4212
www.grangelodgecountryhouse.com
A charming Georgian country house with a garden producing food for the table and flowers for the house. Norah Brown is a renowned cook, and the breakfast is outstanding. **££**

In and around Armagh

Charlemont Arms Hotel
57–65 English Street, Armagh
Tel: 028-3752 2028
www.charlemontarmshotel.com
Old-fashioned city-centre hotel, run by one family for three generations. The bar and restaurant are traditional but the bedrooms are contemporary, spacious and comfortable. **££**

Seagoe Hotel
Upper Church Lane, Portadown
Tel: 028-3833 3076
www.seagoe.com
A striking modern hotel with a double-height foyer in its own grounds outside Portadown. It has 34 bedrooms, colour-coordinated in warm reds and yellow, and an airy modern restaurant with a courtyard garden. **££**

County Down

Glassdrumman Lodge
85 Mill Road, Annalong
Tel: 028-4376 8451
www.glassdrummanlodge.com
A small family-run hotel in the foothills of the Mourne Mountains. Renowned hospitality aimed firmly at golfers (10 minutes to Royal County Down) and walkers. Open fires downstairs and spacious bedrooms. **££**

Slieve Donard Hotel
Downs Road, Newcastle
Tel: 028-4372 1066
www.hastingshotels.com
An imposing Victorian mansion in 2.4 hectares (6 acres) of public grounds, built specifically for holidaymakers right on beach. Indoor pool, spa and pitch-and-putt on-site, and superb views of the Mourne Mountains. **£££**

County Antrim

Bayview Hotel
2 Bayhead Road, Portballintrae
Tel: 028-2073 4100
www.bayviewhotelni.com
A landmark hotel on a bluff above the picturesque harbour village of Portballintrae. Bedrooms are unfussy and contemporary, and have large windows with amazing

View over the Slieve Donard Hotel grounds

Atlantic views. Good restaurant and lively bar. **££–£££**

Bushmills Inn
9 Dunluce Road, Bushmills
Tel: 028-2073 3000
www.bushmillsinn.com
Conveniently near the world's oldest whiskey distillery: an old country inn of character, with a distinctive whitewashed circular bay, and an excellent restaurant. Bedrooms are individually decorated, some with four-posters. **£££**

RESTAURANTS

With superb local meat and a thriving fishing industry, it is no surprise that Northern Ireland has produced more than its quota of brilliant chefs. Standards are high at all levels, whether it's modern cooking or old favourites.

Restaurant price categories
Prices are for a standard two-course meal with a beer or glass of wine:

£ = below £15
££ = £15–25
£££ = £25–40
££££ = over £40

Derry/Londonderry
Browns Restaurant, Bar and Brasserie
1–2 Bond's Hill
Tel: 028-7134 5180
www.brownsrestaurant.com
A relaxed, unfussy space behind a double shop front, the city's leading contemporary restaurant offers consistently good food. **££**

Mange 2
110–115 Strand Road
Tel: 028-7136 1222
www.mange2derry.com
Top-quality French-inspired cuisine in the heart of Derry, with views of the river. A changing menu features unpretentious dishes that make the most of local produce. **£££**

Inland to Tyrone and Fermanagh
Café Merlot
6 Church Street, Enniskillen
Tel: 028-6632 0918
This informal bistro is a popular new venture from the Blakes of the Hollow pub team. Creative modern food and a cosy dining room. **££**

Oysters Restaurant
37 Patrick Street, Strabane
Tel: 028-7138 2690
www.tyronegoodfoodcircle.com
Oysters is worthy of its fine-dining reputation. A creative chef offers Irish favourites with a modern twist, served by attentive staff. **££**

In and around Armagh
Manor Park Restaurant
2 College Hill, The Mall, Armagh
Tel: 028-3751 5353
www.manorparkrestaurant.co.uk
French through and through (staff, menus, cuisine), albeit with a pride in local Irish ingredients, which are treated with care and cooked with skill by chef James Nelly. **£££**

County Down
Portaferry Hotel
10 The Strand
Tel: 028-4272 8231
www.portaferryhotel.com
Spacious restaurant with an open fire in a beautifully renovated 18th-century hotel overlooking Strangford Lough. Local seafood

is a great strength of the menu, which also features Ulster beef and Mourne lamb. **££**

Restaurant 23
Balmoral Hotel, 13 Seaview, Warrenpoint
Tel: 028-4175 3222
www.restaurant23.com
Small modern restaurant, relaxed and informal with a loyal local clientele, serving fusion and classic dishes in hearty portions. **£££**

County Antrim
The Cellar Restaurant
11b The Diamond, Ballycastle
Tel: 028-2076 3057
www.thecellarrestaurant.co.uk
A delightful surprise in the town centre: a bustling restaurant with church pews, stained glass and cosy snugs. Menus favour seafood with steaks and vegetarian options. **££–£££**

Lynden Heights Restaurant
97 Drumnagreagh Road, Ballygally
Tel: 087-1703 1161
Located on the Antrim coastal drive, there are great sea views. Carefully sourced seafood and game in season feature, along with generous portions and efficient service. **££**

NIGHTLIFE AND ENTERTAINMENT

Thanks to government investment, every community in Northern Ireland has a lively arts centre. Music in pubs is less widespread than in the Republic so ask locally.

Pubs
Denvir's Hotel
English Street, Downpatrick
Tel: 028-4461 2012
www.denvirshotel.com
Old coaching inn with live music in bar.

The House of McDonnell
Ballycastle
Tel: 028-2076 2975
Traditional pub with traditional Irish music every Friday.

Theatre and arts
Burnavon Arts and Cultural Centre
Cookstown
Tel: 028-8676 7994
www.burnavon.com
Multipurpose arts centre for mid-Ulster.

Market Place Theatre & Arts Centre
Market Street, Armagh
Tel: 028-3752 1820
Lively local arts centre.

Millennium Forum Theatre
Newmarket Street, West Bank, Derry
Tel: 028-7126 4455
www.millenniumforum.co.uk
Touring theatre, music and comedy.

SPORTS AND ACTIVITIES

Golf and angling are the traditional sporting pursuits in this neck of the woods.

Angling
County Fermanagh, with its large lakelands offering coarse and game fishing, is a big draw. The Waterways Ireland Classic Fishing Festival is held in spring (tel: 028-6632 3110; **www.fermanaghlakelands.com**).

Golf
NI has many 18-hole golf courses, most less expensive than these two legendary ones.

Royal County Down
Newcastle

Tel: 028-4372 2419
www.royalcountydown.org

Royal Portrush
Tel: 028-7082 2311
www.royalportrushgolfclub.com

Horse racing
Down Royal Racecourse'
Tel: 028-9262 1256
www.downroyal.com
This Lisburn course holds 12 meetings a year.

Walking
The two main mountain ranges, the Mourne Mountains and the Sperrins, have waymarked routes and festivals.
www.sperrinstourism.com
www.visitnewryandmourne.com

A walking festival in County Antrim's Glens

Numerous short looped walks run through woodland, country parks or in the beautifully managed estates owned by the National Trust: **www.nationaltrust.co.uk; www.walkni.com.**
Individual walking itineraries are available from guides. Details at: **www.antrimhills. com** or **www.northcoastwalks.co.uk.**

TOURS
Perhaps because public transport is good in Northern Ireland, there is not a great choice of tours outside Belfast.

City tours
Derry Visitor and Convention Bureau
Tel: 028-7126 7284
www.derryvisitor.com
Take a walking, bus or taxi tour.

Bus tours
Allen's Tours
Tel: 028-9091 5613;
www.allentours.co.uk
Full-day tours to the Giant's Causeway.

FESTIVALS AND EVENTS
St Patrick is closely associated with several places in Northern Ireland and his feast day is widely celebrated, while the Oul Lammas Fair day is a unique experience.

March
St Patrick's Festival
www.armagh.co.uk; www.downdc.gov.uk
Celebrate the saint on his home territory in Armagh and Downpatrick.

April
City of Derry Jazz Festival
www.cityofderryjazzfestival.com
Northern Ireland's biggest jazz festival.

June
Mourne International Walking Festival
www.mournewalking.co.uk
Walk in company by day, free entertainment in Newcastle and Warrenpoint by evening.

August
Oul Lammas Fair
www.moyle-council.org/tourism
Ireland's oldest market fair, in Ballycastle.

PRACTICAL ADVICE

Accommodation – *p.258* **Transport** – *p.261*
Health and safety – *p.268* **Money and budgeting** – *p.270*
Responsible travel – *p.273* **Family holidays** – *p.274*

Accommodation

After the boom years, Ireland has a large surplus of hotel rooms; standards have risen, while prices have dropped. B&Bs have had to invest to compete, ensuring that most rooms now have en suite showers or baths. Places with character and friendly management are doing well at all price levels. Holiday resorts get booked up in advance for bank holiday weekends, during major festivals, and in July and August. Some hotels insist on a two-night minimum stay. Many smaller places in coastal areas close from late October to mid-March or Easter.

HOTELS

Both the Irish Republic and Northern Ireland classify hotels on broadly the same grading system from five- to one-star, as follows:

★★★★★ Top-grade hotels, some in former castles; large rooms with private bathrooms and suites available. High-quality restaurant.

★★★★ Hotels, ranging from modern, purpose-built premises to converted period houses, offering a high standard of comfort and service, and often indoor leisure facilities too. All rooms have private bathrooms.

★★★ Medium-priced hotels, ranging from small, family-run places to larger, more commercial operations. Most rooms have private bathrooms.

★★ Smaller, mostly family-run hotels in small towns, with limited facilities. Some rooms have private bathrooms.

★ Simple but satisfactory accommodation, often come with shared bathrooms.

The Irish Hotels Federation (www.irelandhotels.com) and the Northern Ireland Hotels Federation (www.nihf.co.uk) have excellent websites covering hotels and guesthouses throughout the country. Book rooms

The bar at Inchydoney Island Lodge Spa, Clonakilty, west Cork

Hotel listings	Page
Dublin	88
The southeast	107
County Cork	123
The southwest	142
Limerick and the Shannon	165
The west – Galway and Mayo	182
Inland Ireland	198
The northwest	213
Belfast	229
Northern Ireland	252

either directly with the hotel or through www.discoverireland.com or www.discovernorthernireland.com/accommfinder. If money is no object, plan your stay around the luxurious and characterful heritage properties listed in Ireland's Blue Book at www.irelandsbluebook.com, or those listed on www.gulliver.ie, a dedicated accommodation website that charges a €5 booking fee.

If you are booking directly, check out the hotel's website for special offers. Owing to the current economic climate, a wide range of offers are available. Some offers may require you to stay two or more nights; most are only available online.

The Slieve Bloom B&B in Killarney, Co. Kerry

BUDGET ACCOMMODATION

B&B or guesthouse accommodation is on offer both in towns and in the countryside (if a B&B has more than five rooms, it is officially a guesthouse). In recent years, Irish B&Bs have increased greatly in professionalism. The new type of B&B is often purpose-built with en suite bathrooms, and differs from budget hotels only in that it doesn't usually have a bar or restaurant. Evening meals can, however, sometimes be provided if notice is given before noon.

B&Bs offer good value for money, and the home-made breakfast is usually far superior to the breakfast in a budget hotel. B&B room rates currently average about €35–40 per night, with some more upmarket places charging €50–60 in high season. Do bargain if you are staying more than one night.

B&B Ireland (www.b&bireland. com) is the main association, and also produces a printed guide. Farmhouse B&Bs offer excellent value and can provide a memorable experience of rural life – though many farmhouses are actually modern bungalows. See www.irishfarmholidays.com for a selection of over 300. Family Homes of Ireland (www.familyhomes.ie) is an association of people offering accommodation in their family home; many are places of great character.

OTHER ACCOMMODATION

The Irish student and youth travel company USIT runs **Kinlay House year-round centres** (www.kinlayhouse. ie) in Dublin (tel: 01-679 6644), Galway (tel: 091-565 244) and Cork (tel: 021-450 8966). Prices start at €16 per night. During the long vacation, from mid-June to mid-September, they also offer self-catering apartments in **UCD Village**, Belfield Campus, Dublin 4 (tel:

Camping near Leenane, Galway

01-269 7111). **Brookfield Holiday Village** also offers apartments at College Road, Cork (tel: 021-434 4032). Prices start at €25 per night.

YOUTH HOSTELS

Ireland has two kinds of hostel: those belonging to An Oige, and independent hostels. All independent hostels are privately owned, and can vary from scenic organic farms to tiny townhouses stacked with bunk beds. They are generally relaxed places with cooking facilities and no curfew. Prices range from €15 to €25 for a dormitory bed, though Dublin is more expensive. Note that in July and August, and at festival times, hostels can fill up quickly. An umbrella organisation for about 125 privately owned hostels is **Independent Holiday Hostels of Ireland (IHH)**; tel: 01-836 4700; www. hostels-ireland.com.

The **Irish Youth Hostel Association (An Oige)**, 61 Mountjoy Street, Dublin 7; tel: 01-830 4555; www.

irelandyha.org, has 23 hostels in the Republic, with rates varying from €18 to €25 per person per night, with a €2 discount per night for members (adults: €20 per year). Hostels in Northern Ireland are run by **Hostelling International Northern Ireland** (www.hini.org.uk). Members of the International Youth Hostel Federation can use any of these.

CAMPING

Camping is a seasonal activity in Ireland. It's not advisable between October and April. Many farmers let campers stay on their property, but always ask first, and offer a few euros. Prices at campsites vary, but are usually around €10–15 to pitch a tent, and €2–6 per person in addition. Lists of camping and caravanning parks and their facilities are available from tourist information offices or the **Irish Caravan and Camping Council** (www.camping-ireland.ie). In Northern Ireland see www.discov ernorthernireland.com/camping.

SELF-CATERING

This is available in houses, cottages, apartments, caravans and even castles. If you are looking for a traditional Irish cottage, note that many are newly built in clusters and used solely for holiday rentals. Bargains can be found off-season, but in July and August expect to pay around €650 a week for a 4-bed cottage. For listings and information, contact the **Irish Self-Catering Federation**; tel: 08-1830 0186; www.iscf.ie; or the **Northern Ireland Self-Catering Holiday Association**; tel: 028-9043 6632; www.nischa.com.

Transport

GETTING TO IRELAND
By air

The main carriers from Britain are Aer Arran (www.aerarran.com), Aer Lingus (www.aerlingus.com), bmi (www.flybmi.com), bmibaby (www.bmibaby.com), easyJet (www.easyjet.com) and Ryanair (www.ryanair.com).

There are flights from Britain and Europe to Belfast, Dublin, Cork and Shannon airports, with over 30 airlines flying from 70 destinations. The flight time from London to Dublin and Belfast is about 1 hour and 10 minutes; to Cork it's 1 hour. The flight time from Amsterdam to Dublin is 1 hour and 45 minutes, and from Paris 1 hour and 30 minutes. If you plan to visit mainly the southwest of Ireland, use Cork Airport. There are also frequent flights from British airports to regional airports in Kerry, Galway, Waterford and Knock (County Mayo).

There are direct flights from the US to both Dublin and Shannon airports and Belfast International Airport. The main carriers are Aer Lingus (www.aerlingus.com), American Airlines (www.aa.com), Continental Airlines (www.continental.com), Delta Airlines (www.delta.com) and US Airways (www.usairways.com). There are direct flights from Boston, Chicago, New York, Newark, Orlando and Philadelphia. The flight time from New York to Dublin is 5 hours and 30 minutes, from Boston 7 hours, and from Chicago 8 hours.

Travel from Australia, New Zealand and South Africa is generally via London or one of the European or Gulf cities that have direct flights to London (eg Frankfurt or Abu Dhabi). From Australia or New Zealand it takes more than 24 hours to reach Ireland. From South Africa it takes at least 13 hours.

The best way to get a cheap flight from the UK or the European mainland to Ireland is to book online as far ahead as possible. Competition is intense, and prices can be very low – often below €50 each way. On the other hand, booking at the last minute can mean that the same flight will cost you around €180 each way.

Ireland's main airports are:
Dublin Airport (DUB); tel: 01-814 1111; www.dublinairport.com; 10km (6 miles) north of the city centre. Transatlantic flights and flights from

Flights from the UK and elsewhere in Europe come into Cork Airport

A flock of sheep causes a hold-up in County Antrim, in Northern Ireland

Europe and the UK; domestic and holiday charters.

Cork Airport (ORK); tel: 021-431 3131; www.corkairport.com; 5km (3 miles) south of the city centre. Flights from the UK and the rest of Europe; domestic and holiday charters.

Shannon Airport (SNN); tel: 061-712 000; www.shannonairport.com; situated on the west coast, 25km (16 miles) to the west of Limerick. Transatlantic flights, and flights from Europe and the UK; domestic and holiday charters.

Ireland West Airport (NOC); tel: 094-936 7222; www.irelandwestairport.com; 40km (30 miles) south of Ballina; 55km (34 miles) southeast of Sligo. Daily flights from the UK (8 destinations), flights to summer-sun hotspots, and holiday charters.

Belfast International Airport (BFS); tel: 028-9448 4848; www.belfastairport.com; at Aldergrove, 24km (15 miles) from the city. Local and UK flights, and all international traffic.

By sea

If you are visiting mainly the southwest of Ireland, Rosslare is the best port to use. The longer sea crossing from Swansea to Cork saves a considerable amount of driving on both sides. For the rest of the Republic of Ireland use Dublin or Dun Laoghaire. For Northern Ireland, head for Belfast or Larne.

The main ferry routes include Dublin/Dun Laoghaire to Holyhead (Wales) or Liverpool (England); Rosslare to Pembroke or Fishguard (Wales), Roscoff and Cherbourg (France); Larne to Fleetwood, Cairnryan or Troon (Scotland); Belfast to Stranraer (Scotland); and Cork to Swansea (Wales). Many routes vary by season; seas can be rough in winter.

The main ferry operators are:

Irish Ferries; www.irishferries.com; tel: 08717-300 400. *Services*: Holyhead–Dublin North Wall, two crossings daily (3 hours 15 minutes); Holyhead–Dublin, fast service, four crossings daily (1 hour 49 minutes); Pembroke–Rosslare (3 hours 45 minutes). There are also sailings every second day between Rosslare and Roscoff and Cherbourg.

Stena Line; www.stenaline.co.uk; tel: 01-204 7700 in Dublin, 08705-707 070 in the UK. *Services*: Holyhead–Dublin (3 hours 15 minutes); Holyhead–Dun Laoghaire (1 hour 39 minutes); Fishguard–Rosslare (3 hours 30 minutes or 1 hour 50 minutes); Stranraer–Belfast (1 hour 45 minutes); Larne–Fleetwood (8 hours).

Fastnet Line; www.fastnetline.com; tel: 021-437 8892 in Cork, 0844-576 8831 in the UK. *Services*: Swansea–Cork (10 hours).

P&O Irish Sea Ferries; www.poirish sea.com; tel: 0871-664 4777 in the UK. *Services*: Cairnryan–Larne (1 hour 45 minutes); Troon–Larne (1 hour 49 minutes, mid-Mar–mid-Oct); Liverpool–Dublin (8 hours).

By bus

Bus companies run through services from various locations in England and Wales via the ferries. The ride to Galway from London, for example, takes around 17 hours by **Bus Éireann/National Express**, tel: 01-836 6111 in Dublin or 08705-808 080 in Northern Ireland; www.buseireann.ie or www.nationalexpress.com.

GETTING AROUND IRELAND

Public transport provision is not comprehensive. While there are plenty of intercity trains and buses, local services within each region are minimal. The best way to get around Ireland is therefore by car. Without a car, the best bet is to base yourself in a

Picturesque coastal drive on Achill Island, Co. Mayo

regional city and use public transport for day trips into the hinterland.

In the Republic, there are two national bus service providers: **Bus Éireann Expressway** (serving provincial areas nationwide) and **Iarnród Éireann** (operating intercity trains as well as the **DART**, the Dublin Area Rapid Transit system).

For information on bus travel within Dublin, contact **Dublin Bus**, tel: 01-873 4222; www.dublinbus. ie. Buses are plentiful, and dedicated bus lanes keep the traffic moving. The **LUAS** tram system, tel: 1-800-300 604; www.luas.ie, offers a handy connection between Connolly and Heuston train stations. **Aircoach.ie**, tel: 01-844 7118; www.aircoach.ie, has daily services from Dublin Airport via the city centre to Cork. **Citylink**, tel: 091-564 164; www.citylink.ie, links Dublin Airport to Cork and to Galway via Shannon Airport.

Eurailpasses are valid for bus and train travel in the Republic, excluding city services. Reduced-rate Rambler passes provide unlimited travel on buses and trains (excluding city services) for either 8 or 15 days. Tickets can be bought from any bus or train station in the Republic, or through a travel agent in your home country.

Domestic flights

There is a limited network of domestic flights linking Dublin with Cork, Shannon and the following regional airports: City of Derry, Donegal, Galway, Ireland West, Kerry, Sligo and Waterford. There are flights from Cork to Dublin, Donegal, Galway and Ireland West. Flight times for most

Boats moored at Banagher harbour, in County Offaly

as little as €10 each way off-peak, compared to the standard fare of €71 return. Full-rate tickets can be bought immediately before travel from the ticket offices at stations. For information on rail travel, contact **Iarnród Éireann**, tel: 01-836 6222; www.irishrail.ie.

In Northern Ireland, trains run from Belfast northwest to Derry via Ballymena and Coleraine, east to Bangor and south to Dublin via Newry. For rail information, call **Translink** in Belfast, tel: 028-9066 6630; www.translink.co.uk.

Intercity coaches

The state-owned bus company, Bus Éireann, is the major operator of intercity coaches. Express bus time-tables are sold in newsagents. Most towns have a central bus station, which can often be found adjacent to the rail station. Bus fares are generally much cheaper than rail fares, but the journey time is longer. Cork to Dublin by bus takes up to 5 hours, and costs about €18, compared to 2 hours 50 minutes by train at a standard fare of €66 one way (cheaper deals can be found online, and return fares offer better value for money).

Once off the main routes, small towns and villages may only be served by a couple of buses a week. The Bus Éireann website is excellent for route planning and also provides information on fares. For details of Expressway services, contact **Bus Éireann** at tel: 01-836 6111; www.buseireann.ie.

Other coach operators include: **Citylink.ie,** tel: 091-564 164; www.citylink.ie, a private bus company

domestic routes are around 30 to 40 minutes. The main operators are Aer Arran, Aer Lingus and Ryanair.

Trains

Trains in Ireland are clean and well run, and generally arrive on time. Trains radiate from Dublin on different lines, terminating in Waterford, Cork, Tralee, Limerick, Galway, Westport, Ballina and Sligo. The journey from Dublin to Tralee takes approximately 4 hours, and the route from Dublin to Sligo about 3½ hours. A new line links Limerick and Galway via Ennis, and there are commuter lines from Cork to Cobh and Midleton, and from Dublin along the coast.

In most cases, however, it is cheaper – and a more flexible option – to travel around a region using bus services. All the same, booking online with Irish Rail can lead to worthwhile savings if you can book early and travel at off-peak times. Trains from Dublin to Cork, for example, can cost linking Cork to Galway and Clifden via Shannon Airport.

Aircoach.ie, tel: 01-844 7118; www.aircoach.ie, runs daily services from Dublin Airport via the city centre and six stops en route to Cork.

In Northern Ireland buses are operated by the state-owned Ulsterbus service, with good links to those towns not served by trains. An Irish Rover bus ticket from Ulsterbus can be used in both Northern Ireland and the Republic, and costs about £56 (€64) for 3 days, and £127 (€146) for 8 days. It also includes city centre bus travel everywhere but Dublin. For more details, contact **Ulsterbus**, tel: 028-9033 3000; www.translink.co.uk or www.ulsterbus.co.uk.

Boats and ferries

With over 4,800km (3,000 miles) of coastline and 14,480km (9,000 miles) of rivers and streams, Ireland is a boater's paradise. You might rent a fishing boat to take advantage of the excellent freshwater and sea fishing, or enjoy the country's scenic splendours in a rented cruiser (normally available with two to eight berths).

No boating permit is needed for navigating the Shannon, and all companies offer a free piloting lesson. Popular points of departure are Carrick-on-Shannon, Athlone, Banagher and Killaloe.

Reputable boat-hire companies can be found at www.discoverireland.ie and www.discovernorthernireland.com. For information on boating in both the Republic of Ireland and Northern Ireland, contact **Waterways Ireland**, tel: 028-6632 3004; www.waterwaysireland.org.

The rugged islands off the coast of Ireland are rich in folklore, antiquities and spectacular natural wonders (especially birdlife). Fáilte Ireland's publication *Explore Islands of Ireland* lists details of all accessible islands and provides contacts for scheduled ferries. See www.irelandsislands.com.

Cycling

Ireland is a good destination for cyclists, and many enthusiasts visit the country to take to its highways and byways. For those to do come, it is vital to bring wet-weather gear – and to be prepared for hilly roads.

Throughout the Republic, rent-a-bike outlets hire out sturdy Raleigh Tourer bicycles, which can sometimes be delivered to airports. Expect to pay upwards of €70 a week for rental. For a list of Raleigh rent-a-bike dealers, see www.raleigh.ie. In Dublin, you can hire bicycles and accessories from **Cycleways**, 185–186 Parnell Street;

Cycling and fine coastal views in The Burren in County Clare

Approaching the Errigal Mountains, in Co. Donegal

Transport

tel: 01-873 4748; www.cycleways.com. Another organisation is **Dublin Bikes** (www.dublinbikes.ie). Their bicycles can be hired and returned to 44 stations around the city. A three-day ticket costs €2, payable by credit card.

Organised cycling holidays are increasingly popular, either travelling in a group with a back-up van, or cycling independently to pre-booked accommodation, with baggage transfer. **Irish Cycle Hire** (tel: 041-685 3772; www.irishcyclehire.com) will rent you a bike, as well as offering self-guided tours with luggage transfer. Dublin-based **Irish Cycling Safaris** (tel: 01-260 0749; www.irish-cyclingsafaris.com) offer routes on the Antrim coast, the highlands of Donegal, the Ring of Kerry, Wicklow and west Mayo.

Ireland has a strong tradition of road racing, and there are races most weekends, organised by **Cycling Ireland** (tel: 01-855 1522; www.cyclingireland.ie).

DRIVING

Outside the cities, Ireland's roads are still amongst the least congested in Europe – although it's hard to believe it when stuck in a traffic jam in Dublin's ever-expanding suburbs or on the ring roads of Galway, Cork or Killarney. Irish drivers – especially outside Dublin – are generally courteous.

Road conditions

Roads linking the main cities are mainly motorway or dual carriageway. Most secondary and regional routes are smaller, two-lane roads (one in each direction).

There are toll charges for using the M50 Dublin orbital motorway, the M1 northern motorway, the Limerick tunnel plus three roads outside the Dublin area. Visit www.eflow.ie for information on barrier-free tolling.

In some areas finding a petrol station open on a Sunday morning may be a problem, so it's best to top up on Saturday for weekend excursions. Petrol (gas) is sold by the litre.

Regulations

The rule on both sides of the border is to drive on the left and give way to traffic coming from the right. Drivers and front-seat passengers must wear seat belts; back-seat passengers must also wear belts if they are fitted.

In the Republic, the speed limit is indicated in kilometres, and is 45kmh, 60kmh or 80kmh (28mph, 37mph or 50mph) in urban areas, and 80kmh or 100kmh (50mph or 62mph) on National Routes (green signposts), with 120kmh (75mph) permitted on motorways. Remember when

Approximate driving times
Dublin–Limerick – 3 hours
Dublin–Galway – 3 hours
Dublin–Belfast – 2 hours
Dublin–Waterford – 2½ hours

entering Northern Ireland that speed limits are indicated in miles – 30mph (48kmh) in built-up areas, 60mph (96kmh) on country roads and 70mph (113kmh) on motorways and dual carriageways. On-the-spot fines can be issued for speeding offences. Drink-driving laws are strict. It is an offence to drive with a concentration of alcohol exceeding 80mg per 100ml of blood.

Motoring associations

The Automobile Association of Ireland is affiliated to its UK counterpart, and has a reciprocal membership agreement, so if you are a member, be sure to take your AA card with you. Otherwise, contact your car-rental company for assistance. In the Republic, AA Ireland can be contacted at tel: 01-617 999; www.aaireland.ie. Contact details in Northern Ireland are tel: 0800-887 766; www.theaa.com.

Car hire

If visiting in July and August, be sure to book in advance. Car hire is expensive in Ireland, and advance booking as part of a fly-drive or train-ferry-drive package often leads to a better deal, as does booking online. Drivers under 25 and over 70 may have to pay a higher rate. Most companies will not rent cars to people over 76. If you intend to drive across the border, inform your rental company beforehand to check that you are fully insured. The big international car-hire companies have offices in all major cities, airports and ferry terminals. Local and international car hire companies in both the Republic and Northern Ireland are listed on www.carhireireland.com.

ACCESSIBILITY

Ireland is still introducing facilities such as ramps and toilets that are accessible for people with disabilities. Public transport also lags behind, especially outside Dublin. However, visitors with disabilities often find that people's helpfulness makes up for the lack of amenities. The key organisation to contact for practical information, including wheelchair sales and rental, parking permits and holidays is the Irish Wheelchair Association, Ara Cuchulainn, Blackheath Drive, Clontarf, Dublin; tel: 01-818 6400; www.iwa.ie.

The official government body responsible for the rights of people with disabilities is the National Disability Authority, 25 Clyde Road, Ballsbridge, Dublin 4; tel: 01-608-0400; www.nda.ie. They will have up-to-date information on disability issues. The Head Office of Fáilte Ireland can advise on attractions and accommodation suitable for disabled visitors: 88–95 Amiens Street, Dublin 1; tel: 01-884 7700; www.discoverireland.ie. In Northern Ireland the campaigning body Disability Action also offers practical advice: 2 Annadale Avenue, Belfast; tel: 028-9029 7880; www.disabilityaction.org.

Health and safety

MEDICAL CARE

Both Ireland and Northern Ireland are part of the European Union, and have standard reciprocal healthcare arrangements. Australian Medicare has an arrangement with Ireland and Britain (Northern Ireland) that covers emergency hospital treatment but not GP surgery visits, which cost on average around €50 per consultation. None of these reciprocal arrangements will cover all medical costs, or repatriation, so it is advisable to take out travel insurance. Most travel policies exclude certain adventure sports unless an extra premium is paid: take note if you intend to go horse riding, kayaking, mountaineering, diving or windsurfing while in Ireland.

Ireland has a similar standard of medical care to the rest of western

Emergency contacts

Ambulance: 112 or 999
Fire service: 112 or 999
Police: 112 or 999
Coastguard: 112 or 999
Northern Ireland: dial 999 for all services

Europe. General practitioners expect payment in cash or by credit card at the conclusion of the appointment, as do the out-of-hours services that operate in most areas. Pharmacies generally display a green cross. Pharmacists or your accommodation providers will recommend a doctor. Treatment in one of the 35 public hospital accident and emergency units is free to those who have been referred by a GP, and to those who are entitled to hospital services under EU regulations or other reciprocal agreements. Others may be charged €100. If you are admitted to a public hospital, normal charges of €75 per day apply.

Condoms can be purchased at supermarkets and in pharmacies and in pub toilets across Ireland. The pill, including the morning-after pill, is only available on prescription. Note that abortion is illegal in Ireland.

Major hospitals

Dublin: Mater Misericordiae University Hospital, Eccles Street; tel: 01-803 2000; www.mater.ie.
Belfast: Royal Victoria Hospital, 274 Grosvenor Road, Belfast; tel: 028-9024 0503; www.belfasttrust.hscni.net.
Cork: University Hospital, Wilton;

Police officer patrolling the beach at Portrush, Co. Antrim

Minihans Chemist on Cork City's pedestrianised Oliver Plunkett Street

tel: 021-454 6400; www.cuh.hse.ie.
Limerick: Limerick Regional Hospital, Dooradoyle; tel: 061-301 111; www.hse.ie.

Natural hazards

Lifeguards are only on duty at Blue Flag beaches during the summer months. In their absence, ask other surfers or swimmers for local knowledge about safe places to surf or swim, riptides and other hazards. Do not attempt to surf near the Cliffs of Moher and the Aran Islands without local knowledge; the water is dangerously shallow.

Be sure to carry a mobile phone when walking: coverage is good even in relatively remote areas. Check the forecast before setting out, as weather can change dramatically in a very short time owing to the Atlantic weather systems. The most reliable meterological service is the official state one, Met Eireann – www.met.ie.

Irish way-marked routes are often in remote parts of the country, and way-marks can become hidden by vegetation. Walkers are advised to carry a compass and a detailed map. Be sure to wear strong hiking boots or shoes.

CRIME

In Ireland the police are known as Garda Síochána – Guardians of the Peace – and in the normal course of duty they do not carry arms. In Northern Ireland policing is carried out by the Police Service of Northern Ireland. All officers are routinely armed. In Dublin, report any crime to Store Street Garda Station, tel: 01-666 8109. In Northern Ireland contact the local police station or tel: 0845 600 8000; www.psni.police.uk.

Health and safety

Embassies and consulates

Australia: Fitzwilton House, Wilton Terrace, Dublin 2; tel: 01-664 5300; www.ireland.embassy.gov.au
Britain: 29 Merrion Road, Dublin 4; tel: 01-205 3700; www.britishembassyinireland.fco.gov.uk
Canada: 7–8 Wilton Terrace, Dublin 2; tel: 01-231 4000; www.canada.ie

New Zealand: None. See www.nzembassy.com/united-kingdom
South Africa: 2nd Floor, Alexandra House, Earlsfort Centre, Earlsfort Terrace Dublin 2; tel: 01-661 5553; www.dfa.gov.za/foreign/bilateral/ireland.html
US: 42 Elgin Road, Dublin 4; tel: 01-668 8777; www.usembassy.ie

Money and budgeting

CURRENCY

Currency: Euro € notes in denominations of 500, 200 100, 50, 20, 10, 5; coins are 1 euro, and 50 cents, 20, 10, 5, 2, 1. Exchange rates are US$ = €0.75, and GB£ = €1.15.

Northern Ireland uses the British pound. In border areas, both currencies are accepted at most large establishments including petrol stations and supermarkets.

Amounts of currency that exceed €10,000 must be declared on arrival or departure.

CASH AND CARDS

Banks and their ATMs are the best places to get money. Major Irish banks have 24-hour ATMs in cities and larger towns. In rural areas you may find ATMs in supermarkets, convenience stores and petrol stations; they are supplied by the major banks, and do not charge extra commission. You are able to use an international PIN to access money from international bank accounts using these machines.

MasterCard and Visa are widely accepted (American Express less so, and Diners Club rarely), although it's cash only at smaller pubs and cafés, take-aways and some B&Bs. Traveller's cheques can be exchanged at bureaux de change and major banks.

ATM-related scams using skimming machines to collect credit-card numbers are becoming more prevalent. Try to use an ATM that is located in a well-lit branch lobby. Be sure to keep your PIN details concealed when entering them on the ATM keyboard.

Some of the more expensive hotels may levy an additional service charge as a percentage on top of the room

Pulling a pint of one of the country's best exports

Money-saving tips

- Buy a heritage card at the first state-owned site you visit (€21, €16 seniors, €8 students).
- Always ask if there is a price for seniors (often called golden years), generally defined as being over 55.
- Make midday lunch your main meal, not dinner, and eat it at a pub carvery.
- In Dublin buy a visitor's bus travel pass for 1, 3 or 7 days.
- Look out for 'kids go free' offers for attractions and cruises.
- Book a family room, for two adults and two children.
- Buy air, rail and bus tickets online as far ahead of travel as possible.
- Plan your day around free activities: beaches, country walks, national parks, self-guided city walks.
- Visit the Tourist Information Office first, and stock up on free maps and brochures.

Ireland may be fairly pricey, given the euro exchange rate, but bargains can still be had

bill; be sure to enquire when booking. Some restaurants add a service charge and also expect tips. If there is a service charge, tipping is at the customer's discretion, and should only be done if the service was exceptionally good.

Tipping in restaurants and cafés is common, but not obligatory; about 10 percent of the bill is standard. Bar staff do not expect tips, and most people do not tip when served bar food. The exception is Dublin lounge bars, where drinks are brought to your table, and a small tip (20–50 cents) is expected. Tipping taxi drivers is optional; about 10 percent of the fare, or rounding up to nearest full euro is the norm.

TAX

VAT is charged at 21 percent for goods in the luxury category and 13.5 percent for most other goods and services (but only 9 percent in the tourism sector). Certain goods and services are zero-rated. VAT is generally included in prices. Note that rates may change as Ireland combats the economic downturn; check www.revenue.ie to confirm the latest rates. Non-EU visitors can claim back sales taxes on purchases made in the Republic. Participating stores have a 'Tax Free Shopping' sign in the window. You must complete a tax refund document, and present this and the goods at customs on departure. Some airports will refund you on the spot; otherwise, mail the validated document back to the store, and a refund will be issued.

Enjoying the view at the Cliffs of Moher, one of Ireland's most popular sights

BUDGETING FOR YOUR TRIP

Ireland is generally an expensive destination for visitors coming from the UK and the US, and also for visitors from elsewhere in the Eurozone. Alcohol and tobacco are far more expensive than in the rest of the Eurozone; eating out also tends to work out to be relatively pricey.

A cheap return flight from the UK costs approximately £60 (€69); a standard flight costs around £90 (€103). There are currently no business-class flights on this route.

A cheap return flight from the US costs approximately US$460 (€320); a standard flight costs around US$870 (€605) and a first-class flight in the region of US$2,900 (€2,016).

For a budget, backpacker-style holiday you will need to set aside €490 (£430/US$693) per person per week. A standard family holiday for four will cost around €2,400 (£2,106/US$3,393) per week. A luxury, no-expense-spared break can cost over €3,600 (£3,159/US$5,050) per person per week.

Budgeting costs

Top-class/boutique hotel: €160–220 for a double room
Standard-class hotel: €90–120 for a double room
Bed & breakfast: €80–90 for a double
Youth hostel: €15–20 per person
Campsite: €10–15 per tent
Domestic flight: €50 Dublin–Cork
Intercity coach ticket: €15 Dublin–Cork, €18 Dublin–Galway
Intercity train ticket: €51 round-trip Dublin–Cork, €35 round-trip Dublin–Galway
Car hire: €35 per day
Petrol: €1.50 a litre
10-minute taxi ride: €12
Airport shuttle bus: €6
Short bus ride: €1.80
One-day travel pass: €10

Breakfast: €8.50
Lunch in a café: €8
Coffee/tea in a café: €2.20
Main course in a budget restaurant: €12
Main course in a moderate restaurant: €20
Main course in an expensive restaurant: €35
Bottle of wine in a restaurant: €20 and up
Beer in a pub: €5
Museum admission: €4–16
Day trip from Galway to the Cliffs of Moher: €25
Half-day guided kayak tour: €35
One hour's horseback riding: €35–40
Theatre/concert ticket: €25 (theatre), €80 (big-name music act)
Shopping item: €40 and upwards for a woollen sweater
Nightclub entry: €8–25

Responsible travel

GETTING THERE

Perhaps the greenest way to get to Ireland is by ferry. Services operate from the UK, Roscoff and Cherbourg *(see pp.262–3)*. The carbon footprint of a return flight to Ireland from London is approximately 0.2519 tons of carbon. A return flight from New York to Dublin generates 2.2906 tons of carbon.

To offset your carbon footprint by contributing to a renewable energy or reforestation project, see www.sustainabletravelinternational.org. The suggested contribution to offset a return flight from London to Dublin is US$6.39 (roughly £4), and for a New York to Dublin flight is $58.07 (roughly £35).

ECOTOURISM

Ecotourism is slow in coming to Ireland. For details of green breaks and activity holidays contact **Green Box**, based in Leitrim (tel: 071-985 6898; www.greenbox.ie). It offers breaks with eco-friendly accommodation in the North and Northwest of Ireland (Leitrim, Sligo, Donegal, Fermanagh, Cavan and Monaghan), including organic gardening and cookery courses, spa breaks and cycling trails. The Green Box site also has details of a Green Travel App for Ireland by author and TV presenter Catherine Mack. This includes details of over 120 green places to stay, and activities such as hiking, biking and canoeing in the whole of the rest of Ireland.

At the time of writing only one company offers yurt holidays in Ireland, but its success makes it likely that others will quickly follow. The yurts are on Cape Clear Island, a delightful destination for walkers and bird watchers, 40 minutes from Baltimore on the coast of west Cork. See www.yurt-holidays-ireland.com.

For details of how to have a working holiday on an organic farm in Ireland, see www.wwoof.ie. Membership of the organisation is the first condition, and costs €20 per person or €25 for two people or a family. Hosts all over Ireland can be previewed on the website.

Responsible travel

Farmstays and holidays working on farms are increasingly popular in Ireland

Family holidays

PRACTICALITIES

The Irish have a welcoming attitude towards families, children and babies. Irish cities and towns are well provided with facilities for travellers with children: nappy-changing facilities are widely available, all supermarkets sell a range of nappies and other baby essentials, and most hotels are hospitable to families, for example. All major car-hire companies will supply and fit baby car seats, though sometimes there is an additional charge for this service. Bring pushchairs and carrier backpacks with you, however, as they are generally not readily available for hire.

ACCOMMODATION

The majority of accommodation in Ireland is child-friendly. The rare exceptions ('not suitable for under 12s') are usually upmarket hotels or guesthouses with antiques, or else spas and other places that offer quiet retreats for stressed-out executives.

On the other hand, most mid-range hotels in seaside resorts with leisure facilities offer kids' clubs during Irish school holidays. In summer these run from June to August, with children returning to school in the first few days of September. If there is no formal babysitting arrangement, hotel receptions can usually find someone with whom you can make a private arrangement. Cots are widely available, and most leisure centres have a children's pool, to be used under adult supervision. Children under 16

are not allowed to use facilities such as saunas, Jacuzzis or steam rooms.

Most farmhouse B&Bs make a special point of welcoming children and making sure that they are entertained. Caravan parks and clusters of self-catering cottages often present children with the opportunity to meet other kids. Irish children tend to mix very easily with other children of all ages, and often the older children automatically look after any younger children in the group.

FOOD AND DRINK

Most places – even pubs – have children's menus, or will serve smaller

A young musician playing the fiddle

portions of the adult menu. High chairs are widely available in most daytime restaurants. Children are generally welcome in restaurants. In pubs, children are generally allowed in all areas, though they are expected to be under appropriate adult supervision. There are usually designated (normally outside) areas for children to play in. Many landlords like children to be off the premises by 7pm; it is illegal for under 18s to be in a bar after 9pm (10pm May–Sept). Consult www.drinkaware.ie for further details.

ATTRACTIONS AND ACTIVITIES

Children are welcomed at activity centres that offer climbing, zip wires and other activities – after all, their main business in the off-season is school trips. For kayaking, horseback riding and other adventure activities, children under 16 are expected to be accompanied, unless they are taking a specific children's course. Similarly, most Irish visitor centres and museums have been designed with children in mind, and there is often a special self-guided children's tour or project, or a children's room with crayons and colouring books; ask at the entrance.

The following highlights are guaranteed to keep kids amused. Of course, the numerous sandy beaches around the coast are also a good bet.
Dublin: The Viking Splash Tour; Dublinia; Temple Bar is packed with shops selling the kind of souvenirs children like to buy.
The Southeast: Irish National Heritage Park, Wexford; Waterford Museum of

A glorious sandy beach at Connemara, Co. Galway

Family holidays

Treasures; Dunbrody Famine Ship.
County Cork: Blarney Castle; Fota Wild Life Park.
Southwest: Seafari Ecotour, Kenmare; jaunting car ride, Killarney; Kerry Bog Village Museum, Glenbeigh.
The Shannon Region: Bunratty Castle and Folk Park; the Cliffs of Moher.
The West: Salmon Weir, Galway City; Lough Corrib cruise, Cong or Oughterard; Westport House and Pirate Adventure Centre; National Museum of Country Life, Castlebar.
The Northwest: the beach at Strandhill, County Sligo; the seafront, Bun doran, County Donegal.
Belfast: Belfast Titanic Centre; Botanic Gardens; Ulster Folk and Transport Musuem.
Northern Ireland: Giant's Causeway; Carrick-a-Rede Rope Bridge; Old Derry Walls.

SETTING THE SCENE

History – *p.278* **Culture** – *p.286* **Food and drink** – *p.292*

History

EARLY HISTORY

Stone Age relics reveal that the first inhabitants arrived in Ireland some time after 8000BC. The first settlers probably travelled on foot from Scandinavia to Scotland – England was linked at that time to Northern Europe by land – then across what was a narrow sea gap to Ireland.

During the late Stone Age, inhabitants began to settle down and farm. Tombs and temples from this period can be found across the country. These monuments range from simple stone tripods in the middle of a farmer's field to sophisticated passage-graves built on astronomical principles and decorated with mysterious spiral and zigzag engravings.

New settlers introduced Bronze Age skills from Europe, but by the time of the Iron Age Ireland was lagging behind the Continent. Iron Age technologies only reached the island in the last years of the pre-Christian era, thanks to the migration of Celtic tribes from Central Europe.

The Roman legions that marched across Western Europe and into Britain stopped short at the Irish Sea. The island was therefore left free to develop its own way of life during the centuries of the great Roman Empire. Although Irish society was decentralised in scores of bickering mini-kingdoms, nevertheless, a single culture did evolve. Druids and poets told legends in a common language that is clearly recognisable as the Irish version of Gaelic.

ST PATRICK

The Celts frequently staged raids on Roman Britain for booty and slaves. During one 5th-century raid, they rounded up a large number of captives. One of these 'immigrants', a 16-year-old boy named Patrick, later became Ireland's national saint. After spending a few years as a humble shepherd, he escaped to Britain, became a monk, and finally returned to convert the 'heathens' to Christianity.

The early Christians developed a system of monasteries to serve as the centre for all Church activities. This suited life in Ireland – a rural, sparsely populated island. While the rest of Europe crawled through the Dark Ages, the Irish monasteries kept the flame of Western culture alight. Scholarly minds from different regions of Europe converged on the island to participate in its religious and intellectual life. The monks of the 'island

Statue of the Irish patron saint, Patrick, at the pilgrimage site of Croagh Patrick, Mayo

of saints and scholars' dutifully created illuminated manuscripts. These books remain some of Ireland's most valuable works of art.

THE VIKINGS

At the turn of the 9th century, well-armed warriors sailed in from Scandinavia aboard sleek boats. The undefended Irish monasteries, full of relics and treasures, were easy targets. The shallow-draught ships moved in and attacked virtually at will, making their way around the Irish coast and up its rivers as well. This danger inspired tall 'round towers', which variously served as watchtowers, belfries, storehouses and escape hatches. Dozens still stand. But plunder wasn't the only thing on the Viking agenda: they soon added trading colonies around the coast and founded the first towns on the rural island – Dublin, Waterford and Limerick.

The Irish learned sailing, weaponry and metalworking from the Norse, but resented their presence. In the end, the natives ousted the Vikings, with the last struggle taking place in 1014 at the Battle of Clontarf, when the High King of Ireland, Brian Ború, defeated the tough Norse and their Irish allies, although he himself was killed in the battle.

RIVALRY AND REVENGE

Ireland's next invasion was motivated by jealousy. In 1152, the wife of Tiernan O'Rourke, an Irish warrior-king, was carried off by rival Dermot MacMurrough of Leinster. Allegedly, she was a willing victim, and possibly even the instigator. Regardless,

St Mary's church roof and tiny round tower, Glendalough, Co. Wicklow

O'Rourke got his queen back a few months later, but wasn't about to forgive and forget. He forced Dermot to flee, in 1166, first to England and then France. But from there, Dermot was able to shape an alliance with a powerful Norman nobleman, the Earl of Pembroke. The Earl, known as Strongbow, agreed to lead an army to sweep Dermot back to power. In exchange, the Earl was to be given the hand of Dermot's daughter and the right to succeed him to the Leinster throne. The hardy Normans – the elite of Europe's warriors – won the Battle of Waterford in 1169, and Strongbow married his princess.

In the years following his decisive victory, Strongbow tightened his grip using the Norman war machine, and local Irish forces were stunned and swiftly defeated. Indeed, things went so well for Strongbow that his overlord, King Henry II of England, arrived in 1171 to assert his sovereignty.

Painting depicting the legendary Battle of the Boyne, which took place in 1690

THE ENGLISH ASCENDANCY

The Anglo-Norman occupation brought profound and long-lasting changes. Towns, churches and castles were built alongside institutions for feudal government. There was much resentment among the Irish, but for the colonial rulers the challenge of revolt was less serious than the danger of their own cultural assimilation. With settlers adopting the ways of the natives, rather than the other way round, the Statutes of Kilkenny were introduced in 1366, banning inter-marriage and forbidding the English from speaking Gaelic.

English control was consolidated when the House of Tudor turned its attention to Ireland. Henry VIII, the first English monarch to be titled 'King of Ireland', introduced the Reformation to Ireland as well as England, but the new religion of Protestantism took root only in the Pale (the area around Dublin) and in the large provincial towns under English control. In the rest of Ireland, Catholic monasteries carried on as before, as did the Irish language.

From the mid-16th century, the implementation of the so-called plantation policy heralded the large-scale redistribution of wealth. Desirable farmland was confiscated from Catholics and given to Protestant settlers. During the reign of Elizabeth I revolts were widespread, but the most unyielding resistance was in the northeastern province of Ulster, where chiefs formed an alliance with Spain – England's bitterest enemy. In 1601, a Spanish mini-armada sailed into the southern port of Kinsale. The English defeated the invaders and the Ulstermen who attempted to join them. Leading Ulster aristocrats, now defeated, abandoned their land for European exile, and the 'plantation' programme continued. During the reign of James I, most of what is now Northern Ireland was confiscated and 'planted' with thousands of Scots and English, who changed the face of the province. After the English Civil War, Oliver Cromwell, England's ruler, ruthlessly massacred the garrisons at Drogheda and Wexford as the price for their support of Charles I, and pursued his own colonisation of Ireland. From 1654, Catholics were only allowed to hold land west of the River Shannon, much of it scarcely habitable. 'To Hell or Connaught' was the slogan used to sum up the alternatives for the dispossessed.

In 1690, the Protestant King William III of England defeated his rival claimant for the throne, the former King James II, at the decisive Battle of the Boyne. In the aftermath, the Irish

Catholic majority suffered further persecution. Penal Laws were introduced by the all-Protestant Irish parliament in order to keep Catholics away from positions of power and influence.

REVOLUTIONARY IDEAS

It took the American Revolution to provoke daring new thinking in Ireland. Henry Grattan, a Protestant of aristocratic heritage, led agitation for greater freedom and tolerance, and staunchly defended the rights of all Irishmen in the House of Commons in London. Further pressure came from an Irish Protestant, Theobald Wolfe Tone, a young lawyer campaigning for parliamentary reform and the abolition of anti-Catholic laws. In 1798, with the United Irishmen in rebellion, a French squadron came to their aid off the coast of Mayo. It was swiftly intercepted by British naval forces and Wolfe Tone was captured on board the flagship. Convicted of treason, he cut his own throat before his sentence of death by hanging could be carried out.

In 1801 the Irish parliament voted itself out of business by approving the Act of Union, which established the United Kingdom of Great Britain and Ireland. To help shape a common economic and political destiny for the two islands, all Irish MPs would now sit at Westminster. In 1823 Daniel O'Connell founded the Catholic Association to work for emancipation, and five years later, he won a landslide victory to become an MP. However, because he was a Catholic he was legally unable to take his seat. To prevent conflict, parliament finally passed the Emancipation Act in 1829, thus removing the most discriminatory laws.

STARVATION AND EMIGRATION

One of the worst disasters of 19th-century Europe was the great Irish Famine. The problem emerged in September 1845, when potato blight was found on farms in the southeast of Ireland. The next crop failed nationwide, wiping out the staple food of the Irish peasant. Cruel winter weather and the outbreak of disease added to the horror of starvation. Believing that they should not interfere with free market forces, the British government did not provide relief.

Survivors fled the stricken land aboard creaking 'coffin ships'. Irish refugees swamped towns such as Liverpool in England, and, across the Atlantic, Halifax, Boston and New York. The famine reduced the population of Ireland by 2 million – half dying, the rest emigrating. It took another century for the decline in population figures to be reversed and the flow of emigrants to be stemmed.

Irish Famine victims receive help at Kilrush, in 1849

FRUSTRATION AND REVOLT

Nationalist sentiment continued to grow throughout the second half of the 19th century, and in 1905 a number of nationalist groups were consolidated in a movement called Sinn Féin ('We Ourselves').

As Britain entered World War I, activists planned a revolt. During the Easter Rising of 1916, rebels seized the General Post Office in Dublin and declared Ireland's independence from Britain. The authorities crushed the revolt, which had lacked a broad base of support, but the authorities' pitiless execution of the ringleaders reversed public opinion. The war of independence had begun.

At the next general election the nationalist Sinn Féin, led by Eamon de Valera, won by a landslide. The newly elected Sinn Féin parliamentarians refused to fill their posts in the Commons in London, but set themselves up in Dublin as Dáil Éireann, the new parliament of Ireland.

More than two years of guerrilla warfare followed, until the partition of Ireland was agreed in December 1921. Under the terms of the treaty, the six northern counties of Ulster – Antrim, Down, Tyrone, Fermanagh, Armagh and Derry – where the Protestant majority rejected rule from Dublin, were allowed to remain part of the United Kingdom. The other 26 counties had a Catholic majority and became the Irish Free State (Éire), a dominion within the British Empire. The British hoped that the two sides would soon patch up their differences, but few Republicans accepted the settlement and a bitter civil war broke out in the South. Among the many casualties was Michael Collins (1890–1922), memorably portrayed by Liam Neeson in Neil Jordan's eponymous film. He had been one of the heroes of the 1916 Rising, and, as an important member of the first Sinn Féin government, had helped to negotiate the 1921 Anglo-Irish Treaty. A group of Republicans who saw this as a betrayal of their ideals ambushed and shot him dead on 22 August, 1922, not far from his birthplace in County Cork.

FINE GAEL AND FIANNA FÁIL

The civil war ended in 1923 with the effective surrender of Eamon de Valera's anti-treaty forces, but the tensions of the war were to dominate every aspect of political life in the Free State for the next half-century. The country's two main political parties, Fine Gael (Tribe of Ireland) and Fianna Fáil (Warriors of Ireland) are direct descendants of the pro- and anti-treaty forces. In 1927, de Valera entered parliament (the Dáil) at the head of Fianna Fáil. He came to power in the 1932 election, vowing to reinstate the ancient Gaelic language and culture, ushering in a new era of pious respectability, based firmly on Catholic values. Meanwhile, emigration, mainly to England and America, claimed yet another generation of younger sons unable to inherit the family farm and younger daughters unable to find husbands. In the early 1920s, an astonishing 43 percent of Irish-born men and women were living abroad.

In 1937, de Valera produced a constitution that abolished the oath of allegiance to England's king, claimed sovereignty over all 32 counties of Ireland and underlined the influence of the Roman Catholic Church. When Britain declared war on Germany in 1939, the 26 counties remained neutral and formally became an independent republic – Eire – in 1949.

In post-partition Northern Ireland, although the Unionists were content to remain an integral part of Britain, Prime Minister Lloyd George decided instead to give the six counties their own parliament. The result was Stormont, situated on the outskirts of Belfast and built in the style of Buckingham Palace, only grander.

POST-WAR IRELAND

Britain left Northern Ireland to its own devices and its own government, but many Catholics did not recognise the province's legitimacy, and many Protestants responded by ensuring that jobs and public housing went

A Catholic mural in Belfast

mainly to Protestants. In 1969, civil rights marches against these injustices were repressed, unleashing old hatreds. A reluctant British government sent troops onto the streets of Derry and Belfast, where the violence was concentrated. It was intended to be a temporary arrangement, but caused the Irish Republican Army to be resurrected.

Terrorism and internecine violence were to last for three decades. The IRA's armed offensive gathered pace, spreading terror by means of snipers' bullets, booby-trapped vehicles and bombs in crowded bars. Protestant vigilante and terrorist groups such as the Ulster Defence Association and the Ulster Volunteer Force began to match violence with violence. The situation worsened dramatically after 30 January 1972, known as 'Bloody Sunday', when shooting broke out at an anti-internment rally in Londonderry. At the end of it, 13 civilians lay dead, shot by paratroopers. The following month, as a reprisal, a bomb exploded at Aldershot Barracks in England, killing seven. Britain abolished the 50-year-old Stormont parliament, imposing direct rule from London, and tried unsuccessfully to persuade Protestant and Catholic leaders to set up a power-sharing executive. As atrocities multiplied, an entire generation reached adulthood without ever having known peace.

BOOM AND BUST

As violence dragged on from the 1970s into the 1980s, the South left the North to fight its ancient battles and looked instead to Europe,

Queen Elizabeth II is entertained on a visit to Cork city's English Market

Periods of partial self-rule alternated with direct rule from Britain. Then, in 2005, the IRA declared a permanent ceasefire and decommissioned its weapons, and in May 2007, a new united government was formed.

Back in the South, in 2008, Bertie Ahern, president of the Republic of Ireland, resigned after nearly 11 years as leader. Soon afterwards, the first rumblings of trouble in the Republic's financial sector surfaced, and before long the nation was engulfed in a full-blown economic crisis.

It emerged that Irish banks were massively under-capitalised and had been operating in a regulatory environment that was too lax. Reckless speculation by property developers had been encouraged, and leading builders were now in dire trouble. Thousands of workers were laid off, leaving few if any buyers for the thousands of houses and offices built during the boom. In a desperate measure to save the banks that had lent money so freely during the boom, the government nationalised them. Pay and pension cuts were imposed on public sector workers, and a host of other measures were imposed to put the country back on course economically. The beleaguered government of Brian Cowen called a general election, and the opposition Fine Gael party under Enda Kenny won a landslide victory.

A ray of optimism was brought by the state visit of Queen Elizabeth II in May 2011, the first visit by a British monarch since George V in 1911. It was an unexpected success, and brought a sense of reconciliation after years of hostility and resentment.

overhauling its economic and social values. Following a period of cuts in public services and soaring unemployment, the '90s were ushered in with the election of Mary Robinson as Ireland's president. A left-wing lawyer and feminist, she proved a popular success and a force for social change.

The European Union was largely responsible for the economy's upturn. Jobs were created and roads built as billions of pounds poured into the country from the European social fund. A sharp fall in interest rates gave rise to a boom in property development and construction. Tourism benefitted as Ireland suddenly became a chic tourist destination among Europeans. In 2002, Ireland became one of the first 12 countries to adopt the euro.

In Northern Ireland, the Good Friday Agreement, signed in 1998, established the framework for a self-governing Northern Ireland with power-sharing. Many Protestant politicians refused to cooperate with their nationalist counterparts until the Irish Republican Army disarmed.

Historical landmarks

c.8000BC
Date of earliest archaeological evidence.

c.500BC
Celts migrate to Britain. Ireland's Iron Age.

c.432
St Patrick returns to Ireland as a missionary.

1014
Brian Ború, High King of Ireland, defeats the Vikings near Clontarf.

1366
Statutes of Kilkenny forbid English to intermarry or speak Gaelic.

1541
Henry VIII declares himself King of Ireland.

1607
The most powerful Irish princes flee to Spain (Flight of the Earls).

1608
James I moves Protestant Scots and English to Ulster Plantation.

1649
Oliver Cromwell conquers Ireland in a merciless campaign.

1690
William of Orange defeats England's Catholic King James II at the Battle of the Boyne. 'Protestant Ascendancy' begins.

1801
Act of Union makes Ireland part of the United Kingdom.

1845–51
The Great Potato Famine; 1 million die.

1905
Sinn Féin ('We Ourselves') is formed.

1916
1,800 people take part in the 'Easter Rising', occupying public buildings.

1918–23
Sinn Féin wins a landslide election victory, with 73 of Ireland's 105 seats, and announces formation of Irish parliament in Dublin. After the 1919–21 Anglo-Irish War, the treaty creates the Irish Free State, excluding the six counties of Northern Ireland, which had Protestant majorities.

1937
The Free State, Eire, adopts its own constitution.

1949
Having remained neutral in World War II, Eire leaves the British Commonwealth and becomes the Republic of Ireland.

1972
British soldiers shoot dead 13 demonstrators on 'Bloody Sunday'. Belfast's parliament is dissolved. Northern Ireland is ruled from London.

1973
The Republic of Ireland joins the EU.

1998
The Good Friday Agreement is signed in Northern Ireland.

2002
The Republic of Ireland adopts the euro.

2007
A united government is formed in Northern Ireland.

2008
Ireland goes into a deep recession in the wake of the global financial crisis. The property boom finishes with a crash.

2011
Republican dissidents kill a Catholic police officer in Omagh. Landslide victory for Enda Kenny and the Fine Gael party signals a change in outlook after years of Fianna Fáil-led coalitions. Successful state visit by Her Majesty Queen Elizabeth II.

History

Culture

Céad Mile Fáilte: a hundred thousand welcomes! An alluring marketing brand has been created for Ireland over the years, portraying an unspoilt green land with hospitable people, and a leisurely pace of life. But then Ireland always has been known for its fairy tales…

While the image is not all makebelieve, the truth is more complicated. To start with, there are two Irelands: Northern Ireland, with its British-facing Protestant majority and Ulster Scots heritage; and the Republic of Ireland, traditionally Catholic, and until the late 20th century an economically deprived, priest-dominated country whose major export was emigrants.

In 1973, however, Ireland joined the European Union, or EU (at that time the EEC), and took full advantage of its subsidies. Adopting the euro in 2003 distanced Ireland decisively from its old imperial master, Britain, which clung to sterling. Irish culture, it found, travelled well, whether in the form of the 'Irish pub' which was exported to over 42 countries, or as slickly modernised traditional music and dance, *Riverdance*-style. The global success of Bob Geldof's Live Aid and stadium rockers U2 gave Dublin a hip new identity. From being a dull provincial backwater, Dublin became a city where it was fun to be young.

A job market flooded with well-educated, energetic graduates, coupled with generous tax breaks encouraged multinationals – Google and Microsoft among them – to establish Irish operations. Emigrants from Eastern European countries and elsewhere flocked to Ireland to take up the lower-paid jobs that no one else wanted, diversifying the formerly homogeneous population.

Recently, however, the 26-county Republic has endured a dramatic cycle of boom and bust. From being the economic wonder of the EU, Ireland has fallen dramatically into recession, leaving a legacy of an excess of hotel rooms, untenanted office blocks and unsold apartments and houses on 'ghost estates'. It subsequently emerged that a cabal of bankers, property developers and politicians had been flouting the usual regulatory processes in search of ever-bigger

At Curragower Bar in Limerick; the classic Irish pub is a major export internationally

profits. In response, the government increased taxation, cut public sector pay and reduced social welfare, requiring ordinary people to tighten their belts to pay off the glut of debt.

While other European countries faced with similar scenarios took to the streets and protested, the Irish, with characteristic good humour, talked a lot about how unfair it was, then carried on as normal. The political party that had presided over the boom years – and the cronyism that characterised that era – was voted out, and life went on.

IRELAND TODAY

In the Republic, the centuries-old dominance of the Catholic Church has been eroded by child abuse scandals and revelations of the sexual activity of priests and bishops. While many people continue to attend Sunday Mass, others are seeking alternative spiritual paths, through yoga and other therapies, which have become extremely popular.

Northern Ireland, on the other hand, is more conservative, and there has been little change in its traditional Protestant communities. The victory of William of Orange at the Battle of the Boyne is celebrated as enthusiastically as ever on 12 July with parades and drums.

Since the early 1990s, the Republic has developed an increasingly suburban commuter lifestyle, and has become more like everywhere else. But enough people have realised the danger of losing Ireland's unique cultural identity, and are working hard to promote a pride in all things

At a florist's in Co. Wicklow

Irish, including the language, the music and even the football team. Visitors, once they have recovered from the shock of the high prices, are likely to find that the traditional hospitality has survived.

Indeed, it is not surprising that Ireland has one of the highest use of mobile phones per capita in Europe: the Irish love to talk, and have a natural, informal friendliness. People are constantly striking up conversations with total strangers: at the bus stop, in the supermarket queue, on the train. Join in, and soon you'll be having the proverbial 'grand old time.'

LANGUAGE

English is spoken everywhere in Ireland – though English as spoken in Ireland (Hiberno-English) has a few variations on standard English, influenced by both the structure and vocabulary of Irish.

In the Gaeltacht areas of the west and south of the country, the principal language is Irish, though most people speak English too. Bilingualism is officially encouraged. Many people choose to study at an Irish-speaking school, and take their final exams 'through Irish', as it increases their chances of interesting employment and is still required for entrance to the civil service.

The Irish language radio station Radio na Gaeltachta was joined in 1996 by an Irish-language television station, TG4 (www.tg4.ie), broadcasting from studios in the Galway Gaeltacht. The imaginative programming (in Irish with English subtitles) has helped make the Irish language 'cool' among the younger generation.

GOVERNMENT ARTS POLICY

Aosdána, an association of writers and artists, was set up in 1981 by the Taoiseach, Charles J. Haughey (1926–2006), who had already introduced tax exemption for writers and artists. The aim was to lure home Irish artists living abroad. The scheme was named in honour of the Celt's high regard for the *áes dána* – the people of talent.

Membership, limited to 250 people, includes most but not all of Ireland's artistic elite: Seamus Heaney is in, but John Banville opted out. To ensure that a new generation did not suffer the poverty of their predecessors – many of whom, like James Joyce and Samuel Beckett, chose to emigrate – members can claim an annuity of around €20,000 to work full-time on creative projects.

This has given a great boost to the arts in Ireland, both directly and indirectly. Many Irish writers and artists living abroad returned to Ireland, and others stayed, often participating in events at community level, and greatly enriching the local arts scene. Apart for Aosdána, the Arts Councils of Ireland and Northern Ireland both work hard to provide facilities for all the arts, including new venues and budgets for touring.

LITERATURE

Part of Ireland's love of talk is evident in its love of storytelling. This is one of the reasons Irish writers are so popular all over the world, and why an evening in a Dublin pub can be so entertaining. It's not only the storytelling that attracts admiration. The Irish are also admired for their imaginative, even magical, ability with words. Before the written word, travelling storytellers

Ireland has produced a disproportionately large – and impressive – number of novelists

(*seanchaí*) are said to have entertained beside the fire. The tradition of impromptu verbal wit lives on today with Irish comedians and broadcasters. Ireland also has a disproportionately large number of novelists, including international prize winners John Banville, Sebastian Barry, Roddy Doyle, Anne Enright, Colm McCann, Edna O'Brien and Colm Tóibín, to name but a few. Dubliners enjoy the work of Joseph O'Connor (Sinead's brother) – try *Ghost Light*.

Literary festivals are convivial, informal events, where authors and the reading public mingle freely. The biggest one is Bloomsday (16 June), a four-day event that commemorates James Joyce's *Ulysses* (1922) in its Dublin setting (see www.visitdublin.com).

The Irish are also great readers: most small towns have a bookshop, and most people read a daily paper. *The Irish Times* is the newspaper of record, while *The Irish Independent* is good for political gossip and general features. *The Ticket*, a supplement in Friday's *Irish Times*, lists arts and music events for the forthcoming week. In Dublin, buy the *Evening Herald*, and in Cork and Limerick the *Evening Echo*, on sale daily from about noon. Alternatively, go online and consult www.entertainment.ie.

Inside Belfast's Grand Opera House, designed *c.*1895 by Frank Matcham

Culture

THEATRE

Ever since the Abbey Theatre's production of *The Playboy of the Western World* by John M. Synge in 1907 caused a riot (people reacted violently to its use of the word 'shift', referring to a female undergarment), Dublin has had an exciting theatre scene. It also offers great value for money, with tickets at the Abbey (at around €25) often available at short notice. Productions from the Gate Theatre, which fostered the work of Brian Friel, regularly transfer to New York.

Belfast, Wexford, Kilkenny, Waterford, Cork, Galway and Sligo all have reputable theatres that host touring productions and mount their own productions. Galway's Druid Theatre Company has successfully transferred productions to Broadway, including Martin McDonagh's *The Cripple of Inishmaan*. Other younger playwrights to look out for are Marina Carr, Conor McPherson, Mark O'Rowe and Enda Walsh *(Disco Pigs)*.

FILM

Ireland had no film studio until 1958, when Ardmore Studios opened in Bray, County Wicklow. It was thus left

Still from the 2006 film *The Wind That Shakes the Barley*

Englishman, Ken Loach. *The Wind That Shakes the Barley* (2006) is set in 1920 and was filmed on location in rural Cork.

Although film is very popular in Ireland, there are few art-house cinemas outside Dublin; look out instead for screenings at local arts centres.

MUSIC

Apart from the thriving traditional music scene, Ireland also has a lively classical music scene, and many people – both players and audiences – retain an interest in both. The uncrowned king of the classical music world is pianist John O'Connor, best known for rescuing the work of the Irish composer John Field (1782–1837) from oblivion. Younger pianists such as Belfast-born Barry Douglas and Finghin Collins are also making international names.

to Hollywood to portray Ireland to the world, and it did so by targeting the huge audience of Irish-Americans who had a sentimental attachment to the pastoral ideal most potently portrayed in John Ford's *The Quiet Man*. The film's star, Maureen O'Hara, lives in Glengarriff and celebrated her 92nd birthday in 2011 by revealing an ambitious plan for an Irish Academy of Film, to be based in the village. The legacy of *The Quiet Man* (Hollywood Blarney or cinematic masterpiece?) is entertainingly explored by documentary filmmaker Sé Merry Doyle in *Dreaming The Quiet Man* (2010). It includes contributions from Martin Scorsese and O'Hara herself.

Ireland is a small country, and most of its filmmakers leave to work abroad – though some, including Neil Jordan (whose film *The Crying Game* was one of the few made about the Troubles), return constantly to Irish themes. The best recent film about the Irish civil war, though, was made by an

Among Ireland's composers are Gerald Barry (b.1952), whose operas include *Intelligence Park* and *The Bitter Tears of Petra von Kant*, and Raymond Deane (b.1953), known for his chamber music. The Crash Ensemble specialises in new music, while the Vanbrugh Quartet has worked from its Cork base for over 25 years. Composer and performer Julie Feeney is one of a growing number of musicians who move freely between classical, pop and new music and sound art.

The RTE Symphony Orchestra performs mainly at the National Concert Hall, touring the provinces twice yearly. The Sligo Festival of Baroque Music, the Festival of Music in Big Houses, the West Cork Chamber Music Festival and numerous other events ensure that there's a lively calendar for classical music fans.

Dublin has over 120 clubs and live music pubs. The club scene is mainly for the under 30s who flock to the city from all over Europe in search of a good time. This was where artists such as Sinead O'Connor, Westlife and Imelda May got their first break. Limerick is the home of the Cranberries, and more recently the Rubberbandits. Enya is from a Donegal family of musicians, and Dolores Keanc is from Galway. Their younger counterparts are gigging all around the country. The magazine *Hot Press* aspires to be the Irish equivalent of *Rolling Stone*; it's worth checking its pages for reviews of up-and-coming talent.

Belfast is intensely proud of its superstar Van Morrison, who was born there in 1945. There are plenty of venues for traditional music in the city centre, with a burgeoning bar scene in the Cathedral quarter and shabby-chic music clubs in the student areas of the south of the city.

One of Belfast's most famous sons

CONTEMPORARY ART

Ireland's ancient tradition of visual art was largely neglected in the 20th century, but a new generation of painters and sculptors has recently been making more of an impact. Irish art colleges are now heavily over-subscribed, with the University of Ulster at Coleraine having a particularly high reputation for contemporary art practice. The Irish Museum of Modern Art opened in 1991, and has helped raise the profile of Irish artists with its steadily growing collection. Irish artists Sean Scully and Felim Egan have gained international reputations as abstract artists, while sculptors such as Maud Cotter, Vivienne Roche and Eilis O'Connell have achieved high reputations both at home and abroad.

Admittedly, many of the younger generation of artists – Clare Langan, Linda Quinlan and Amanda Coogan, for example, working respectively in video, installation art and performance – produce work that fits seamlessly with their contemporaries in London, Paris or New York. Others, however, continue to be inspired by the Irish landscape, even though their work may use forms and styles belonging to the international contemporary art scene; important work includes Sarah Walker's coolly modernist wild flower grids, Charles Tyrrell's rigorous abstracts and Gary Coyle's dramatic photographs of Dublin Bay. Others paint in the traditional style, and interesting original works can be found for sale in the many small galleries around the country, with prices ranging from as little as €150 upwards.

Culture

Food and drink

NATIONAL CUISINE

Traditionally, Irish food was plain but hearty. Bread and potatoes accompanied the main meal – a meat stew if you were lucky, or fish on Fridays. Vegetables were boiled to a pulp and salads were a rare summer treat. Garlic, avocados and aubergines were unheard of in most homes. However, in one generation Irish cooking has changed beyond all recognition. There is a new awareness of the excellent raw materials available to chefs in the form of grass-fed beef and lamb, fresh seafood from the Atlantic, abundant dairy produce and home-grown vegetables and salads. Even the humble Irish soda bread, made without yeast or other additives, and once considered inferior to shop-bought white bread, has come to be valued for its unadulterated wholesomeness.

The same holds true for Northern Ireland, where the chefs are if anything even more innovative than in the south. There are minor differences in the two cuisines – for example, at breakfast in Northern Ireland you will probably get a potato farl (fried potato bread) with your Ulster Fry, while down south, there'll be white pudding with the Full Irish, as it's known (bacon, eggs, sausages, black pudding, fried tomato and sometimes mushrooms).

Traditional Irish dishes usually include some form of potato, while most main courses are served with at least one kind of spud, and sometimes three – for example, mashed, roast and *dauphinoise*. Cabbage with bacon remains a firm favourite, and is usually served with unpeeled potatoes on a side dish, their skins bursting open. Another favourite is Irish stew – onions, potato, carrots and lamb, boiled together, seasoned with salt and pepper and parsley. Dublin coddle – ham, sausage, potato and onion cooked on the stove top in a broth – is a great comfort food. In Cork, tripe and drisheen (cows' intestines and blood pudding) is a traditional dish, and one stall at the entrance to the famous market on Princes Street sells nothing else. Pig's trotters (feet) are popular in both Cork and Dublin; both dishes are on the menu at Cork's Farmgate Café *(see p.124)*.

The Irish are also great cake makers: try a slice of tea brack (a light fruit

A hearty Irish stew, made of lamb, potatoes, carrots and onions, and carefully seasoned

cake in which the fruit has been soaked overnight in tea), or a slice of traditional fruit cake – still one of the most popular options on Irish Rail's tea trolley.

THE NEW IRISH CUISINE

Ireland's high-quality produce is imaginatively prepared by today's chefs to emphasise its freshness, flavour and texture. Ireland's chefs work closely with artisan food producers, who use traditional methods to smoke fish and make charcuterie and farmhouse cheeses. Besides excellent smoked salmon, you will also encounter smoked trout, mackerel and eel. Many restaurants grow their own salads and herbs, or have an arrangement with a local grower. When people eat out, they have come to expect a high standard of cuisine, whether at an expensive restaurant or at the local café.

Irish chefs are trained in the classic tradition, and most go abroad for a few years and bring back culinary influences from their travels – generally Mediterranean, but sometimes eastern – adapting them to the Irish market. This eclectic approach is also followed by Ireland's private cookery schools, of which by far the best known is Ballymaloe Cookery School near the famous country-house hotel in County Cork. Darina Allen, its director, has been preaching the doctrine of using fresh local produce, treated with simplicity and respect, since 1983, and has trained many of today's Irish chefs. Her mother-in-law, Myrtle Allen, who started advocating this philosophy back in the 1960s at

Seafood at Smugglers Creek Inn at Rossnowlagh, near Donegal Bay

Food and drink

her restaurant in Ballymaloe House, is active alongside Darina in the highly successful Irish Slow Food movement (www.slowfoodireland. com). Meanwhile, up in the north, on the fast-growing restaurant scene of Belfast, young chefs vie for the privilege of working in the kitchen of Paul and Jeanne Rankin, pioneers of new Irish cuisine, at their flagship Cayenne restaurant (see p.230).

All meat in Ireland is now traceable back to the farm, and the flavour of locally reared and butchered meat comes as a pleasant surprise. The Irish Food Board runs a programme, Féile Bia, encouraging restaurants to source as much of their food as possible from local suppliers, and to pass on the information about its provenance to their customers. 'Bia' is the Irish word for food, and 'féile' means both festival and celebration. If you see these words

Traditional fish and chips on the pier at Schull, a village in west Cork

on the menu, it means that the restaurant is committed to serving carefully sourced fresh local produce. This reliance on Irish suppliers of meat means that restaurant menus will change according to the season. There will often be game in the autumn and winter, including venison, pheasant, duck and woodcock. New season spring lamb is eagerly awaited, especially in Connemara and Kerry, and is usually on the menu by Easter.

Irish fish comes straight from the Atlantic, and in places such as Kinsale, Dingle and Galway, which have their own fishing fleet, most restaurants buy direct from the boat. The difference is remarkable. Be sure to sample a fresh crab open sandwich, lobster, brill, john dory, tuna and monkfish in summer, and oysters and mussels from September to April (although they are sold all year round, this is the traditional season).

Irish restaurants have also increasingly turned their attention to the quality of their bread, which is usually served with butter on the side. Most places now either bake their own or buy it in from an artisan baker.

Of course, in addition to the new wave of restaurants, there remain many that continue to service the old culinary habits. Many Irish people like to order steak when they eat out, and it will be found on even some of the fancier menus. Pubs advertising 'carvery lunches' offer roast meat carved to order at a self-service counter, with traditional vegetables and, of course, at least two kinds of spuds. Another favourite is fish and chips, traditionally eaten as a takeaway in the street, but now served even in some upmarket restaurants, including Kinsale's Fishy Fishy *(see pp.124–5)*.

WHERE TO EAT
Fine dining

Some 50 years ago, there were hardly any restaurants in Ireland apart from hotel dining rooms, especially in provincial towns. Even today, some of the best restaurants are still to be found in hotels, such as the Park Hotel Kenmare *(see p.143)* on the Ring of Kerry and Gregan's Castle *(see p.166)* in County Clare. Even in Dublin, hotel restaurants are chic, none more so than The Tea Room *(see p.92)* at the U2-owned Clarence Hotel (which has drastically reduced its prices since first opening). Many hotels have two or more restaurants, one for fine dining and another for informal meals. Hotels also have the advantage of being open daily, whereas many Irish restaurants close after Sunday lunch and do not serve dinner on Sunday or Monday.

Booking is advisable at most upmarket restaurants. Even the best, including Dublin's top places, Restaurant Patrick Guilbaud (see p.92) and Chapter One (see p.93), are relatively informal, specifying only 'smart casual' at dinner. If you want to treat yourself, remember that lunch is generally less expensive than dinner. Some restaurants also have reduced-price 'early bird' menus for diners who arrive before 7 or 7.30pm. Since the recession, many restaurants serve a value-for-money menu – often three courses for €25 – at other times too.

Bistros, wine bars and brasseries

The Irish have an idiosyncratic way with these terms, all of which can be interpreted as an 'informal, fun place without tablecloths'. A high rate of VAT and stiff overheads make it very difficult to run a stylish and good-value establishment, but people do try. The Pearl Brasserie in Dublin (see p.92), The Chart House in Dingle town (see p.146) and the Café Paradiso in Cork (see p.124) are good examples. An increasingly popular way of keeping prices down is to offer a tapas menu, where dishes can be shared. Northern Ireland is better value, especially for those living in the sterling zone; in Belfast, seek out the brasseries along Botanic Avenue for good-quality food at democratic prices.

Pubs

Since the introduction of the smoking ban and drink-driving laws, pubs have had to diversify. Nearly everywhere now serves tea and coffee, with espresso machines commonplace in city pubs. More are serving food, often with an all-day menu that may feature soups, sandwiches, salads and a couple of hot dishes. Others offer a self-service 'carvery', which may offer salads as well as the 'roast of the day'.

The best pub food is usually found in places that offer daily specials at lunchtime and in the early evening. Most pubs stop serving food at about 9pm, to make more room for drinkers. Some pubs have effectively turned into restaurants that also serve drinks, with waiter service at all tables. Children are welcome in most food-serving pubs during the daytime, and some even have play areas and children's menus.

Daytime cafés

Since the Irish acquired a taste for real coffee, cafés have bucked up no end. They usually offer some form of home-baking, often the humble scone

Food and drink

Not all Irish bars are traditional – there are plenty of fashionable wine bars too

or a warm slice of quiche, as well as sandwiches, salads and home-made soups and cakes.

Most towns now have at least one Chinese takeaway, but prices are high compared to elsewhere in Europe and the UK. Indian restaurants, when they can be found, generally offer basic surroundings but good food. However, there is neither the choice nor the quality that can be found in the UK.

Most people rely on convenience stores (small supermarkets with generally higher prices) and petrol stations for quick, takeaway snacks – sandwiches, wraps, and a limited selection of hot food, usually roast chicken, sausages and pies. The quality is generally low. A better bet is to visit the local farmers' market, where producers sell directly to the public. These are ideal for picnic food, offering local farmhouse cheeses and charcuterie. Traditional breads and baking are also a strong point, as are jams, chutneys and fresh organic salads, fruit and vegetables. For an up-to-date list of markets, see www.countrymarkets.ie.

Many people still eat their main meal – 'dinner' – at midday, which is why pub lunches are so hearty and filling. But increasingly, for urban dwellers, lunch is a sandwich at the desk, and the more important meal is eaten in the evening. Most Irish restaurants stop serving new customers by about 9.30pm, and pubs close the kitchen by 10pm, but this is more flexible in summer.

DRINKS

Irish pubs sell the usual range of beer and lager, bottled and on tap,

The Irish have a taste for coffee of all styles

in measures of a pint or half-pint, but the one that every visitor has to try (as Barack and Michelle Obama did in 2011) is stout, a strongish black beer with a creamy white head. Murphy's is brewed in Cork, but the most famous stout is undoubtedly Guinness, which has been brewed in Dublin since 1759.

Great care is taken in serving Guinness; about half a glass is poured and left to 'settle' for a minute, then topped up with the trade-mark creamy head. Try a half-pint to start with, referred to as a 'glass'. In a good Irish pub it will taste smooth as velvet, bearing little relation to the Guinness served in Britain or America.

Irish whiskey is spelt differently from Scotch 'whisky' and tastes different too, as it is distilled from a mixture of malted and unmalted barley grains. The most popular brands are Bushmills, Jameson and Paddy, and all have a slightly different flavour. The fine old single malts are generally taken neat or with a splash of water as a digestif. Irish whiskey is also used in Irish coffee, a hot, sweet coffee spiked with whiskey and topped with cream, a delicious way to end a meal.

Irish pubs are expensive. A pint of beer in Dublin will set you back about €5 (compared to about €4.20 in a rural pub), and a soft drink can cost €2.50. Wine by the glass goes from about €4.50 in a country pub to €9 or more in a fancy Dublin hotel, with €5 being the average. Try to be philosophical: you are not just paying for the drink, you are paying for the experience of being in a real Irish pub. With any luck, you will also get some free live music (most likely after 10pm), or some witty conversation.

By far the most popular non-alcoholic drink in Ireland is tea, usually black tea, served with a dash of milk. However, green tea and herbal infusions are growing in popularity, and can be found in more cosmopolitan urban centres such as Dublin, Galway, Kenmare and Kinsale. Decent coffee is also much easier to come by than in the past, but outside urban areas an espresso can be hard to find.

Irish whiskey is distinguished from its Scottish equivalent with an 'e' – and more besides

Index

A

accessibility 267
accommodation **258–60**, 274
  Belfast 229–30
  County Cork 123–4
  Dublin 88–90
  Inland Ireland 198
  Limerick and the Shannon 165–6
  Northern Ireland 252–3
  Northwest 213–14
  Southeast 107–8
  Southwest 142–4
  The West 182–3
Achill Island 17, **181**
Act of Union 281
Adare **154–5**, 165, 166, 168
Adfert 141
age restrictions 11
Ahakista 118
Ahern, Bertie 284
Aillwee Cave 161, **164**
Air India Memorial 118
air travel 261–2, 263–4
ancient sites 32–7
angling **26–7**, 126, 147, 168, 200, 216, 254
Anglo-Irish Treaty 282
Anglo-Norman occupation 280–1
Annestown 100
Antrim 17, **248–51**, 252–3, 254
Aran Islands 170, **173–4**, 182, 184, 185
Aranmore island 211
Ardara **211**, 216
Ardfert **141**, 146
Ardmore **37**, 107, 109
Armagh **242–3**, 245, 252, 253, 254, 255
art 291
arts policy 288
Ashford Castle 175
Ashley Park House **195**, 198
Athlone **188–9**, 198, 199, 200, 201
ATMs 270
Avoca **84–5**, 90
Avondale 84

B

B&B 259
Ballina **181**, 184
Ballinasloe 189
Ballinskelligs Bay 136
Ballybunion **141**, 147
Ballycastle 15, **250**, 254, 255
Ballycroy National Park 48
Ballydehob 121
Ballygalley **249**, 254
Ballyhack 98–9
Ballyheighue Strand 141
Ballyholme Bay 247
Ballymote Castle 209
Ballyvaughan 161, **164**, 166, 169
Bangor 247
Banna Strand 141
Bantry **122**, 124, 126
Bantry Bay 118–19, **122**
Beara Peninsula **122**, 123, 126, **131**
Beckett, Samuel 55, 56, 288
beer 296–7
Behan, Brendan 55, 56
Belfast 17, **218–33**, 283
  accommodation 229–30
  cafés 227
  festivals and events 15, 59, 233
  nightlife and entertainment 231–2
  pubs 52, **231**
  restaurants 230–1
  sports and activities 232
  tours 233
  transport 221
  Albert Memorial Clock 223
  Big Fish 223
  Botanic Gardens 224, **227–8**
  City Hall 219
  Crown Liquor Saloon 222
  Custom House 223
  Donegal Quay 223
  Grand Opera House **222**, 232
  Linen Hall Library 219
  McHugh's Bar **223**, 231
  Metropolitan Arts Centre 223
  Northern Bank 223
  The Odyssey 226
  Ormeau Baths Gallery 221
  Parliament Building (Stormont) **228**, 283
  Queen's University 224–5, **227**
  Royal Belfast Academical Institution 223
  Royal Ulster Rifles Museum 223
  St Anne's Cathedral 223
  St George's Market 226
  Titanic Belfast 226
  Ulster Hall **221**, 232
  Ulster Museum 224, **228**
  Waterfront Hall **226**, 232
Belfast Lough 247–8
Belvedere House and Gardens **193**, 194, 195
Ben Bulben 17
Bennettsbridge 102
Birr 189, **190–1**, 198, 199, 200, 201
Blakes of the Hollow (Enniskillen) 241
Blarney Castle 16, **116–17**
Blasket Islands 140
Bloody Foreland 17, **217**
Bloody Sunday 283
boat trips 127, 149, 169, 187, 200, 265
bogs 48, 188, **191**
books 19, 58
bookshops **57**, 289
Boyne, Battle of the 280, 287
Boyne Valley 85–6
Brian Ború 37, 279
Brittas Bay 84
budgeting 272
Bundoran **207**, 217
Bunmahon 100
Bunratty Castle and Folk Park 16, **156**, 168
Burren National Park 34, 150, **160–4**, 168–9
Burtonport 211
bus travel 263
Bushmills 17, **251**, 253

C

cabaret 42
cafés 295–6
Caherconnell 163
Caherdaniel 136
Cahersiveen **132**, 143
Cahir **105**, 108
camping 260
car hire 267
Caragh Lake **132**, 143
Carnlough 249
Carrick 211
Carrick-a-rede Rope Bridge 250–1
Carrick-on-Shannon **207**, 213, 215, 216
Carrickfergus 249
Carrowmore 34, 203
Casement, Roger 141

Cashel 16, **105**, 108, 109
Castle Coole 241
Castle Espie 247
Castlebar 180
Castlecove 136
castles and fortifications 208–9
Castletown House 87
Castletownshend 121
Castlewellan Forest Park 246
Catholics
  Emancipation Act 136, 281
  persecution of 280–1
  role of church 287
Causeway Coastal Road 249
Cavan 197
Céide Fields 181
Celts 208, 278
Charleville Forest Castle 193
children 274–5
Christianity 32–3, 99, 244, 278–9
Clare, County **155–64**, 165–6, 167–8
Clare Island 180
Clarinbridge 173
Clew Bay 180
Clifden 17, **175**, 184, 186, 187
Cliffs of Moher 16, 150, **158–9**
climate 12–13
clocháns (beehive huts) 139
Clonakilty **120**, 125, 127
Clonea 100
Clonmacnoise 36–7, 189, **190**
Clonmel 101, **104**
Clontarf, Battle of 279
coach travel 264–5
Cobh **116**, 125, 127
Collins, Michael 120, 127, 282
Comber 247
Cong **175**, 183
Connemara 17, 170, **175–7**, 179, 182–3, 185
Connemara National Park 175
Coolbanagher Church 193
Cork 16, **112–15**
Cork, County 112–27
country houses 194–5
Cowen, Brian 284
crafts 85, 101
credit cards 270
crime 269
Croagh Patrick 17, 44, 171, **177**, 245
Cromwell, Oliver 104, 105, 134–5, 280
cruising 200, 201

Cultra 247–8
culture 286–91
Curracloe Strand 97
Curragh 87
currency 10, 270
Cushendall 250
Cushendun 250
cycling **29–30**, 111, 126, 148, 168, 186, 200, 216, 232, **265–6**

D

Dáil Éireann 282
dance 38, **42–3**, 157, 169
de Valera, Eamon 282, 283
Derry/Londonderry 17, **234–9**, 283
Derrynane House 136
Devenish Island 33
Dingle **138–9**, 144, 146, 147, 148, 149
Dingle Peninsula **138–40**, 143–4
disabled travellers 267
diving 169
dolphin watching 169
Donard Forest Park 246
Donegal **210**, 213, 215, 216
Donegal, County 17, 202–3, **207–12**, 213–14, 215, 217
Donleavy, J.P. 55
Doo Lough Pass 17, **177**
Doolin **159**, 165, 168, 169
Doolin Cave 159, 162
Down, County **243–8**, 252, 253
Downpatrick 244, **246**, 254, 255
Downpatrick Head 17
drinks 296–7
driving 266–7
Dromahair 205
Drombeg Stone Circle 35, **120**
Dromineer 192
Drumcliff 206
Drumshanbo **207**, 217
Dublin 16, **64–95**
  accommodation 88–90
  excursions 83–7
  festivals and events 14, 15, **95**
  nightlife and entertainment 57, **93–4**
  pubs 51–2, 70
  restaurants 91–3
  tours 78, **94–5**
  transport 68

Abbey Theatre 57, **79**, 94, 289
Bank of Ireland 65
Belvedere College 81
Chester Beatty Library 76
Christ Church Cathedral 77
City Hall 75
Custom House 78
Dublin Castle **75–6**, 77
Dublin City Art Gallery, The Hugh Lane 80
Dublin Writers' Museum 56, **80–1**
Fitzwilliam Square 74
Four Courts 81
Garden of Remembrance 80
Gate Theatre 57, **80**, 94, 289
General Post Office **79**, 282
Georgian Dublin walk 72–3
Glasnevin Cemetery 83
Government Buildings 71
Grafton Street 69
Guinness Storehouse 78
Ha'penny Bridge 74
Henry Street 79
Irish Museum of Modern Art 83
James Joyce Centre 56, **81**
Kilmainham Gaol 83
Leinster House 70
Merrion Square **71**, 73
National Botanic Gardens 83
National Gallery of Ireland 71
National Library 70
National Museum 70–1
National Museum of Decorative Arts and History 82
O'Connell Street 79
Old Jameson Distillery 82
Olympia Theatre **75**, 94
Parnell Square 80–1
Phoenix Park 82
Powerscourt Townhouse Centre 69
St Mary's Pro-Cathedral 80
St Michan's Church 81–2
St Patrick's Cathedral 76–7
St Stephen's Green **69**, 72
Shelbourne Hotel 69
Temple Bar 74–5
Trinity College 56, **65–9**
Dún Aengus 174
Dunbeg Fort 139
Dungarvan **100**, 109, 111
Dungloe 211

Dunluce Castle 251
Dunmore East 100
Dunquin 140
Dunseverick Castle 251
Durrus 118

E

Easky 203
Easter Rising 282
economy 284, 286–7
ecotourism 273
electricity 11
embassies and consulates 18, 269
emergencies 11, 268
emigration 103, 116, 238, 240, 281, 282
Emo Court **192–3**, 194
Ennis 14, **156–8**, 167–8, 169
Enniscrone 203
Enniskillen **241**, 253
entry requirements 18
Erne River 197, 207, 241
European Union 284, 286

F

family holidays 274–5
Fastnet Rock 121
Fermanagh 238, **241–2**, 253, 254
ferries 262–3, 265
festivals and events **14–15**, 41–2, 49, 59
  Belfast 233
  County Cork 127
  Dublin 95
  Inland Ireland 201
  Limerick and the Shannon 169
  Northern Ireland 255
  Northwest 217
  Southeast 111
  Southwest 134–5, **149**
  The West 178–9, **187**
Fianna Fáil 282
film 14, 127, **289–90**
Fine Gael 282, 284
flora 48, 164, 191
Florence Court 242
food and drink 15, 111, 127, 179, 187, 274–5, **292–7**
  see also restaurants
football 22, 23, 24, 232
Fota House 115–16
Fota Wildlife Park 115
Foynes 155

G

Gaelic games 23–4
Gallarus Oratory 139
Galway Bay **173**, 179
Galway City 16, **170–3**
Gandon, James 78–9, 81, 193
Gap of Dunloe 130
Garden of Light (Omagh) 239
Gartan Lough 212
Giant's Causeway 17, **251**
Glandore 120–1
Glen of Aherlow 101, **105**, 108, 110
Glenaan 249
Glenariff 249–50
Glenarm 249
Glenballyeamon 249
Glenbeigh **132**, 149
Glencloy 249
Glencolumbkille **211**, 214
Glencorp 249
Glendalough 36, **84**
Glendun 249
Glengarriff 122
Glenshesk 249
Glentaisie 249
Glenveagh National Park **212**, 217
Glin Castle 155
Goat's Path 119
golf **24–6**, 147, 158, 168, 216, 254–5
Good Friday Agreement 228, 284
Gorey 96–7
Government of Ireland Act 228
Grange Stone Circle 154
Grattan, Henry 281
Great Famine 103, 121, 196–7, 281
guesthouses 259
Guinness 78, **296–7**

H

Haughey, Charles J. 288
health and safety 268–9
Heaney, Seamus 55–6, 288
Henry II of England 279
Henry VIII of England 280
high/low season 13
Hill of Tara 34, **85**
Hilton Park **195**, 198, 201
history 278–85
Hook Head Peninsula **98**, 107
horse racing 14, **24–5**, 149, 179, 187, 255
horse riding 15, **27–9**, 87, 179, 186, 187
horse trading **134–5**, 189
hotels see accommodation
hurling 23–4

I

Ilnacullin Gardens (Garinish Island) 122
Inch Strand **138**, 146
Inishmore 174
Inishmurray Island 33
Inland Ireland 188–201
Innisfallen Island 37, **130**
Irish Free State 282
Irish National Heritage Park (Ferrycarrig) 98
Irish Republican Army (IRA) 283, 284
itineraries 16–17

J

Jerpoint Abbey 102–3
Joyce, James 14, 55, **56**, 288

K

Kenmare **137–8**, 143, 145, 148, 149
Kenny, Edna 284
Kerry 128–49
Kilcar 211
Kilcolgan **173**, 184
Kilcrohane 119
Kildare **86–7**, 90, 93
Kilfenora 160, **162–3**, 168
Kilkee **158**, 169
Kilkenny 15, **101–4**, 108, 109, 110, 111
Killala 181
Killarney 16, **128–9**, 142, 144–5, 147, 148, 149
Killarney National Park 129–31
Killary Harbour 177
Killorglin **131–2**, 134–5, 142, 145, 149
Killybegs 211
Killykeen Forest Park 197
Kilmore Quay 98
Kilnaruane Pillar Stone 119
Kilronan **174**, 185
Kilrush **158**, 169
Kinsale **117**, 123, 124, 125, 126, 127
Kinvara **173**, 179, 184, 185

Knocknarea 34, **203**
Kylemore Abbey 177

L

Lahinch **158**, 166, 167, 168,
169
Lake Isle of Innisfree 205
language 58–9, 287–8
Lanyon, Charles **222**, 224,
226, 249
Leamaneh Castle 161, **163**
Leenane 17, **177**, 182–3,
186, 187
Leitrim, County 202, **206–7**,
213, 215
Letterfrack 17, 184, 185
Letterkenny **212**, 214
Limerick 16, **150–3**, 165,
166, 167, 169
Liscannor 161
Lisdoonvarna 160, **162**, 165,
167
Lismore **106**, 109, 111
Lissadell House 205, **206**
Listowel 59, **141**, 146
literature 14, **54–9**, **288–9**
Lough Allen 206–7
Lough Corrib 17, 172, **175**, 187
Lough Derg **191–2**, **210**, 245
Lough Derravaragh 193
Lough Ennel 193
Lough Erne 241
Lough Gill 205
Lough Gur 154
Lough Ree 189, **201**
Louisburgh 177

M

McGahern, John 206
MacMurrough, Dermot 279
Magharee Islands 31, **141**
Mahee Island 247
maps 19
Mayo, County 17, 171,
177–81, 183, 184, 185
Meath **85–6**, 90, 93
medical care 268–9
Mizen Head 118, **121**
Monaghan **197**, 199
monasteries 32–3, **36–7**,
278–9
money 270–1
Moneygall 192
Mount Gabriel 121
Mount Usher Gardens 84
Mourne Mountains **243–6**,

247, 255
Muckross House 129
Muckross Park 129
Mullingar **193**, 200, 201
music **38–43**, 97, 110, 111,
125, 127, 157, 167–8, 169,
173, 217, 232, 233, 255,
290–1

N

National Folklife Collection
180–1
nationalism 282
natural hazards 269
Navan Centre (near Armagh)
243
Nendrum Abbey 247
New Ross 103
Newgrange 33–4, **86**
nightlife and entertainment
Belfast 231–2
County Cork 125–6
Dublin 93–4
Inland Ireland 200
Limerick and the Shannon
167–8
Northern Ireland 254
Northwest 216
Southeast 110
Southwest 147
The West 185
Nore Valley **102–3**, 107, 111
Normans 99, 208, 209, 279
Northern Ireland 17, **218–55**,
283, 284
The northwest 202–15

O

Obama, Barack 192, 296
O'Casey, Sean 55, 56
O'Connell, Daniel 136, 281
Omagh 239–40
opening hours 11
opera 97, 110, 111, 125, 178,
222, 232
O'Rourke, Tiernan 279
Oughterard **175**, 187

P

Parke's Castle 205, 209
partition 282
Patrick, St 177, 210, 243,
244–5, 246, 248, 255, **278**
politics 284
Portmagee **133**, 145, 147
postal services 11

Poulnabrone Dolmen 34–5,
161, **163–4**
Powerscourt House and
Gardens 85
Protestants 194, 280, 283
public holidays 12
public transport 263
pubs 39–41, **50–3**, 241, **295**
Puck Fair (Killorglin) **134–5**,
149

R

rail travel 263, **264**
Rathlin Island 250
responsible travel 273
restaurants
Belfast 230–1
County Cork 124–5
Dublin 91–3
Inland Ireland 199
Limerick and the Shannon
166–7
Northern Ireland 253–4
Northwest 214–15
Southeast 109
Southwest 144–6
The West 183–4
Ring of Beara 122, **131**
Ring of Kerry 16, **131–8**,
142–3, 145–6, 147
road travel 266–7
Rock of Cashel 16, **105**
Roscommon 197
Ross Castle 37, **130**
Rossaveal 173
Rossbeigh 132
Rosscarbery 120
The Rosses **211**, 215
Rosses Point 206
Rossmore Forest Park 197
Rossnacaheragh Stone Circle
119
Rossnowlagh **210**, 214
round towers **35**, 104, 208–9
rugby 22, 232

S

sailing 126, 127, 169, 201
Saltee Islands 98
Scattery Island 33
Schull **121**, 125
sea kayaking **31**, 126
sea travel 174, 262–3
Second World War 283
self catering 260
Shannon River/Estuary 150,

301

Index

151, 153, 155–6, 189, 190, 197, 207
Shannonbridge **190**, 199
Shaw, George Bernard 55
Sheep's Head Peninsula 118, 119, 126
Silent Valley Reservoir 247
Sinn Féin 282
Skellig Michael 37, **133**, 139
Skibbereen **121**, 126, 127
Sky Road **175**, 182
Slane **85–6**, 90
Slea Head 139
Slieve Bloom Way 47–8, **192**, 200–1
Slieve Donard 246
Slieve League **211**, 217
Sligo 17, **202–6**, 213, 214–15
Sligo town **202**, 203, **205**, 213, 214, 216, 217
smoking 11
Sneem **137**, 143
songs, traditional **39**, 169
The Southeast 96–111
The Southwest 128–49
Sperrin Mountains 238, 255
sports and activities **22–31**
  Belfast 232
  County Cork 126
  Inland Ireland 200–1
  Limerick and the Shannon 168–9
  Northern Ireland 254–5
  Northwest 216–17
  Southeast 111
  Southwest 147–8
  The West 186
Staigue Fort 136–7
Statutes of Kilkenny 280
Strangford Lough 246–7
Strokestown Park House and Famine Museum 195, **196–7**
Strongbow 279

surfing **30–1**, 126, 158, 159, 169, 203, 217

T
Tarbert 155
tax 271
telephone numbers 11, 268
terrorism 283
Terryglass 191
theatre 57, 94, 110, 125, 185, 216, 232, 254, **289**
Thomastown **102–3**, 108, 111
time zone 11
Tipperary **104–6**, 108, 109
tipping 271
Titanic 116, 127, 218, 226, 248
Tollymore Forest Park 246
Torc Waterfall 129
Tory Island 209, **212**
tourist information 18–19
tours
  Belfast 233
  County Cork 127
  Dublin 78, **94–5**
  Inland Ireland 201
  Limerick & the Shannon 169
  Northern Ireland 255
  Southeast 110
  Southwest 148–9
  The West 187
Tralee **140–1**, 144, 146, 147, 149
Tramore 100
transport **261–7**
  Belfast 221
  Derry/Londonderry 239
  Dublin 68
the Troubles 235, 239, 240, **283–4**
Tullan Strand 207
Tullynally Castle 193–6
Tyrone, County **238–40**, 252, 253

U
Ulster Folk and Transport Museum (Cultra) 248
Ulster-American Folk Park 238, **240**
Unionists 283

V
Valentia Island **132–3**, 142, 145, 147
Vee Gap 105–6
Ventry 139
Vikings 99, 208, 279
visas 18

W
walking **44–9**, 111, 126, 148, 149, 168–9, 186, 200–1, 217, 233, 255
Waterfoot 249
Waterford **96**, **99–100**, 107, 109, 110, 111
watersports 126, 148, 169, 201, 217
Waterville **133**, 143, 146, 147
weather 12–13
websites 19
The West 170–87
Westport 17, 171, **177–80**, 183, 185, 186
Wexford **97–8**, 108, 109, 110, 111, 178
whiskey 82, 251, **297**
White Bay 249
Wicklow **83–5**, 90, 93
Wilde, Oscar 55, 56, 73
wildlife 45, 48, 191, 248
Wolfe Tone, Theobold 281

Y
Yeats, W.B. 55–6, **57–8**, 79, 205–6, 217
youth hostels 260

Accommodation Index

Abbeyglen Castle (Sky Road) 182
Aberdeen Lodge (Dublin) 88
Adare Guest House (Galway) 182
Adare Village Inn (Adare) 165

Aherlow House Hotel and Lodges (Glen of Aherlow) 108
Ambassador Hotel (Cork) 123
Ard na Breatha Guesthouse (Donegal) 213
Ardtara Country House

(Maghera) 252
Arlington Lodge Town House & Restaurant (Waterford) 107
Ashford Castle (Cong) 183
Ashley Park House (Nenagh) 198

Atlantic Villa (Valentia Island) 142
Avenue Guesthouse (Belfast) 229
Ballinalacken Castle (Doolin) 165
Ballygarry House Hotel and Spa (Tralee) 144
Ballymaloe House (Midleton) 123
Ballynahinch Castle Hotel (Recess) 182
Barberstown Castle (Straffan) 90
Bayview Hotel (Portballintrae) 252–3
Benedicts Hotel (Belfast) 229
Bewley's Hotel Ballsbridge (Dublin) 88
Blarney Castle Hotel 123
Boffin Lodge (Westport) 183
Brook Lane Hotel (Kenmare) 143
Brook Manor Lodge (near Tralee) 144
Burren Hostel (Lisdoonvarna) 165
Bush Hotel (Carrick-on-Shannon) 213
Bushmills Inn (Bushmills) 253
Buswell Hotel (Dublin) 88
Butler House (Kilkenny) 108
Cahernane House Hotel (Killarney) 142
Camera Guesthouse (Belfast) 229
Cappabhaile House (Ballyvaughan) 166
Carrig Country House (near Glenbeigh) 143
Cashel Palace Hotel (Cashel) 108
Central Hotel (Dublin) 88
Charlemont Arms Hotel (Armagh) 252
Charles Stewart Parnell Guest House (Dublin) 90
Clarence Hotel (Dublin) 88
Clarion Hotel (Cork) 123
Clarion Hotel (Limerick) 165
Cliff House Hotel (Ardmore) 107
Delphi Mountain Resort (Leenane) 182–3
Dingle Skellig (An Daingean Harbour) 143
Dooley's Hotel (Waterford) 107

Dromoland Castle (Newmarket-on-Fergus) 166
Duke's at Queens (Belfast) 229
Dunbrody Country House Hotel (Arthurstown) 107
Dunraven Arms (Adare) 165
Dylan Hotel (Dublin) 88
Dzogchen Beara Retreat Centre (Allihies) 123–4
Earls Court House (Killarney) 142
Emlagh House (An Daingean Harbour) 143–4
Eskermore House (Tullamore) 198
Ferrycarrig Hotel (Ferrycarrig Bridge) 107
Ferryport House (Rosslare Harbour) 107
Final Furlong Farmhouse (Cahirsiveen) 143
Fitzgerald's Woodlands House Hotel (Adare) 165
Fitzwilliam Hotel (Belfast) 229
Four Seasons (Dublin) 89
Foxmount Farm and Counrty House (Waterford) 107
Friar's Glen (Killarney) 142
Friar's Lodge (Kinsale) 124
G The 'G' (Galway) 182
Garnish House (Cork) 123
Glassdrumman Lodge (Annalong) 252
Glebe House (Mohill) 213
Glen Country House (Kilbrittain) 124
Grange Lodge (Dungannon) 252
Grapevine Hostel (Dingle) 144
Gregan's Castle (Ballyvaughan) 166
Gresham Hotel (Dublin) 90
Hanorah's Cottage (Ballymacarbry) 107
Harcourt Hotel (Dublin) 89
Harvey's Point Country Hotel (Lough Eske) 213–14
Hayfield Manor Hotel (Cork) 123
Heaton's Guesthouse (Dingle) 144
Hillcrest House (Bantry) 124
Hilton Park (near Clones) 198
Hotel Europe (Killarney) 142
Hotel Isaacs (Dublin) 90
Hotel Kilkenny (Kilkenny) 108
Hotel St George (Dublin) 90

Hyland's Burren Hotel (Ballyvaughan) 166
Ionad Siúl Walking Lodge (Glencolumbille) 214
Jurys Inn Belfast 229
Jurys Inn Christchurch (Dublin) 90
Jurys Inn Limerick 165
Kelly's Resort Hotel (Rosslare Village) 107
Kilcoran Lodge (Cahir) 108
Killarney International Hostel 142
Kilmurvey House (Inis Mór) 182
Kinlay House (Dublin) 90
Lakelands Farm Guesthouse (Waterville) 143
Loch Lein Country House Hotel (Killarney) 142
Malin Hotel (Inishowen) 214
Malmaison Belfast 229
The Maltings (Birr) 198
The Malton (Killarney) 142
Maritime Hotel (Bantry) 124
Markree Castle (Coolooney) 213
Merchant Hotel (Belfast) 229
The Merrion (Dublin) 89
The Millhouse (Slane) 90
The Morrison (Dublin) 90
Mount Juliet Conrad (Thomastown) 108
Moy House (Lahinch) 166
No. 1 Pery Square (Limerick) 165
Number 31 (Dublin) 89
O An Old Rectory (Belfast) 230
Ostan Inis Oirr (Inisheer) 182
Park Hotel (Kenmare) 143
Park House Hotel (Galway) 182
Parknasilla Resort (Sneem) 143
Pier House (Kinsale) 124
Radisson Blu (Limerick) 165
Radisson Blu Roe Park Hotel (Limavady) 252
Rathmullan House (Letterkenny) 214
Riverside House (Cootehill) 198
Riverside Suites Hotel (Sligo) 213
St George Guest House (Wexford) 108
Sand House Hotel (Rossnowlagh) 214
Sandymount Hotel (Dublin) 89
Seagoe Hotel (Portadown) 252

Seaview House Hotel (Bantry) 124

Shelbourne Hotel (Dublin) 89

Sheraton Athlone Hotel (Athlone) 198

Sleepzone (Leenane) 183

Slieve Donard Hotel (Newcastle) 252

Slieve Russell Hotel & Country Club (Ballyconnell) 198

Sligo Southern Hotel (Sligo) 213

La Stampa (Dublin) 89

Tara Lodge (Belfast) 230

Temple House (Ballymote) 213

Ten Square Hotel (Belfast) 229

Trident Hotel (Kinsale) 124

Waterside (Graiguenamanagh) 108

Wellington Park Hotel (Belfast) 230

Westbury Hotel (Dublin) 89

Westport Plaza and Castlecourt Hotel (Westport) 183

Wineport Lodge (Athlone) 198

Woodenbridge Hotel (Arklow) 90

Zuni Townhouse (Kilkenny) 108

Credits for Berlitz Handbook Ireland

Written by: Alannah Hopkin
Series Editor: Tom Stainer
Commissioning Editor: Sarah Sweeney
Map Production: Phoenix Mapping and Apa Cartography Department
Production: Linton Donaldson, Rebeka Ellam
Picture Manager: Steven Lawrence
Art Editors: Richard Cooke and Ian Spick
Photography: Alamy 97B, 268, 269; Courtesy Ashford Castle 183; Courtesy Chapter 40 145; Corbis 9LM, 52, 281; APA Kevin Cummins 2R, 4B, 5BL, 10/11, 16, 17, 113T, 119, 129T, 133, 199, 219B, 223, 224, 225, 226, 227, 228, 231, 241, 242, 243, 245T, 250, 271, 283, 286, 288, 291, 294; Courtesy Doonbeg Golf Club 168; Fotolia 5BR, 7B/MR, 9BR, 23, 46, 60/61; APA Glyn Genin 2L, 3L, 5TR, 7TL, 36, 45, 55, 69, 70, 72, 74, 83, 99, 100, 113, 115, 116, 117, 125, 126, 131, 137, 138, 139, 140, 151, 153, 155, 157B, 175, 181, 189B, 191, 292; Courtesy Grand Hotel 108; Imagefree.org 280; Istockphoto 163; Kobal Collection 290; Leonardo 143; Courtesy Mahoney's Point 148; NITB 233, 255, 273; Courtesy Out of the Blue 146; Photolibrary 5LM, 9TL, 34, 53, 57, 101, 106, 118, 121, 122, 132, 134, 135/T, 137T, 141, 195T, 197/T, 246, 247, 248, 249, 251, 256/257, 261, 276; Pictures Colour Library 162, 174, 196; Courtesy Slieve Donard Hotel; Tourism Ireland Imagery 8BL/BR/T, 14, 22, 24, 25, 26, 27, 28, 29, 30, 31, 33, 37, 38, 39, 41, 43, 44, 47, 50, 51, 59, 56TR, 75, 78, 81, 82, 86, 87, 88, 91, 92, 95, 97T, 102, 103, 104, 105, 129B, 157T, 158, 164, 171, 177, 178, 179B, 180, 189T, 190, 192, 193, 194, 201, 203, 209B, 210, 212, 215, 222, 235/T, 238, 240, 244, 245B, 258, 259, 260, 262, 263, 264, 265, 266, 274, 275, 278, 284, 289, 295, 297; Courtesy Wexford Opera House 110; APA Corrie Wingate 3R, 4TL/TR, 5TL, 7TR, 9TR, 12, 13, 15, 19, 20/21, 32, 35, 40, 42, 48, 49, 54, 56, 58, 65B, 71, 73, 76, 77, 79, 80. 85, 89, 94, 151T, 154, 159, 160, 161, 167, 171T, 173, 179T, 185, 186, 202T, 205, 206, 207, 208, 209T, 211, 217, 270, 272, 279, 287, 296

Front cover: Corbis **Back cover:** (from left) fotolia; Wingate/APA; fotolia
Printed by: CTPS-China

© 2012 Apa Publications (UK) Limited
First Edition 2012
Berlitz Trademark Reg. US Patent Office and other countries. Marca Registrada. Used under licence from the Berlitz Investment Corporation

Contacting Us
At Berlitz we strive to keep our guides as accurate and up to date as possible, but if you find anything that has changed, or if you have any suggestions on ways to improve this guide, then we would be delighted to hear from you. Write to Berlitz Publishing, PO Box 7910, London SE1 1WE, UK or email: berlitz@apaguide.co.uk

Worldwide: APA Publications GmbH & Co. Verlag KG (Singapore branch), 7030 Ang Mo Kio Ave 5, 08-65 Northstar @ AMK, Singapore 569880; tel: (65) 570 1051; email: apasin@singnet.com.sg
UK and Ireland: Dorling Kindersley Ltd, a Penguin Group company, 80 Strand, London, WC2R 0RL, UK; email: customerservice@dk.com
United States: Ingram Publisher Services, 1 Ingram Boulevard, PO Box 3006, La Vergne, TN 37086-1986; email: customer.service@ingrampublisherservices.com
Australia: Universal Publishers, 1 Waterloo Road, Macquarie Park, NSW 2113; tel: (61) 2-9857 3700; email: sales@universalpublishers.com.au
www.berlitzpublishing.com